THE BROWNS

OF

BEDFORD COUNTY, VIRIGINA

1748-1840

A COLLECTION OF BROWN SURNAME RECORDS
EXTRACTED FROM PRIMARY AND SECONDARY SOURCES

Barbara Brown Eakley

HERITAGE BOOKS
2008

HERITAGE BOOKS

AN IMPRINT OF HERITAGE BOOKS, INC.

Books, CDs, and more—Worldwide

For our listing of thousands of titles see our website
at
www.HeritageBooks.com

Published 2008 by
HERITAGE BOOKS, INC.
Publishing Division
100 Railroad Ave. #104
Westminster, Maryland 21157

International Standard Book Numbers
Paperbound: 978-0-7884-0922-6
Clothbound: 978-0-7884-7051-6

CONTENTS

Contents i

Preface iii

Given names, alphabetical order 1

Bibliography 149

Index - surnames 153

Index - slaves 181

PREFACE

John Brown. Who was John Brown? Who were the ancestors of John Brown? Every Brown researcher can empathize with the dilemmas inherent in tracing that name. It would seem that most villages in early Virginia had a John Brown in every generation. The author's John Brown was said by family tradition to have "come from" Bedford County. Was that true?

Bedford County in Virginia was on the path of the great Wagon Road which led from Philadelphia to Harper's Ferry to Tennessee. Uncounted scores of immigrants moved westward along that road, settling in a county for a few years before moving farther west. Bedford County records reflect that pattern of settling and moving, settling and moving.

Many Brown families passed through Bedford County on their way west, and left recorded evidence of having been there. Many of their family members, slaves, neighbors and business associates were named with them.

Some 606 other surnames are associated with Brown in those records.

The author studied all available records, and was able to rule out that the ancestors of her John Brown were from Bedford County He was the descendant of several generations of pioneer settlers in Montgomery County, Virginia, but had married into a family which had moved there from Bedford County.

Every genealogist knows that to rule out is to get closer to the truth.

This collection of abstracted records is intended as a finding tool for researchers. The abstracts are written in modern English, and place names have been standardized. The serious researcher will remember to look to the original records for final authority.

Barbara Brown Eakley
Coos Bay, Oregon
January 8, 1998

The Browns of Bedford County

AARON

Aaron entered military service from Bedford County in 1776, was born in 1756 at Cumberland County VA. At Monroe County TN in 1833 he received a pension for Revolutionary War service. He died in 1836, leaving widow Nancy and children: Elizabeth Hunly, Dicey Heisel, Mary Christian, Joseph, Phebe Staples, George, Lewcinda, Nancy, Wilson, James, Sarah Purvines, and John. His widow's sister was Dicey Brown. Reel R358 of M804, National Archives. (Wardell 1988, 1:116).

Aaron was sued by Peter Dent and Micajah McCormack on suspicion that he stole leather from Dent, and a bill and collar from McCormack. Bond by Aaron Brown, Absolom Adams and Zachariah Brown. Recorded Aug 1782. (Bedford OB 6:368).

Aaron was indicted and found guilty of grand larceny. Recorded Nov 25, 1782. (Bedford OB 7:13).

Aaron Sr's land was near John Maglothlin, William Maglothlin and John MacPherson. Recorded Mar 12, 1800. (Bedford PRO 1:69).

Aaron Jr's land was near Isaak Bond. Recorded Mar 12, 1800. (Bedford PRO 1:69).

Aaron was the father of Betsy who married Jordan Hundley. Surety was William Corley. Bond dated Oct 24, 1806. They were married by Richard Pope on Oct 27, 1806. (Hinshaw 1969, 6:1938).

AGGY

Aggy married Joseph Wright. Surety was John Brown. Bond dated Jun 26, 1805. (Hinshaw 1969, 6:1021). See SARAH.

ALBERT

Albert G was security with James M Brown for Mary Brown, who was granted letters of administration of the estate of James T Brown, deceased. Recorded May 1840. (Bedford OB 27:68).

The Browns of Bedford County

ALEXANDER aka Alex, Sawney

Alexander married Vilet Barton. Surety was Brer Barton. Bond dated Feb 20, 1791 (sic). (Dennis 1989, 8).

Alexander Brown and John Pate were present when the land of Thomas Brown was processioned. Recorded Apr 26, 1796. (Bedford PRO 1:41).

Alexander Brown and Violet Barton were married by William Johnson on Feb 25, 1797. (Bedford PRO 1:237).

Sawney had 1 male 21+, and 1 horse. Personal Property Tax List of 1800, District 1. (Dorman 1963, 7:66).

Alexander was conveyed a deed from John Pate for 103A on both sides of Falling Creek. Signed Feb 24, 1800. (Bedford DB 11:183).

Sawney's land was near Ebenezer Brown and Anthony Wright. Recorded Jul 20, 1800. (Bedford PRO 1:90).

Alexander was appointed to survey a road from Botetourt County line to Weavers Creek. Recorded Jun 22, 1801. (Bedford OB 12:174).

Alexander was conveyed a deed from Ebenezer Brown and his wife Ruth for 100A on the north side of the Staunton River, near Caniel Corley. Signed Sep 22, 1802 and recorded Sep 27, 1802. (Bedford DB 11:606).

Sawney and his wife Vilet conveyed a deed to Bartholomew Cary for 30A on both sides of Falling Creek, near Matthew Pate and Ebenezer Brown. Signed Sep 24, 1802 and recorded Sep 27, 1802. (Bedford DB 11:616).

Sawney and his wife Violet conveyed a deed to Ebenezer Brown for 50A on the south side of Falling Creek. Signed and recorded Sep 27, 1802. (Bedford DB 11:617).

Sawney was present when the land of Ebenezer Brown was processioned. Recorded Feb 2, 1803. (Bedford PRO 1:114).

Alexander was conveyed a deed from Samuel Morgan for 30A on both sides of Falling Creek, near Matthew Pate, Anthony Wright and Alexander

The Browns of Bedford County

Brown. Witnesses were William Dent, Leroy Jordan and James Johnson. Signed Oct 11, 1810 and recorded Oct 22, 1810. (Bedford DB 13:732).

Alexander was conveyed a deed from Sally Finley for a tract of land on the north side of Staunton River. Witnesses were Matthew Pate, John Pate and David Barton. Signed Dec 24, 1811 and recorded Nov 23, 1812. (Bedford DB 13:774).

Alexander's property on Falling Creek was near Ebenezer Brown and John Pate, per deed from Ebenezer Brown and his wife Ruth to Matthew Pate and Edmund Pate for 50A. Signed Oct 10, 1817 and recorded Oct 1817. (Bedford DB 15:254).

Alexander had 2 males 0-10, 1 male 10-16, 1 male 16-26, 1 male 45+, 2 females 0-10, 1 female 10-16, 1 female 16-26-, 1 female 26-45, and 2 females 45+. (U S Census of 1820, Southern District, p 1).

Alexander was the father of Sarah who married Elijah Hamilton. Surety was Elijah Hamilton. Bond dated Jan 4, 1820. (Hinshaw 1969, 6:927).

Alexander served as a juror with Thomas Brown and others. Recorded Sep 1, 1820. (Bedford OB 18:31).

Alexander conveyed a deed with wife Violet to Samuel Mead for 360A on Staunton River, near Anthony Wright, Pate, Col Dickerson, Hardy, and Beverly Cawley. Witnesses were John Hurt, William Hurt and Wilkins Hunt. Signed Oct 24, 1820 and recorded Nov 27, 1820. (Bedford DB 16:352).

Alexander conveyed a deed of trust secured by a horse to trustee John Patterson for a debt owed Caleb St Clair. Signed Mar 21, 1826 and recorded same date. (Bedford DB 19:375).

Alexander married Polly Lively. Surety was Willis B Lively. Bond dated Apr 25, 1826. They were married by William Harris on Apr 27, 1826. (Hinshaw 1969, 6:884).

Justices of the peace Alexander Brown and Nelson Anderson certified that James Marr and his wife Elizabeth were parties to a deed. Signed and recorded Mar 8, 1833. (Bedford DB 23:287).

3

The Browns of Bedford County

ALICE aka Alce, Alcy, Aley

Alce Beard married Henry Brown in Bedford County VA on Feb 20, 1757. Their children were Lettice, born Dec 3, 1757; Henry, born Aug 10, 1760; Elizabeth, born Jul 20, 1762; Alce, born Nov 10, 1764; Samuel, born Nov 10, 1766; and Daniel, born Dec 18, 1770. Recorded Jan 25, 1773. (Bedford DB 4:455).

Alice and her husband Henry were conveyed a deed from Thomas Brown for 87A on Goose Creek. Recorded 1760 at Augusta County VA DB 8:413. (Kegley 1993, 298).

Alice and her husband Henry of Bedford County VA, conveyed a deed to Thomas Walker for 200A on Goose Creek. Recorded Aug 20, 1760 at Augusta County VA DB 8:403. (Chalkley 1989, 362).

Alice and her husband Henry conveyed a deed to Esther Brown for 54A on Lick Run, a branch of the Roanoke River. Recorded Aug 20, 1760 at Augusta County VA DB 8:408. (Chalkley 1989, 363).

Alice and her husband Henry conveyed a deed to Francis Thorpe for 226A on both sides of Buffalo Creek, a branch of Otter Creek, near Adams. Signed Jun 28, 1779 and recorded Aug 17, 1779. (Bedford DB 6:234).

Aley married Jesse Witt. Surety was Henry Brown. "Consent of Aley, saying she is of age". Bond dated May 6, 1786. (Dennis 1989, 77).

Alcy was the daughter of Henry Brown and Alice Beard. She and her siblings were named in their father's will dated Jan 9, 1796. She inherited furniture by the will. His will was recorded Jun 24, 1799. (Bedford WB 2:261).

Alice Beard Brown was buried at Ivy Hill. Her tombstone is obliterated. (Merrill 1968, chart A).

Alice and her siblings were named in the will of their father Henry Brown. She was bequeathed the house in Lynchburg and 15 bank shares. Her father's will was signed Jan 6, 1837 and recorded Sep 25, 1841. (Bedford WB 10:392).

The Browns of Bedford County

Alice was the daughter of Henry and Frances Thompson Brown of Ivy Cliff. She married William Worthington Jun 27, 1839 at Richmond, VA. (Merrill 1968, 21).

ALLEN

Allen and his brothers, the children of Jennings Brown, were ordered bound out by the overseers of the poor. Recorded Apr 27, 1795. (Bedford OB 10:366).

Allen, the son of Jennings Brown, was ordered by the overseers of the poor to be bound out to Caleb Browning. Recorded Jun 1795. (Bedford OB 11:12).

Allen and John Brown had been soldiers in the Virginia Continental Line, and died intestate. Allen's sole heirs were proven to be Jennings Brown and Robert Brown. Recorded Nov 3, 1826. (Bedford OB 21:60).

ANNE aka Ann, Anna

Anne was the daughter of John Brown and his wife Margaret. She was named in her father's will dated Jan 13, 1774. She was to get three years schooling when she reached age eight years. Executors were Margaret Scruggs and John Holloway. Will dated Jan 13, 1774 and recorded Mar 23, 1778. (Bedford WB 1:286).

Anne married Philip Pankey. Consent of Gross Scruggs. Surety was William Gibson. Bond dated Feb 4, 1788. (Dennis 1989, 54). They were married by James Mitchell on Feb 11, 1788. (Bedford PRO 1:219).

Anne and her siblings were named in the will of their father James. His will was dated Dec 3, 1789 and recorded Jul 26, 1790. (Bedford WB 2:35).

Ann married John Reese. Surety was James Brown. Ann certified that she was of age. Bond dated Dec 5, 1792. (Dennis 1989, 56). They were married by James Mitchell on Dec 6, 1792. (Bedford PRO 1:228).

Ann "Nancy" Brown was born 1795 to Henry and Frances Thompson Brown of Ivy Cliff. Her husband was Dr William Steptoe. She died

5

The Browns of Bedford County

Apr 5, 1817 and was buried at Ivy Hill. (Merrill 1968, chart A).

Ann was the daughter of Henry Brown and Ann Richardson, his first wife. (Merrill 1968, 11). She and her siblings and half-siblings were named in her father's will dated Jan 9, 1796. She inherited 10 shillings by the will. His will was recorded Jun 24, 1799. (Bedford WB 2:261).

Anne and her brothers were named in the will of their father Daniel, dated Jan 6, 1797, recorded Feb 27, 1797. (Bedford WB 2:193). She was the mother of John Ashwell Brown, per her father's will. (Merrill 1968, 7).

Anna Hopkins was the daughter of Price. She married Ethelred Brown, son of John. Surety was Tilson A Pullen. Bond dated Feb 22, 1825. (Hinshaw 1969, 6:884).

Ann Brown, William Hopkins, Sally Walker, John Hopkins and Martha Hopkins were proven to be the children of Elizabeth Hopkins, deceased, who was the daughter of James Turner, deceased, who died intestate. Recorded Aug 3, 1828. (Bedford OB 21:116).

Ann and her husband Ethelred of Franklin County VA conveyed a deed of trust to trustees Pleasant Preston and George Davis for John T Davis, secured by 119 3/4A at Stony Fork near John Walden, Thomas Johnson and Pleasant Dickinson. Signed Oct 29, 1831 and recorded Nov 8, 1831. (Bedford DB 22:474).

Trustees for Ann and her husband Ethelred conveyed a deed to John T Davis for 119 3/4A at Stony Creek. Signed Oct 22, 1832 and recorded Dec 24, 1832. (Bedford DB 23:205).

Anna Brown Reece was a sister of John Brown. She and her siblings were named in his pension application for service in the Revolutionary War. Reel R370 of M804, National Archives. (Wardell 1988, 1:116).

ARABA aka Arab, Arabia, Raba

Arabia entered service from Bedford County in 1777. He was born on Dec 27, 1755, and died on Mar 13, 1844 at Garrard County KY. He married Elizabeth Dooley in 1778. His family bible records were submitted with his pension application, naming children: Stephen, born Jun 25, 1779; --chel,

The Browns of Bedford County

born Sep 18, 1783; Arabia J, born Mar 16, 1785 at Bedford County; Peggy, born Aug 28, 1786; Doshy, born Sep 10, 1788; Stephen U, born Aug 17, 17--; Henry, born May 16, 1792; Elizabeth, born Feb 2, 17--, and other unnamed children. In 1832 he received a pension for service in the Revolutionary War. Reel R359 of M804, National Archives. (Wardell 1988, 1:116).

Raba was conveyed a deed from George Hughes for 150A at Little Otter River. Witness was William Brown. Signed Aug 18, 1778 and recorded Aug 24, 1778. (Bedford DB 6:94).

Araba lived near Brambletts Road near Thomas Brown Sr, John Anthony, Augustine Leftwich, James Brown and William Woodley, per deed to Thomas Brown Sr from Augustine Leftwich Sr for 160A. Recorded Aug 24, 1778. (Bedford DB 6:97).

Araba was surety for the marriage of Thomas White and Jane Lusk. Bond dated Mar 18, 1783. (Dennis 1989, 74).

Araba was conveyed a deed from Robert Mitchell Jr for 200A on both sides of the middle fork of Little Otter River. Recorded May 26, 1783. (Bedford DB 7:206).

Arabia Jackson Brown was born Mar 16, 1785 at Bedford County VA per his father Arabia's pension application for Revolutionary War service. Reel 359 of M804, National Archives. (Wardell 1988, 1:116)

Araba conveyed a deed to Thomas Eidson for 100A on the branches of Little Otter River, near Thomas White. Recorded Jun 27, 1785. (Bedford DB 7:520).

Araba conveyed a deed to Thomas White for 100A on the branches of Little Otter River, near Murphy. Recorded Jun 27, 1785. (Bedford DB 7:528).

Raba was given permission to keep an ordinary at the house where William French formerly lived. Recorded Aug 1785. (Bedford OB 8:193).

Raba and his wife Elizabeth conveyed a deed to Ansalom Goodman for 150A on the Little Otter River. The land was patented by Augustine Leftwich, was sold to Joseph Patterson, then to George Hughes, then to

7

The Browns of Bedford County

Raba Brown. Near John Gallaway and Randolph's old line. Witnesses were William French, Hanner Hanes and Elebeth Eitson. Signed Aug 27, 1786 and recorded Apr 23, 1788. (Bedford DB 8:71).

Araba was conveyed a deed from Benjamin McCraw for 209A on the branches of Little Otter River near Cary, Beard, Brumfield and Dooley. Witnesses were Edward McCraw, George Dooley and Janey Dooley. Signed Jun 19, 1787 and recorded Apr 23, 1792. (Bedford DB 9:48).

Araba Brown of Kentucky gave power of attorney to John Dooley Sr for handling the sale of his 200A on the branches of Little Otter River, near George Dooley, James Turner, John Dooley and William French. Signed Aug 23, 1787, and recorded Jul 23, 1804. (Bedford DB 11:1051).

Arabia's land was near John Dooley. Recorded Feb 19, 1796. (Bedford PRO 1:35).

Araba conveyed a deed by attorney John Dooley Sr to James R Saunders for 157A on Little Otter River, near Walton, Turner and Dooley. Signed and recorded Jun 25, 1798. (Bedford DB 10:469).

Raba conveyed a deed by attorney John Dooley to Charles Marckle for 150A on the branches of Little Otter River, near Murphy. Signed and recorded Dec 23, 1799. (Bedford DB 11:146).

Araba conveyed a power of attorney to John Dooley Sr to sell 200A on branches of Little Otter River, near William French. Recorded 1804. (Bedford DB 11:1051).

Araba of Caldwell County KY was conveyed a deed from Sarah Brown for her 1/3 interest in the estate of the late George Brown in Jefferson County TN. Sarah was the widow of said George Brown, deceased. Witness was J Steptoe Jr. Signed Apr 2, 1814 and recorded same date. (Bedford DB 13:841).

ARCHIBALD

In suit of Archibald Brown v Abraham Bitz, the defendant confessed judgment, and Archibald was awarded $50 plus interest from Sep 20, 1826. Recorded May 3, 1833. (Bedford OB 24:132).

The Browns of Bedford County

BENJAMIN

Benjamin was identified as an idiot, and a resident of Williamson County TN. His guardian William H Allen conveyed power of attorney to Henry Moss to manage Benjamin's property in Bedford County. Signed Apr 24, 1827 and recorded May 30, 1827. (Bedford DB 20:251).

BRAMBLE

Bramble H Brown, Joseph Flood and Greenbury Bowles were ordered to give testimony at the trial of Caleb Brown. Recorded Nov 1816. (Bedford OB 17:284). (Note: Court index reads "William Bramblett Brown").

BROWN & CLAYTOR CO

Henry Brown was a partner with Samuel Claytor in the merchant firm of Brown & Claytor. They were conveyed a deed from William O Hurt for land in the estate of Garland Hurt, deceased. Signed Oct 6, 1821 and recorded Oct 8, 1821. (Bedford DB 17:87).

Henry Brown and Samuel Claytor, as Brown & Claytor, conveyed a deed to Ira Hurt for 103A on Craddock Creek. Witnesses were James Ayers, N Robertson and Harvey Layton. No signing date. Recorded Dec 23, 1822. (Bedford DB 17:347).

Henry Brown and Samuel Claytor, merchants and partners doing business as Brown & Claytor, acted as trustees for John Headen for a debt owed by Benjamin W Crouch. Signed Oct 20, 1827 and recorded same date. (Bedford DB 20:367).

Henry Brown and John P Claytor were merchants and partners doing business as Brown & Claytor. They had been trustees for a deed of trust from Bennett M Murphy, secured by 1) 78A on Mill Creek, 2) 1/8 profits from a grist mill, 3) 50 1/2A on Goose Creek, and 4) 15A on Goose Creek.

The Browns of Bedford County

Bennett Murphy defaulted, and Samuel Claytor conveyed the land and profits to Henry Brown, who was the highest bidder. Signed Nov 19, 1827 and recorded Dec 27, 1827. (Bedford DB 20:432).

Brown & Claytor, Henry Brown, and Samuel Hancock, executors of Daniel Brown, released the indenture of Isham Lawhorn for the tract where he lived. Signed Apr 28, 1828 and recorded May 26, 1828. (Bedford DB 21:43).

Brown & Claytor had been conveyed 6A in Murphy's Mill Tract by debtors Pleasant Murphy and Bennett Murphy, the sons and heirs of John Murphy. Henry Brown conveyed a deed for the land to John Nance. Signed Mar 30, 1833 and recorded same date. (Bedford DB 23:346).

BROWN LEFTWICH & CO

The Brown Leftwich store was near Goose Creek. Daniel Brown, John Newlon, William Hackworth and Elijah Turner were ordered to view a road at the store. Recorded Feb 23, 1801. (Bedford OB 12:146).

The Brown Leftwich & Co store was ordered to be used on the first Thursday of April as a polling place for the election of an overseer of the poor. The 2nd Battalion of the 10th Regiment was to vote there. Recorded Feb 1806. (Bedford OB 13:301).

BROWN McCREDIE & CO

Brown McCredie & Co gave bond as security for trust deed on 237A which James Robertson conveyed to Samuel Read. Near Richard Lee, Archer Payne, Christopher Moore, William Leftwich, John Farris and William Read's heirs. Signed Aug 5, 1800 and recorded Sep 22, 1800. (Bedford DB 11:256).

James Brown conveyed a deed of trust to trustee James C Steptoe for 70A, to secure a debt owed Brown McCredie & Co. Witnesses were Samuel Read, Thomas Miller and Anderson C Fariss. Samuel Read signed for Brown McCredie & Co. Signed Feb 11, 1806 and recorded Jun 23, 1806. (Bedford DB 12:74).

CALEB

The Browns of Bedford County

Caleb was indicted for "maliously setting afire and burning" a corn house and a stable on the property of Joseph Flood. Security bond was given by Caleb Brown, Sarah Brown, William Baber, William Thomas and Gabriel Keath. Bramble H Brown, Joseph Flood and Greenbury Bowles were ordered to give testimony at the trial. Recorded Nov 1816. (Bedford OB 17:284).

CALLAWAY

Callaway was the son of Hezekiah. He married Sarah Lawhorn. Surety was Jabez Brown. Bond dated Dec 23, 1833. They were married by Merryman Lunsford on Dec 23, 1833. (Hinshaw 1969, 6:884).

CATHERINE aka Catharine

Catharine Pollard was the daughter of Catharine. She married Paschal Brown. Surety was Jesse N Pollard. Bond dated Mar 2, 1824. (Hinshaw 1969, 6:884).

Catharine and her husband James of Campbell County VA, with Joshua R C Brown and his wife Jane of Botetourt County VA, were distributors of the estate of Thomas Leftwich. They conveyed a deed to James C Steptoe for 811A at Porter Mountain. Signed Jul 6, 1826 and recorded Aug 28, 1826. (Bedford DB 20:59). Catharine and Jane were cousins. (Prillaman 1995, 283).

CELIA

Celia married Samuel Woodward. Her grandparents were Edward Bright and Mary Ann Bright. Surety was John Consolver. Bond dated Oct 21, 1779. (Dennis 1989, 75).

CHARLES

Charles was conveyed a deed from William D Taylor, Secretary of the Treasury for the State of Virginia, for 100A on Echols Creek. The property was sold for back taxes. Signed Sep 14, 1822 and recorded Dec 20, 1823. (Bedford DB 18:195).

Charles and his wife Mary of Albemarle County VA conveyed a deed to

11

Ebenezer Watkins of Floyd County VA for 100A at Little Otter River.
Signed May 3, 1831 and recorded May 11, 1831. (Bedford DB 22:349).

CLARA

Clara and her siblings were the children of Edward Brown, who qualified to
be their guardian. Recorded May 1821. (Bedford OB 18:99).

CLAYBURN aka Claiborn

Claiborn entered military service from Bedford County, and married Sarah
Harmon there, per his application for pension for service in the
Revolutionary War. Sarah died in Nov 1828 at the home their son Harmon.
Reel R362 of M804, National Archives. (Wardell 1988, 1:118).

Clayburn married Sarah Harmon. Surety was Peter Harmon. Bond dated
Mar 8, 1781. (Dennis 1989, 10).

CLITUS SMITH

Clitus Smith Brown was the son of Mary Ann, and was indentured to James
McClure. Recorded Jan 24, 1803. (Bedford OB 12:341).

CONSTANT aka Constance

Constant Clark married John Brown. Surety was Isham Clark. Bond dated
Sep 23, 1799. They were married by James Turner on Sep 24, 1799.
(Hinshaw 1969, 6:884). They were married by James Turner on Sep 24,
1799. (Bedford PRO 1:242).

Constant and her husband John conveyed a deed to Moses Miller for 97A
on Goose Creek, near Hobbs, Bramblett and Callaway. Witnesses were D
Crescent, J Grey, Jeremiah Lockett and Joseph D Stratton. Signed and
recorded Jul 22, 1822. (Bedford DB 17:235).

Constant and her husband John conveyed a deed of trust to trustee John H
Otey Jr, for debts owed the executors of Isham Clark, secured by 238 1/2A
on the head waters of Wolf Creek. Signed and recorded Oct 1, 1824.
(Bedford DB 19:44).

The Browns of Bedford County

Constance conveyed a deed with her husband John to William Thaxton for 83 1/2A on the head waters of Wolf Creek, near Thaxton, Williams and Jones. Witnesses were Frederick Aunspaugh, Daniel Aunspaugh and Jos Ferguson. Signed Jun 1, 1827 and recorded same date. (Bedford DB 20:258).

Constant and her husband John were conveyed a release of indemnity by trustee John H Otey on behalf of William Cook, Joseph Clark and George Stanley, the executors of Isham Clark, deceased. The debt had been secured by 238 1/4A near Thaxton and Roy Jones. Witnesses were Jos Ferguson and Fredk Aunspaugh. Signed Jun 1, 1827 and recorded Jun 2, 1827. (Bedford DB 20:257).

DANIEL

Daniel was the son of Henry Brown Sr by his second wife. Henry Sr had moved to the present Roanoke VA area from New Jersey. Daniel moved to Bedford County in 1767. (Kegley 1993, 199).

Daniel was born in New Jersey, the son of Henry Brown and his first wife. (Merrill 1968, 3).

Daniel was born Dec 18, 1770, the son of Henry and Alce Brown. Recorded Jan 25, 1773. (Bedford DB 4:455).

Daniel was born Dec 18, 1770 to Henry and Alice Beard Brown of Ivy Hill. He was a merchant in Lynchburg. His wife was Mary Hancock. He died Apr 23, 1817, and was buried at Ivy Hill. (Merrill 1968, chart A).

Daniel witnessed a deed from William Pike to Henry Taylor for 160A on Gills Creek. Other witnesses were Gross Scruggs and John Nowlin. Deed dated ___ 16, 1771 and recorded Apr 28, 1772. (Bedford DB 4:241).

Daniel was conveyed a deed from John Hall for 131A on the north side of Staunton River. Signed May 24, 1773 and recorded same date. (Bedford DB 5:64.

Daniel was conveyed a deed from John Hall for 200A on both sides of Lick Creek, a north branch of Staunton River. Signed and recorded May 24, 1773. (Bedford DB 5:65).

Daniel's 60A were surveyed. The land was on the north branches of Staunton River, near Orick, Price, Walton, and John Mitchell. Survey dated Mar 15, 1774. (Bedford SR 2:259). The land was transferred to Markham in 1775. (Bedford SR 3:14).

Daniel Jr was conveyed a deed from Samuel Morgan and his wife Elizabeth, for land near Thomas Morgan and Hinman Wooster. Witnesses were Daniel Price, Charles Swain, John Lee and Jane Brown. Signed Aug 28, 1779 and recorded Sep 27, 1779. (Bedford DB 6:331).

Daniel married Polly Callaway. Surety was James Steptoe. Bond dated Aug 4, 1781. (Dennis 1989, 7). Daniel married Emily Callaway on Aug 4, 1781. She was born in 1759, the daughter of Col James Callaway and Sarah Tate. (Ackerly 1930, 296).

Dr Daniel Brown had been a surgeon in the Revolutionary War. Polly was the daughter of Col James Callaway and Sarah Tate. (Prillaman 1995, 282).

Daniel's account was allowed for 350 lbs of beef supplied to Christopher Irvine for the Revolutionary army. Recorded Jul 22, 1782. (Bedford OB 6:362).

Daniel and James Brown were chosen for jury, with James Wright, Henry Jeter, Charles Tate, William Cavenaugh, Rowland Wheeler, John Mead, John Bozwell, William Hancock, Marmaduke Dallis and Edward Hors. Recorded Aug 1784. (Bedford OB 8:77).

Daniel was appointed surveyor of a road from Little Otter River to Fuquas Branch at Jos Fuqua's. Recorded Mar 1785. (Bedford OB 8:105).

Daniel Sr had 3 slaves 16+, 4 slaves under 16, 4 horses and 10 cattle. Personal Property Tax List of 1787, List B. (Schreiner-Yantis 1987, 201). He was visited on the same day as William J Brown. (Ibid, 215).

Daniel Jr had 2 slaves 16+, 5 slaves under 16, 4 horses and 11 cattle. Personal Property Tax List of 1787, List B. (Schreiner-Yantis 1987, 200). He was visited on the same day as Benjamin Blankenship and William Hancock. (Ibid, 213).

The Browns of Bedford County

Daniel Jr was conveyed a deed from Thomas Pleasants for 247A near Benjamin Cundiff, Jesse Grubb, John Hall and Daniel Brown. Signed and recorded Jul 27, 1789. (Bedford DB 8:217).

Daniel of Franklin County VA was conveyed a deed from Robert Clark and his wife Elizabeth for 550A known as Mount Pleasant. Witnesses were Samuel Clayton, John Thompson and Alexander Reid. Signed Nov 17, 1790 and recorded May 23, 1791. (Bedford DB 8:447).

Daniel conveyed a deed to John Newlon for 100A on the north branches of Staunton River near Mitchell. Witnesses were John Mitchell Jr, Banner Bentley, John Mitchell Sr and Samuel Banks. Signed Feb 7, 1793 and recorded Jul 22, 1793. (Bedford DB 9:213).

Daniel of Pittsylvania County VA conveyed a deed to Obediah Tate for 65A on Rockcastle Creek near Hancock and Gorden. Witnesses were Samuel Hancock, Robert Harper, William Brown and Thomas Payne. Signed Mar 14, 1795 and recorded Sep 23, 1805. (Bedford DB 11:1317).

Daniel and his wife Lucy conveyed a deed to Hinman Wooster for 169A on Goose Creek, near Gills Creek. Recorded 1795. (Bedford DB 10:43).

Daniel qualified as a lieutenant in a company of light infantry to the second battalion of the 91st regiment. Recorded Jun 1795. (Bedford OB 11:13).

Daniel was the son of Henry Brown and Alice Beard. He and his siblings and half-siblings were named in his father's will dated Jan 9, 1796. Daniel inherited land by the will. His father's will was recorded Jun 24, 1799. (Bedford WB 2:261).

Daniel's land was near Elizabeth Crum, Jesse Gribb, Benjamin Blankenship, Hinsman Wooster and Magdalene Hall. Recorded Feb 15, 1796. (Bedford PRO 1:110).

Daniel, Henry Brown, Abner Early and Roger Williams were appointed to view a road from the Otter River at Abner Early's to the main road at William Lee's. Recorded Dec 1796. (Bedford OB 11:137).

Daniel, father of Elizabeth, gave consent for her marriage to Benjamin Mead. Bond dated Dec 26, 1796. (Dennis 1989, 44).

Daniel's will named his children William, Daniel and Ann. He bequeathed his estate to his friend Anney Hastens, with reversion to his son William. Witnesses were David Hughes, Samuel Hancock, John Mitchell Jr and John Ayres. Will dated Jan 6, 1797 and recorded Feb 27, 1797. (Bedford WB 2:193). His will also mentioned grandson John Ashwell Brown, son of his daughter Ann, and grandson Shadrack, son of his son Daniel. (Merrill 1968, 7).

Daniel Sr's probate was opened and appraisers appointed. John Newlon qualified as executor. Recorded Feb 1797. (Bedford OB 11:147).

Daniel was chosen by Shadrack Brown to be his guardian. Daniel qualified and made bond. Recorded Feb 1797. (Bedford OB 11:151).

Daniel was appointed to view a road with Henry Brown, John Crumpacker and William Austin, from William Lee's and William Austin's to the academy near New London. Recorded Feb 1797. (Bedford OB 11:152).

Daniel's estate was appraised on Mar 1, 1797 by John Ayres, Samuel Hancock, Daniel Hughes and Benjamin Hatcher. Testator was James Steptoe. Recorded Jul 24, 1797. (Bedford WB 2:197).

Daniel had been granted land warrant #1844 for 608A, and had transferred 119A of it to Nathaniel Shrewsberry. The 119A on Beaverdam Creek were surveyed on Apr 15, 1797. (Bedford SR 2:548).

Daniel's slave Polly was acquited on the charge of murdering a female infant. Recorded Nov 30, 1797. (Bedford OB 11:235).

Daniel had been granted land warrant #1844 for 608A, and sold 422A of the land to Henry Brown. The survey for Henry Brown was dated Mar 27, 1798. (Bedford SR 2:549).

Daniel Brown, Hannah his wife, and their children Samuel, Joseph and Elizabeth presented a certificate of removal from Crooked Run Monthly Meeting to Goose Creek Monthly Meeting, The certificate was recorded in the Goose Creek minutes of Mar 31, 1798. (Wright 1993, 54).

The Browns of Bedford County

Daniel, with Henry Brown, Joseph White and Roger Williams, was ordered summoned to court to show cause why a road should not be established from Blackwater Road near Borams Creek, crossing the Otter River at Earlys Fork and into the road leading to New London. Recorded Feb 25, 1799. (Bedford OB 11:311).

Daniel witnessed a deed from William Brown of Albemarle County SC by his attorney William Fergis to Robert Lazenby for 100A on Fish Creek near Newland. Daniel Brown Sr had left the land to his son William Brown by will. Other witnesses were Edward Hore, Julius Saunders and Jeremiah Fergis. Signed Oct 7, 1799 and recorded Oct 27, 1799. (Bedford DB 11:266).

The overseers of the poor bound Jane Hill and John Hill to Daniel Brown. They were the children of Polly Hill. Recorded Oct 28, 1799. (Bedford OB 12:21).

Daniel was conveyed a deed of trust from Francis Wood for 50A at the mouth of Goose Creek near the widow Perrin, David Kesson, Samuel Burnett and Joseph Hackworth, as security for a debt owed Moses Fuqua. Witnesses were William Leftwich, James Leftwich and George Woody. Signed Nov 7, 1799 and recorded Jun 23, 1800. (Bedford DB 11:283).

Daniel Sr had 5 males 21+, 4 horses, and 5 slaves 12+. Personal Property Tax List of 1800, District 1. (Dorman 1963, 7:65).

Daniel Jr had 1 male 21+, and 1 horse. Personal Property Tax List of 1800, District 1. (Dorman 1963, 7:65).

Daniel was a miller, had 1 male 21+, and 1 horse. Personal Property Tax List of 1800, District 1. (Dorman 1963, 7:65).

Daniel's land was near Daniel Carson, Jessie Grubbs, Elisha Hall and Elijah Cundiff. Recorded Jan 1800. (Bedford PRO 1:61-64).

Daniel's land was near Robert Dalis, Elisha Cundiff, John Cundiff and the widow Hall, all near Goose Creek. Recorded Feb 1800. (Bedford PRO 1:111).

Daniel was the father of Lucy. He gave consent for her marriage to Jimmy Cundiff. Surety was Jesse Brown. Bond dated Mar 29, 1800.

17

The Browns of Bedford County

(Dennis 1989, 12).

Daniel's land was near Elisha Hurt and James Lisle. Recorded Apr 28, 1800. (Bedford PRO 1:840).

Daniel, with John Newlon, William Hackworth and Elijah Turner, was ordered to view a road at Brown Leftwich's Store near Goose Creek. Recorded Feb 23, 1801.(Bedford OB 12:146).

Daniel resigned as captain of a light company in the second battalion of the 91st regiment. Recorded Apr 7, 1801. (Bedford OB 12:163).

Daniel married Joicey Snider, daughter of Henry. Surety was William Snider. Bond dated Feb 12, 1802. (Hinshaw 1969, 6:884).

Daniel of Franklin County VA conveyed a deed to his brother Henry Brown for a 1/2 interest in 377 1/2 A left to them by their father's will. Witnesses were Thomas Clayton, Daniel Brown and Arthur Newman. Signed Sep 15, 1802 and recorded Jan 24, 1803. (Bedford DB 11:689).

Daniel of Franklin County VA conveyed a deed with Henry Brown and his wife Fanny to William Thorp for 336A on Orrix Creek, adjacent Robert White and Austin. Signed Jan 20, 1803 and recorded Jan 24, 1803. (Bedford DB 11:691).

Daniel married Polly Hancock, daughter of Samuel. Surety was James Leftwich. Bond dated Jul 15, 1803. Married by John Ayers on Jul 17, 1803. (Hinshaw 1969, 6:884). Daniel was married to Polly Hancock on Jul 17, 1803 in a ceremony by Rev John Ayers, a Methodist minister. (Bedford PRO 1:252).

Daniel was conveyed a deed from William Landsdown and his wife Trifene for 118A near William Mead. Witnesses were Thomas Alexander, James Branch and William Burnside. Signed Aug 29, 1803 and recorded Feb 27, 1804. (Bedford DB 11:954).

Daniel witnessed an indenture of trust from James Brown to John Watson for L39+ owed Watson by James Brown for 136A on both sides of Goose Creek, near Charles Caffey, Joseph Feezel, Jonathan Consolve and

The Browns of Bedford County

Frederick Gooldy. Other witnesses were Jacob Wade and William Burnside. Signed Aug 4, 1803 and recorded Jan 23, 1804. (Bedford DB 11:913).

Daniel's land was near Stephen Morlan and William Mead, all near Brown's mill pond and Goose Creek. Recorded Feb 6, 1804. (Bedford PRO 1:143).

Daniel of Franklin County VA had acted as trustee for a deed of trust from Francis Wood to Moses Fuqua, for 50A on Goose Creek. Francis Wood paid, and the deed was released. Witnesses were J Leftwich, John Claytor, Charles Swayn and Samuel Wilkes. Signed May 10, 1804 and recorded Jun 25, 1804. (Bedford DB 12:25).

Daniel of Pittsylvania County VA and his wife Lucy conveyed a deed to Thomas Stewart for 200A on the road from Hales Ford to the meadows of Goose Creek, near Lewis Turner, David Kerson, the old mill road and Hancock. Witnesses were Arthur Goolsley, Shadrack Brown, Wiatt Brown and Samuel Murphy. Signed Jun 24, 1805 and recorded Jul 22, 1805, (Bedford DB 11:1282). Lucy released dower Sep 2, 1805 and recorded same on Sep 28, 1807. (Bedford DB 12:250).

Daniel conveyed a deed of trust to trustee Josiah Auld for a debt of L308.4 owed William Davis Jr, executor of the estate of Samuel Davis, deceased. The deed of trust was secured by 25A on Goose Creek, with a merchant and saw mill. Signed Mar 25, 1806 and recorded Sep 2, 1806. (Bedford DB 12:122).

Daniel Jr was conveyed a deed by James Boyd and his wife Milley for 100A on Craddock Creek. Date of signature is unreadable. Recorded Sep 22, 1806. (Bedford DB 12:105).

Daniel was conveyed a deed from the heirs of Samuel Davis, deceased, for 4A on Goose Creek where mills had been erected, and for 20A on Goose Creek where the mill dam abutted, near Elisha Hurt. Witnesses were John Richards, John Richards Jr, Francis Gilpin, John Landon, John H Trent, John Hylton and Henry Davis. Signed 1808 and recorded Apr 25, 1808. (Bedford DB 12:335). Wives of the heirs released dower rights on Jun 30, 1809. (Bedford DB 13:431).

The Browns of Bedford County

Daniel and his wife Hannah conveyed a deed to Abijah Richards for 118A on the north side of Meads Road. Date of signature is unreadable. Recorded Jul 25, 1808. (Bedford DB 12:363).

Daniel and his wife Hannah conveyed a deed to William Dickerson for 4A on Goose Creek where the mills were located, and 20A with a mill dam on Goose Creek, near Elisha Hurt. Signed and recorded Jul 25,1808. (Bedford DB 12:371).

Daniel's land was near Elizabeth Homan, Solomon Hoard and Nicholas Overfelt. Recorded Feb 27, 1809. (Bedford PRO 1:194).

Daniel's land was near Polly Brown, William Leftwich and Jesse Leftwich. Recorded Mar 1809. (Bedford PRO 1:207).

Daniel's land was near Joel Hudson, John Hook, Jonathan Cundiff and Solomon Hardy. Recorded Mar 23, 1809. (Bedford PRO 1:202).

Daniel was present as a justice at August 1809 Court. (Bedford OB 15:120).

Daniel had 2 males 0-10, 1 male 26-45, 4 females 0-10, and 1 female 26-45. (U S Census of 1810).

Daniel of Franklin County VA was chosen by James English to be his guardian. Recorded Nov 1810. (Bedford OB 15:299).

Daniel Brown and John Bird were sureties for the marriage of Joel Chambers and Rhoda Brown, daughter of William and Saray. Bond dated Dec 9, 1811. (Hinshaw 1969, 6:891).

Daniel Brown and Henry Brown were bonded to insure Gov Barbour that John Claytor would perform the duties of sheriff. Recorded 1813. (Bedford DB 14:1, 2, 3).

Capt Daniel Brown was erroneously assessed for delinquent taxes on 50A for the years 1807, 1809, 1813 and 1814, but proved there was "no such land". Recorded 1816. (Bedford OB 17:237).

The Browns of Bedford County

Daniel was appointed to survey a road from the crossing at Staunton River at Anthonys Ford to the fork crossing at Greers Ford. Recorded Nov 1816. (Bedford OB 17:286).

Daniel died Apr 28, 1817, age 41 years, 7 months, 20 days. Gravestone inscription at the Thompson Brown Family Cemetery near New London Academy. (Daughters 1970, 81).

Daniel was appointed with William Kasey to view a road from Overfelt's to Thomas Stewart's. Recorded Jan 1819. (Bedford OB 17:562).

Daniel had 4 males 0-10, 1 male 45+, 2 females 0-10, 1 female 10-16, 1 female 16-26, and 1 female 26-45. (U S Census of 1820, Southern District, p 61).

Daniel was conveyed a deed from Julious Saunders for 49 1/2A on Craddock Creek, near Alexander Hudson, Daniel Brown, Polly Johnson, Jeremiah Furgerson and Judith Johnson. Signed Nov 19, 1821 and recorded Nov 26, 1821. (Bedford DB 17:147).

Daniel Brown and Robert Freeman and Freeman's wife Nancy conveyed a deed to Jeremiah Furguson for 49 1/2A on Craddock Creek, near Judith Johnson, Joseph Furguson and Polly Johnson. Signed Dec 26, 1821 and recorded Mar 25, 1823. (Bedford DB 17:188).

Daniel was a trustee with Chiswell Dabney for a deed of trust from Alexander Henry to Nathaniel Manson for a debt secured by 100A on Judith Creek. Signed May 9, 1822 and recorded May 27, 1822. (Bedford DB 17:219).

Daniel Brown and John Headen as trustees were conveyed a deed of trust from Mark Anthony for a debt owed Galt Bullock & Co, secured by slaves. Signed Jan 16, 1824 and recorded Jan 21, 1824. (Bedford DB 18:154).

Daniel married Lucy Moon. Surety was Thomas Steptoe. Bond dated Aug 31, 1824. They were married by John Ayers on Aug 30, 1824. (Hinshaw 1969, 6:884).

21

The Browns of Bedford County

Daniel was a justice of the peace for the Corporation of Lynchburg. He acknowledged that Henry Clark was party to a deed for land at the Otter River in Bedford County. Signed Dec 18, 1824 and recorded Dec 23, 1824. (Bedford DB 19:86).

Daniel was conveyed a deed from John Ferguson and wife Mary for 12A at Craddock Creek near Johnson and Saunders. Witnesses were James Ayers, William D Martin, Lewis Wingfield and Elijah Murdock. Signed Jun 10, 1825 and recorded Nov 27, 1825. (Bedford DB 20:123).

Daniel was conveyed a deed from John Ferguson and his wife Mary for 75A at Craddock Creek near James Barberry, Abner Anthony, William Dickinson, Jouleus Saunders and Amy Plymale. Witnesses were James Ayres, William D Martin, Lewis Wingfield and Elijah Murdock. Signed Jun 10, 1825 and recorded Jul 23, 1828. (Bedford DB 21:176).

Daniel was buried at the Thompson Brown Family Cemetery. His gravestone reads: Died Aug 10, 1826, age 25 years. (Daughters 1970, 81).

Daniel's executors Brown & Claytor, Henry Brown, and Samuel Hancock released the indenture of Isham Lawhorn for the tract where he lived. Signed Apr 28, 1828 and recorded May 26, 1828. (Bedford DB 21:43).

Daniel had 1 male 5-10, 2 males 10-15, 1 male 15-20, 1 male 60-70, 1 female 5-10, 2 females 15-20, 1 female 20-30, 1 female 50-60, and no slaves. He was near Archibald Overstreet and William Booth. (U S Census of 1830, p 167).

Daniel owned land at Craddock Creek, near Waggoner and Boyd, per a deed from Jonathan Cundiff and his wife Mary S to William Preston and his wife Susanna. Signed Apr 7, 1832 and recorded Apr 22, 1832. (Bedford DB 23:53).

Daniel was deceased. Permenus English qualified as administrator of his estate, and appraisors were appointed. His widow Joyce Brown was alloted her dower in his real and personal estate. Recorded Mar 1834. (Bedford OB 24:266).

Daniel's estate was inventoried and appraised by Lewis Wingfield, James M Headen and Lewis C Arthur, as requested by his executor Parmenas

The Browns of Bedford County

English. Value of the household and farm equipment was $367.10. Dated May 16, 1834 and recorded Aug 25, 1834. (Bedford WB 8:383).

Daniel married Eliza Ann Arnold. Surety was Mosby Arnold. Bond dated Oct 12, 1835. They were married by Robert J Carson on Oct 21, 1835. (Hinshaw 1969, 6:884).

DAVID

David was the son of James Brown and his wife Jinnet. He and his siblings were named in their father's will dated Dec 3, 1789, and recorded Jul 26, 1790. (Bedford WB 2:35).

David's land was near James Brown Jr, James Moorman, Buford, William Thomas, John Otey and James Petross. Recorded Feb 1796. (Bedford PRO 1:25).

David married Nancy Fuqua, daughter of Anna. Surety was John Fuqua. Bond dated Jan 22, 1803. (Hinshaw 1969, 6:884).

David was conveyed a deed from Ruel Shrewsbury and his wife Sally for 80A on Shockoe Creek, near Eads, Brian and Bramblett. Signed Sep 22, 1805 and recorded Sep 23, 1805. (Bedford DB 11:1330).

David had 2 males 0-10, 1 male 26-45, 1 female 0-10, and 1 female 16-26. (U S Census of 1810).

David was surety for the marriage of James T Brown and Polly Preas. Bond dated Apr 15, 1812. (Hinshaw 1969, 6:884).

David and his wife Nancy and Thomas Brown conveyed a deed to William O'Brian for 90 1/2A on Shockoe Creek, near Preas, David Brown and Thomas Brown. Witnesses were A P Agee, Robert Campbell and John Thomas. Signed Jun 22, 1812 and recorded same date. (Bedford DB 13:726).

David was conveyed a deed from William O'Brian and his wife Rhoda for 90 1/2A on Boreauger Creek. No signature date. Recorded Jan 25, 1813. (Bedford DB 13:791).

The Browns of Bedford County

David and his wife Nancy conveyed a deed to William O'Brian for 45A on Shockoe Creek, near William O'Brian and Christopher Clark. Signed Dec 16, 1814 and recorded Dec 26, 1814. (Bedford DB 14:243).

David and his wife Nancy conveyed a deed to the heirs of Jeremiah Hatcher Jr for 45 1/2A on Boreauger Creek. Witnesses were __rin Jeter and Pleasant Jeter. Signed Oct 10, 1816 and recorded Oct 28, 1816. (Bedford DB 15:95).

David had 2 males 0-10, 2 males 10-16, 1 male 26-45, 1 female 0-10, 1 female 10-16, and 1 female 26-45. (U S Census of 1820, Southern District, p 63).

David had been granted two land office warrants: 1) warrant #7081 was granted May 15, 1821 for 14A, and 2) warrant #7283 was granted May 3, 1822 for 70A on Shockoe Creek. His 64A were surveyed Jul 12, 1822. (Bedford SR 4:74).

David had been granted land office warrant #7081 May 15, 1821 for 14A on Boreauger Creek. 12 1/4A of that land was surveyed Jul 9, 1821. (Bedford SR 4:71). David was granted a patent for 12 1/4A on the waters of Boreauger Creek. Recorded Oct 10, 1822. (Bedford PB 71:285).

David was granted a patent for 64A on Shockoe Creek. Recorded Sep 13, 1823. (Bedford PB 72:430).

David Brown, James Williams, Seay Jones, Samuel Jones and James E Bouty were appointed to view a road from the main western road to Boreauger Road. Recorded Feb 16, 1824. (Bedford OB 19:103).

David and his wife Nancy conveyed a deed of trust to trustees Peachy R Gilmer and William R Porter for a debt owed Fleming and Edwin James & Co, secured by 1) land at Boreauger Creek near Hatcher and O'Briant, and 2) by 64A at Shockoe Creek near John Pointer, Matthias O'Bryant and the estate of Samuel Griffin. Trustees to auction the properties. Witnesses were Thomas Preston, Robert C Mitchell Jr and Charles Markle. Signed Jun 12, 1824 and recorded Jun 14, 1824. (Bedford DB 19:135).

David had been granted land office treasury warrant #7253 on May 13, 1822 for 70A. He had been assigned 1 3/4A of land office warrant #2418 for 100A on Shockoe Creek that was granted to Sampson Sharp on Mar 4,

The Browns of Bedford County

1822. He had a survey made of a total of 9 1/2A on Shockoe Creek, which included 7 3/4A of his own warrant, and 1 3/4A of Sharp's warrant. Survey dated Oct 2, 1824. (Bedford SR 4:79).

David conveyed a deed of trust to trustees William R Porter and Elliott Jeter for a debt owed William Fuqua, secured by farm animals, tools and household furniture. Witnesses were G A Wingfield, R C Mitchell and Edw Phillips. Signed Feb 4, 1826 and recorded Mar 27, 1826. (Bedford DB 19:376).

David was conveyed a deed from Christopher Clark for 80A at Boreauger Creek. Signed Nov 29, 1826 and recorded Jan 25, 1840. (Bedford DB 28:436).

David was conveyed a release of deed of trust from trustee James Bullock for 80A at Boreauger Creek which David had purchased from Christopher Clark on Nov 29, 1826. Witnesses to release were James Oney and Edward Phillips. Signed Nov 30, 1826 and recorded Sep 6, 1841. (Bedford DB 29:140).

David was a brother of John Brown. He and his siblings were named in John's pension application for service in the Revolutionary War. Reel R370 of M804, National Archives. (Wardell 1988, 1:116).

DOSHY

Doshy was born Sep 10, 1788, per her father's Arabia's pension application for service in the Revolutionary War. Reel R359 of M804, National Archives. (Wardell 1988, 1:116).

DOUGLAS

Douglas and his siblings were the children of Edward Brown, who qualified to be their guardian. Recorded May 1821. (Bedford OB 18:99).

DYCEY aka Dicey

Dycey and her husband Jesse Brown conveyed a deed to Samuel Oliphant for 175A on the south side of Beaverdam Creek. Recorded Sep 25, 1797. (Bedford DB 10:364).

Dicey Brown Heisel was the daughter of Aaron Brown, who had entered military service from Bedford County in 1776. She was named in his death report of 1836. Reel R358 of M804, National Archives. (Wardell 1988, 1:116).

EBENEZER aka Abenizer, Ebenizer

Ebenezer's 240A were surveyed. The land was on Falling Creek, near Weaver. Survey dated Mar 15, 1775. (Bedford SR 3:39). The land was transferred to George Hawkins. (Bedford SR 2:276).

Ebenezer's 100A were surveyed. The land was on the north side of Staunton River, near Kary Cowley and widow Brown. Survey dated Oct 18, 1793. (Bedford SR 2:607).

Ebenezer's 153A were surveyed. The land was on Falling Creek. Ebenezer was an assignee of John Hawkins, and Ebenezer assigned to Caniel Cowley. Survey dated Apr 8, 1794. (Bedford SR 2:605).

Ebenezer was granted a patent for 100A on the north side of Staunton River. Recorded Aug 22, 1794. (Bedford PB 30:355).

Ebenezer's 100A were processioned, with him present. Recorded Apr 1796. (Bedford PRO 1:41).

Ebenezer had 1 male 21+, and 2 horses. Personal Property Tax List of 1800, District 1. (Dorman 1963, 7: 66).

Ebenezer's land was near Anthony Wright and Sawny Brown, all south of Pates Road. Recorded Jul 20, 1800. (Bedford PRO 1:90).

Ebenezer and his wife Ruth conveyed a deed to Alexander Brown for 100A on the north side of the Staunton River, near Caniel Corley. Signed Sep 22, 1802 and recorded Sep 27, 1802. (Bedford DB 11:606).

Ebenezer was mentioned as a neighbor in a deed from Sawney Brown and his wife Vilet to Bartholomew Cary for 30A on Falling Creek near Matthew Pate. Signed Sep 24, 1802 and recorded Sep 27, 1802. (Bedford DB 11:616).

The Browns of Bedford County

Ebenezer was conveyed a deed from Sawney Brown and his wife Violett for 50A on both sides of Falling Creek, near William Pate. Signed and recorded Sep 27, 1802. (Bedford DB 11:617).

Ebenezer's land was processioned, with Sawny Brown present. Recorded Feb 2, 1803. (Bedford PRO 1:114).

Ebenezer was conveyed a deed from Bartholomew Currey and his wife Razene for 30A on both sides of Falling Creek. Signed and recorded Feb 22, 1804. (Bedford DB 11:927).

Ebenizer was surety for the marriage of Michael Vieley and Lucy Brown. Bond dated Sep 14, 1807. (Hinshaw 1969, 6:1009).

Ebenezer was surety for the marriage of James Bandy and Nancy Brown. Bond dated Apr 12, 1808. (Hinshaw 1969, 6:875).

Ebenezer and his wife Ruth of Montgomery County VA conveyed a deed to Matthew Pate and Edmund Pate for 50A on Falling Creek, near Alexander Brown and John Pate. Signed Oct 18, 1817 and recorded Oct 1817. (Bedford DB 15:254).

EDITH aka Edy, Eady, Edithe

Edy was the daughter of Thomas. She married Ancel Goodman in Bedford County in 1777. From John Craig's pension papers, Reel R676 of M804, National Archives. (Wardell 1988, 1:257).

Edy married John Grant. There was no surety. Bond dated Jul 19, 1794. (Dennis 1989, 25). Eady Brown married John Grant on Jul 22, 1794 in a ceremony by Rev John Ayers, a Methodist minister. (Bedford PRO 1:229).

Edith W Minor married John Brown. Surety was William Minor. Bond dated Feb 2, 1805. (Hinshaw 1969, 6:884).

Edith was the former Edith W Miner, and administratrix of Gabriel Miner. She and her husband John Brown were ordered summoned to show cause why they should not give William Miner counter security. Recorded Dec 24, 1805. (Bedford OB 13:293).

The Browns of Bedford County

Edith was the former Edithe Minor, widow of Gabriel Minor. She was returned her allotment of dower in his estate. Recorded Mar 1814. (Bedford OB 17:332).

Edith W with her husband John R conveyed a deed of trust to trustee Lodowick McDaniel for debt owed Tubal Early, secured by 214A on Echols Creek. Witnesses were Adam Elliott, V K Leftwich and John T Sale. Signed Dec 10, 1835 and recorded May 31, 1836. (Bedford DB 25:299).

Edith W with her husband John R conveyed a deed to Joseph A Brown for 214A at Echols Creek, near Walker, Joel Early and Mrs Early. The land had been conveyed to John R Brown by Tubal Early on Dec 10, 1835. Signed and recorded Aug 24, 1838. (Bedford DB 27:241).

Edith was the wife of John. The case brought by administrator of Gabriel Minor was dismissed. Recorded Nov 7, 1838. (Bedford Chancery OB 1:299).

EDWARD

Edward witnessed a deed from John Simmons to Sheldrake Brown for 100A on Mollys Creek near James Millwood, Shildrake Brown and Josias Bullock. Other witnesses were Richard Stith, John fitchPatrick, R Brown and Vineyard Brown. Signed Feb 5, 1778 and recorded Aug 28, 1780. (Bedford DB 7:18).

Edward witnessed a deed from James Milwood and his wife Anne to William Brown for 100A near Thomas Hayth, William Brown, Shildrake Brown, John Simmons and Ruffin. Other witnesses were Sheldrake Brown, R Brown and Temperence Brown. Signed Apr 6, 1779 and recorded Oct 25, 1779. (Bedford DB6:362).

Edward was appointed by the overseers of the poor to have the child Wiatt Baber bound to him. Recorded May 1819. (Bedford OB 17:618).

Edward qualified as guardian of Sarah Ann, Elizabeth, Clara, Edward, Thomas and Douglas Brown, who were his own children. Recorded May1821. (Bedford OB 18:99).

Edward Brown of Campbell County VA was the brother of Henry Brown,

The Browns of Bedford County

who entered military service from Bedford County in 1779. Edward was named in Henry's pension application for service in the Revolutionary War. Reel R365 of M804, National Archives. (Wardell 1988, 1:118).

ELEANOR

Eleanor Custis Lewis Carter was the wife of Henry Brown Jr, son of Henry Brown of Ivy Hill. (Merrill 1968, chart A).

E C L Carter married Henry Brown Jr. They were married by Rev William S Reid in Mar 1823, as recorded in the Marriage Book of Lynchburg. (Hinshaw 1969, 6:884).

ELIZA

Eliza and her siblings were named in the division of their father Reuben's slaves. Division was made May 25, 1835 and recorded Jun 22, 1835. (Bedford WB 9:47).

Eliza A and William H Brown were orphans of Reuben Brown. Betsy Brown was qualifed as their guardian. Recorded 1834. (Bedford OB 25:125). They chose her as their guardian. John S Brown and Spotswood Brown gave security bonds. Recorded Aug 1835. (Bedford OB 25:125).

Eliza Ann Arnold married Daniel Brown. Surety was Mosby Arnold. Bond dated Oct 12, 1835. They were married by Robert J Carson on Oct 21, 1835. (Hinshaw 1969, 6:884) .

Eliza and her siblings, the heirs and legatees of Reuben S Brown, deceased, were conveyed a deed from William C Leftwich for 51A at Elk Creek, near Howards Branch. Signed and recorded May 1, 1837. (Bedford DB 26:151).

ELIZABETH aka Betsy, Betsey, Betty, Eliza

Elizabeth was born Jul 20, 1762, the daughter of Henry and Alce Brown. She and her siblings were named when their parent's marriage was recorded Jan 25, 1773. (Bedford DB 4:455).

The Browns of Bedford County

Elizabeth Dooley Brown was the wife of Arabia Brown. She and their children were named in his pension application for service in the Revolutionary War. She was born in 1757, and married Arabia in May 1778. Reel R359 of M804, National Archives. (Wardell 1988, 1:116).

Elizabeth and her husband Raba conveyed a deed to Ansalom Goodman for 150A on Little Otter River near John Galloway. Witnesses were William French, Hanner Hanes and Elebeth Eitson. Signed Aug 27, 1786 and recorded Apr 23, 1787. (Bedford DB 8:71).

Elizabeth married William Ferguson. She was the daughter of William Brown, who gave consent. Surety was Jeremiah Ferguson. Bond dated Mar 7, 1787. (Dennis 1989, 21).

Betty married William King. Betty and Zachariah Brown gave consent. Surety was James King. Bond dated Feb 26, 1788. (Dennis 1989, 38).

Elizabeth was named as Elizabeth Jones in the will of her father James, dated Dec 3, 1789. His granddaughters Rebekah Jones and Peggy Jones were also named. The will was recorded Jul 26, 1790. (Bedford WB 2:35).

Elizabeth Best married George Thomas Brown. She was the daughter of Druzilla, who gave consent. Surety was Levi Best. Bond dated Nov 1792. (Dennis 1989, 5). Elizabeth Best married George Thomas Brown. She was the daughter of Druzilla, who gave consent dated Nov 24, 1792. Levi Best was surety. They were married by John Ayers on Dec 13, 1792. (Hinshaw 1969, 6:884).

Elizabeth Best married George Brown on Dec 13, 1792 in a ceremony by Rev John Ayers, a Methodist minister. (Bedford PRO 1:226).

Elizabeth married Israel Jarred. Surety was Henry Preas. Bond dated Jan 27, 1794. (Dennis 1989, 36).

Elizabeth Woody married James Brown. She was the daughter of William, who gave consent. Surety was James Brown Jr. Bond dated May 13, 1794. (Dennis 1989, 10). They were married by James Turner on May 15, 1794. (Bedford PRO 1:230).

Elizabeth married John Walker. Elizabeth was "of full age". Surety was Thomas Andrews. Bond dated Dec 29, 1794. (Dennis 1989, 74). Elizabeth was the daughter of Henry Brown and Alice Beard. (Merrill, chart A).

Elizabeth and her husband James and Sarah Brown conveyed a deed to John Reese for 110A on the waters of Little Otter River near Galloway. Signed Jun 22, 1795 and recorded Jun 27, 1795. (Bedford DB 9:541).

Elizabeth Eckovey married Rhodam Brown. She was the daughter of Mathias. Surety was John James. Bond dated Jun 24, 1795. (Hinshaw: Encyclopedia, 6:884). Bond dated Aug 24, 1795. (Dennis 1989, 6).

Elizabeth was named in the will of her husband Joseph. Their children were Jesse Dent, Rhodham, Joseph, Hezekiah, Orpah, Sarah and Margaret. Joseph's will was dated Aug 22, 1795 and recorded Oct 26, 1795. (Bedford WB 2:163).

Elizabeth was the daughter of Henry Brown and Alice Beard. She and her siblings and half-siblings were named in their father's will dated Jan 9, 1796. She inherited furniture by the will. His will was recorded Jun 24, 1799. (Bedford WB 2:261).

Elizabeth married Benjamin Mead. She was the daughter of Daniel, who gave consent. Surety was John Leftwich. Bond dated Dec 26, 1796. (Dennis 1989, 44). They were married by Alderson Weekes on Dec 29, 1796. (Bedford PRO 1:236).

Elizabeth and her husband Jennings conveyed a deed to Hezekiah Meador for 110A at the mouth of Beaverdam Creek, near Stephen Goggins, Spradling, James Board, Elijah Dowell, Jumping Run and the Staunton River. Signed Sep 23, 1797 and recorded Sep 25, 1797. (Bedford DB 10:359).

Elizabeth and her siblings were the children of Daniel and Hannah Brown who presented a certificate of removal from Crooked Run Monthly Meeting to Goose Creek Monthly Meeting. Recorded in the Goose Creek minutes of Mar 31, 1798. (Wright 1993, 54).

The Browns of Bedford County

Elizabeth and her husband James conveyed a deed to his brothers Larking Brown and John Brown, the sons of Linah Brown, for 42A on Meadows Creek. Signed and recorded Jun 25, 1798. (Bedford DB 10:485).

Elizabeth and her husband James conveyed a deed to his sister Sarah Brown for 8A on Meadows Creek. Signed and recorded Jun 25, 1798. (Bedford DB 10:486).

Elizabeth and her husband William, with James Payne and his wife Anny, conveyed a deed to Charles Anthony for 150A near Burr Barton, Tommy Wright, John Wright, the Pates Road, James Seal and William Brown. Witnesses were Robert Nimmo, Joseph Johnson, Jesse Johnson and James Johnson. Signed Aug 21, 1798 and recorded Sep 24, 1798. (Bedford DB 11:181).

Elizabeth had 1 white male 21+ and 3 horses. Personal Property Tax List of 1800, District 1. (Dorman 1963, 7;65).

Elizabeth and her husband Rhodham conveyed a deed to Isaac James for 92 1/2A on the branches of Beaverdam Creek, near Cavender. Witnesses were Lawrence James, Joseph Brown and Hezekiah Brown. Signed Mar 14, 1800 and recorded Apr 28, 1800. (Bedford DB 11:205).

Betsey McGehee married Reuben Brown. Surety was David Saunders. Bond dated Mar 25, 1800. (Dennis 1989, 5). They were married by James Mitchell on Mar 27, 1800. (Bedford PRO 1:246).

Elizabeth Payne married Jesse Brown. She was the daughter of Thomas. Surety was Dabney Grubb. Bond dated Nov 1, 1801. (Hinshaw 1969, 6:884).

Elizabeth Peryire married Jesse Brown on Nov 12, 1801 in a ceremony by Rev John Ayers, a Methodist minister. (Bedford PRO 1:248).

Elizabeth and her husband James and his mother Sarah Brown conveyed a deed to Thomas Scruggs for land on the Little Otter River near Charles Marckel, Thomas, Mary Ann Brown, Sally Brown, John Fisher and Benjamin Rice. Signed Oct 1803 and recorded Jan 23, 1804. (Bedford DB 11:909).

The Browns of Bedford County

Betsey and her husband James conveyed a deed to Adam Boyer for 97A on Goose Creek, near Hobbs, Bramblett, Callaway and Reuel Shewsbury. Signed Sep 20, 1804 and recorded same date. (Bedford DB 11:1171).

Elizabeth and her husband Thomas conveyed a deed to James Brown Jr for 70A on the Little Otter River, near John Otey, Joseph Fuqua and William R Jones. Witnesses were Aaron Fuqua, John Wright and Thomas Milller. Signed Sep 1, 1805 and recorded Sep 23, 1805. (DB 11:1300).

Elizabeth and her husband James conveyed a deed to Thomas Brown for a tract on the waters of Shockoe Creek, near Shrewsbury, Brian, Simmons and Hobbs. Witnesses were Thomas Miller, Aaron Fuqua and James Miller. Signed Sep 21, 1805 and recorded Sep 23, 1805. (DB 11:1299).

Elizabeth and her husband William conveyed a deed to John Blankenship for 116A on the head branches of Kates Creek. Witnesses were William Halladay, William Maddera and John Dent. Signed Jan 15, 1796 and recorded Feb 24, 1806. (Bedford DB 12:184).

Betsey married Jordan Hundley. She was the daughter of Aaron Brown. Surety was William Corley. Bond dated Oct 24, 1806. They were married by Richard Pope on Oct 27, 1806. (Hinshaw 1969, 6:937). Betsy Brown and Jordan Hunley were married by Richard Pope on Oct 29, 1806. (Bedford PRO 1:259).

Elizabeth Thornhill married Walker Brown. She was the daughter of William. Surety was Jacob Wade. Bond dated Feb 26, 1809. They were married by William Leftwich. (Hinshaw 1969, 6:884). Elizabeth Thornhill and Walker Brown were married by William Leftwich in Nov 1790. (Bedford PRO 1:264).

Elizabeth had 1 male 16-26. (U S Census of 1810).

Elizabeth married John Bird. Surety was William Brown. Bond dated Nov 9, 1810. They were married by John Ayers on Nov 15, 1810 (sic). (Hinshaw 1969, 6:879). They were married on Nov 13, 1810 in a ceremony by Rev John Ayers, a Methodist minister. (Bedford PRO 1:266).

The Browns of Bedford County

Elizabeth conveyed a deed to William Miller for 200A on Stony Fork of Goose Creek. Witnesses were N Shrewsbury, Israel Jared, William Cavanaugh and Jesse Cadwallader. Signed and recorded Feb 25, 1811. (Bedford DB 13:582).

Elizabeth Hurt married William H Brown. Surety was A I Agee. Bond dated Sep 27,1819. (Hinshaw 1969, 6:884).

Betsey and her husband Reuben conveyed a deed to John Lowry for 168A on Big Otter River, near William Lowry, William Boothe and Jesse Noell. Witnesses were John L Cobbs, Thomas Kerr and Robert Steptoe. Signed Sep 30, 1819 and recorded Oct 25, 1819. (Bedford DB 16:58).

Elizabeth and her siblings were the children of Edward Brown, who qualified to be their guardian. Recorded May 1821. (Bedford OB 18:99).

Betty, the former Betty McGhee, with her husband Reubin S and other heirs of Samuel McGhee, deceased, conveyed a deed to John Ryan for 70A on Little Otter River, near Lindsey Stinnett, Thomas Powell, Thomas Edgars and David Saunders. Witnesses were Daniel Hoofman, John Flower, Thomas Otey, Alexander Burton and William Cook. Signed Nov 20, 1822 and recorded Aug 9, 1823. (Bedford DB 18:229).

Betsy McGhee Brown and her husband Reuben S and other McGhee heirs conveyed a deed for land at the north side of Little Otter River to William McGhee. Betsy's and Reuben's signature were signed by their attorney in fact, Thomas Saunders. Signed Jan 26, 1829 and recorded Mar 25, 1833. (Bedford DB 23:306).

Elizabeth married Jonas Jones. She was the daughter of John. Bond dated Apr 2, 1832. They were married by William Harris on Apr 5, 1832. (Hinshaw 1969, 6:943).

Betsy Brown Jones was a sister of John Brown. She and her siblings were named in his pension application for service in the Revolutionary War. Reel R370 of M804, National Archives. (Wardell 1988, 1:116).

Elizabeth and her husband Jesse conveyed a deed to John Kasey Jr for 65 3/4A on Rockcastle Creek, near Thomas Stewart. Recorded 1834. (Bedford DB 24:88).

The Browns of Bedford County

Betsy was qualified as the guardian of the orphans of Reuben S Brown. Recorded 1834. (Bedford OB 25:125).

Betsey was a purchaser at the slave auction conducted by the administrators of Reuben S Brown. Auction was Jan 15, 1835 and recorded Sep 26, 1836. (Bedford WB 9:186).

Elizabeth, the widow of Reuben S, deceased, was alloted her dower in his slaves, and divided the slaves among his children. Recorded Mar 1835. (Bedford OB 25:62).

Elizabeth Brown Hunly was the daughter of Aaron, who had entered military service from Bedford County in 1776. She was named in his death report of 1836. Reel R358 of M804, National Archives. (Wardell 1988, 1:116).

Elizabeth, the widow of Reuben S Brown, was given a life estate in 1/3 of his slaves, with the remainder of the slaves divided among children John S, Granville S, Harriet, Matilda C, Spotswood D, William, Eliza and Mary E. Division made May 25, 1835 and recorded Jun 2, 1835 (sic). (Bedford WB 9:47).

Elizabeth Jane Ewing married Spotswood Brown. She was the daughter of Nancy. Surety was Richard Hobson Jr. Bond dated Nov 16, 1835. (Hinshaw 1969, 6:884).

Elizabeth was the mother of Harriett Brown who married Capt Thomas Robertson. Surety was William H Brown. Bond dated Jan 3, 1838. (Ricks 1939, 135).

Elizabeth J and her husband Spotswood conveyed a deed to Littleberry Carter for 214 1/4A at Ewings Creek, Lot 4, from the estate of her father Mitchell Ewing. Signed Nov 13, 1839 and recorded Nov 23, 1839. (Bedford DB 28:203).

Elizabeth had 1 male 5-10, 2 males 20-30, 2 females 10-15, 1 female 15-20, and 1 female 50-60. She was near James C Robinson and Anderson N Everitt. (U S Census of 1840, p 23).

The Browns of Bedford County

Elizabeth, deceased, had been the wife of Aaron Allred. They were named in a suit brought by John Brown, Thomas M Brown and William H Brown, deceased, by his administrator William Hurt. The case was dismissed. Recorded Oct 5, 1840. (Bedford Chancery OB 1:422).

ELVIRA

Elvira and her husband Sanford Brown Jr, with Lyman Brown and his wife Frances, and Roswell Brown of Sandsfield in Berkshire County MA, conveyed a deed to Charles B Reynolds for 924A on the James River between the Rockbridge County line and the foot of Irish Falls near Balcony Falls and Snow Creek. Signed Jul 6, 1829 and recorded Mar 9, 1830. (Bedford DB 22:75).

EMILY

Emily Callaway married Dr Daniel Brown on Aug 4, 1781. She was born in 1759, the daughter of Col James Callaway and Sarah Tate, and died in 1831. (Ackerly 1930, 296).

ENOCH

Enoch was conveyed a power of attorney from his father Marmaduke Brown to sell all the goods and chattels left to Marmaduke by his father George Brown of Stafford County VA. Witnesses were Jacob White and Charles Gwatkins. Signed Apr 20, 1805 and recorded Sep 23, 1805. (Bedford DB 11:1309).

Enoch of Culpepper County VA was given a power of attorney by Sarah Brown to collect rents and debts, and to sell her life estate in land that had been leased in 1776 to Marmaduke Brown and his wife Sarah by John Davies. Signed Dec 1812 and recorded Jan 25, 1813. (Bedford DB 13:663).

ESTHER

Esther was conveyed a deed from Henry Brown and his wife Alice for 54A on Lick Run, a branch of Roanoke River. Recorded Aug 20, 1760 at Augusta County VA in DB 8:408. (Chalkley 1989, 363).

The Browns of Bedford County

ETHELRED

Ethelred married Anna Hopkins, daughter of Price. Ethelred was the son of John. Surety was Tilson A Pullen. Bond dated Feb 22, 1825. (Hinshaw 1969, 6:884).

Ethelred was conveyed a deed from John Walden and his wife Patsy for 119 3/4A at Stony Fork near Johnson and Dickinson. Signed Oct 28, 1829 and recorded Nov 8, 1831. (Bedford DB 22:475).

Ethelred had 1 male 40-50, 2 females 0-5, 1 female 20-30, and no slaves. He was near Jesse Stanley and Dabney Martin. (U S Census of 1830, p 142).

Ethelred and his wife Ann of Franklin County VA conveyed a deed of trust to trustees Pleasant Preston and George Davis for John T Davis, secured by 119 3/4A on Stony Fork near John Walden, Thomas Johnson and Pleasant Dickinson. Signed Oct 29, 1831 and recorded Nov 8, 1831. (Bedford DB 22:474).

Trustees, acting for Ethelred Brown and his wife Ann, conveyed a deed to John T Davis for 119 3/4A at Stony Fork. Signed Oct 22, 1832 and recorded Dec 24, 1832. (Bedford DB 23:205).

FRANCES aka Fanny

Fanny Thompson married Henry Brown. She was the daughter of John, who gave consent. Surety was John Patrick. Bond dated Jan 7, 1792. They were married by James Mitchell on Jan 10, 1792. (Hinshaw 1969, 6:884). The marriage was recorded. (Bedford PRO 1:225).

Frances Bruce married Rhodham T Brown. She was the daughter of David. Surety was William Bruce. Bond dated Jan 17, 1801. (Hinshaw 1969, 6:884). They were married by Henry Hatcher on Jan 20, 1801. (Bedford PRO 1:248).

Fanny and her husband Henry and Daniel Brown conveyed a deed to William Thorp for 336A on Orrix Creek, near Robert White and Austin. Signed Jan 20, 1803 and recorded Jan 24, 1803. (Bedford DB 11:691).

The Browns of Bedford County

Fanny and her husband Henry conveyed a deed to Henry Crumpton for 43A on Johnson Creek at the top of Johnson Mountain. Signed Jun 10, 1818 and recorded May 27, 1820. (Bedford DB 16:184).

Fanny and her husband Henry conveyed a deed to James Boatright for 142A on Johnson Creek, near Henry Crumpton and David Crumpton. Signed May 20, 1820 and recorded May 27, 1820. (Bedford DB 16:29).

Frances and her husband Henry conveyed a deed to Henry Crumpton for 43A at Johnsons Creek, at the top of Johnsons Mountain. Signed May 25, 1820 and recorded May 27, 1820. (Bedford DB 16:128).

Frances was buried at the Thompson Brown Family Cemetery. Her gravestone reads: Jun 1, 1775-Aug 11, 1822. (Daughters 1970, 81).

Frances and her husband Lyman Brown, and Sanford Brown Jr and his wife Elvira, and Roswell Brown of Sandsfield in Berkshire County MA, conveyed a deed to Charles B Reynolds for 924A on the James River between the Rockbridge County line and the foot of Irish Falls, near Balcony Falls and Snow Creek. Signed Jul 6, 1829 and recorded Mar 9, 1830. (Bedford DB 22:75)

Frances married Edwin Robinson. She was the daughter of Henry. Surety was Alexander Irvine. Bond dated Oct 5, 1836. They were married by William S Reid on Oct 6, 1836. (Hinshaw 1969, 6:986).

Frances and her siblings were named in their father Henry's will dated Jan 6, 1838. She was bequeathed 65 shares in the Bank of Virginia. His will was recorded Sep 25, 1841. (Bedford WB 10:392).

FRANCIS

Francis was exonerated from erroneously assessed delinquent taxes on 142A, because the report was "improperly returned by the sheriff". Recorded 1816. (Bedford OB 17:237).

The Browns of Bedford County

GARRETT

Garrett was the son of Joycy. He married Irenia Plymale, daughter of Thomas. Surety was Wyatt Truman. Bond dated Oct 17, 1838. They were married by William Leftwich on Oct 26, 1838. (Hinshaw 1969, 6:884).

GEORGE

George married Sarah Brown, the daughter of Sarah Brown, who gave consent. Surety was Julius Jones. Bond dated Nov 24, 1783. (Dennis: 1989, 10).

George had 2 horses. Personal Property Tax List of 1787, List B. (Schreiner-Yantis 1987, 200). He was visited the same day as Sarah Brown and William Hurt. (Ibid, 214).

George Thomas Brown married Elizabeth Best, daughter of Druzilla, who gave consent. Surety was Levi Best. Bond dated Nov 1792. (Dennis 1989, 5). They were married on Dec 13, 1792 by Rev John Ayers, a Methodist minister. (Bedford PRO 1:226).

George had 1 male 21+, and 1 horse. Personal Property Tax List of 1800. (Dorman 1963, 7:66).

George's widow and relict Sarah conveyed a deed to Araba Brown of Caldwell County KY for her 1/3 interest in the estate of said George Brown in Jefferson County TN. Witness was J Steptoe Jr. Signed and recorded Apr 2, 1814. (Bedford DB 13:841).

George's 120A were erroneously assessed for delinquent taxes in his name for years 1784, 1785, 1789 and 1790, but he was exonerated when no records could be found in the clerk's office. Recorded Aug 1816. (Bedford OB 17:234).

George was the son of Aaron, who had entered military service from Bedford County in 1836. He was named in Aaron's death report of 1836. Reel R358 of M804, National Archives. (Wardell 1988, 1:116).

The Browns of Bedford County

GRANVILLE

Dr Granville L Brown was born Sep 10, 1813 in Bedford County, and died in 1876. He married Elizabeth Callaway, the daughter of John Callan Callaway and Lucinda Saunders. (Ackerly 1930, 311).

Granville S made a trip to Philadelphia in the fall of 1834. Those expenses were paid from the estate of Reuben S Brown, as shown in an accounting of the estate made Sep 1, 1836 and recorded Oct 26, 1836. (Bedford WB 9:199).

Granville S was the son of Reuben S Brown. He and his siblings were named in the division of their father's slaves. Division was made May 25, 1835 and recorded Jun 22, 1835. (Bedford WB 9:47).

Granville and his siblings, the heirs and legatees of Reuben S Brown, deceased, were conveyed a deed from William C Leftwich for 51A at Elk Creek, near Howards Branch. Signed and recorded May 1, 1837. (Bedford DB 26:151).

Granville L was conveyed a deed from James Leftwich and his wife Mary E, for all their interest in the estate of Reubin S Brown, deceased. Signed and recorded Jan 24, 1839. (Bedford DB 27:375).

HANNAH

Hannah Mitchell and Shadrack Brown were married by James Mitchell on Oct 18, 1787. (Bedford PRO 1:219).

Hannah was the daughter of Henry Brown and Ann Richardson, his first wife. (Merrill 1968, 11). She and her siblings and half-siblings were named in their father's will dated Jan 3, 1796. She inherited 10 shillings by the will. His will was recorded Jun 24, 1799. (Bedford WB 2:261).

Hannah and her husband Daniel, and their children Samuel, Joseph and Elizabeth, presented a certificate of removal from Crooked Run Monthly Meeting to Goose Creek Monthly Meeting. Recorded in the Goose Creek minutes of Mar 31, 1798. (Wright 1993, 54)

The Browns of Bedford County

Hannah and her husband Daniel conveyed a deed to Abijah Richards for 100A on the north side of Meads Road. Date of signature is unreadable. Recorded Jul 25, 1808. (Bedford DB 12:363).

Hannah and her husband Daniel conveyed a deed to William Dickerson for 4A with a mill on Goose Creek where the mills were, and for 20A with the mill dam on Goose Creek near Elisha Hurt. Signed and recorded Jul 25, 1808. (Bedford DB 12:371).

HARMON

Harmon was the son of Claiborn Brown and his wife Sarah Harmon. He was named in his father's pension application for service in the Revolutionary War. Reel R361 of M804, National Archives. (Wardell 1988, 1:118).

HARRIETT

Harriett was the daughter of Reuben S. She and her siblings were named in the division of her father's slaves. Division was made May 25, 1835 and recorded Jun 22, 1835. (Bedford WB 9:47).

Harriett married Thomas Robinson. Surety was William H Brown. Bond dated Jan 3, 1838. (Hinshaw 1969, 6:986).

HENRY

Henry was born 1712 in New Jersey, and died Nov 14, 1798. (Merrill 1968, 3). His wives were Ann Richardson, whom he married 1735 in New Jersey, and Alice Beard, whom he married 1757 in Bedford County. (Ibid, 11). His home was Ivy Hill, which he built with money awarded him for killing an Indian chief. (Ibid, 10).

Henry Jr was the son of Henry Sr, who had come from New Jersey and settled on the Roanoke River by 1742. Henry Jr married Alice Beard and lived in Bedford County VA from the time of his father's death in 1757. His brother was Daniel Brown of Bedford County VA. (Kegley 1993, 199). (For more about Henry Sr, see Chalkley 1989, 3:313, and Merrill 1968, 1-10).

Henry Jr was granted a patent for 200A on the south side of Goose Creek.

The Browns of Bedford County

Recorded on Aug 10, 1756 in Land Grants Book 34:125. (Kegley 1993, 109).

Henry Brown and Alce Beard were married Feb 20, 1757 in Bedford County "by parson of Bedford County". Their children were Lettice, born Dec 3, 1757; Henry, born Aug 10, 1760; Elizabeth, born Jul 20, 1762; Alce, born Nov 10, 1764; Samuel, born Nov 10, 1766; and Daniel, born Dec 18, 1770. Recorded Jan 25, 1773. (Bedford DB 4:455).

Henry and his wife Alice were conveyed a deed from Thomas Brown for 87A on Goose Creek. Recorded 1760 in Augusta County VA DB 8:413. (Kegley 1993, 298).

Henry was the son of Henry and Alce Brown. He was born Aug 10, 1760. He and his siblings were named when their parents' marriage was recorded Jan 25, 1773. (Bedford DB 4:455).

Henry Sr was born Aug 10, 1760 at Bedford County, and entered military service from there. In 1832 he applied as Henry Sr for a pension for service in the Revolutionary War. He died in 1841. Reel R365 of M804, National Archives. (Wardell 1988, 1:118). Henry was drafted as a militia man to fight the British who had invaded Portsmouth VA. He guarded British prisoners, served in NC with Col Washington's corps of light horse, and was wounded at the battle of Guilford. See National Archives, pension file S-8098. (Merrill 1968, 161).

Henry was buried at the Thompson Brown Family Cemetery. His gravestone reads: Aug 10, 1760 - Aug 13, 1841. (Daughters 1970, 81).

Henry and his wife Alice of Bedford County VA conveyed a deed to Thomas Walker for 200A on Goose Creek. Recorded Aug 20, 1760 at Augusta County VA DB 8:403. (Chalkley 1989, 3:362).

Henry's wife Alice of Bedford County conveyed a deed to Dr Thomas Walker for land in Augusta County VA. Recorded Aug 20, 1760 in Augusta County VA court records. (Kegley 1993, 296).

Henry was conveyed a deed from William Irvine and his wife Elizabeth for 180A on the north side of Otter River including the mouth of Gladys Creek and Lick Run. The land had been surveyed for William Callaway, patent bearing date Jun 1, 1750. Recorded Jan 1, 1761. (Bedford DB A-1:320).

The Browns of Bedford County

Henry witnessed a deed from Phillip Preston and wife his Mary to John Ward for 200A on the south side of Otter River and on both sides of Island Creek, near Womack and Thomas Halsey. Other witnesses were George Grundy and Robert Allen. Recorded Jan 25, 1763. (Bedford DB 2:138).

Henry was ordered to handle the estate of John Nance. Recorded 1763. (Bedford OB 3:24).

Henry was conveyed a deed from James French for 100A at the head of the south fork of Mollys Creek near Gallaway. Chain of title: this land was part of 3,150A patented by John Ornsby, deeded successively to John Fitzpatrick, to John Simmons, to James French. Recorded Mar 18, 1767. (Bedford DB 3:100).

Henry was conveyed a deed from Obediah Woodson for 190A on both sides of Sick Run, near Newline. Witnesses were __Callaway Jr, John Smith, Moses Fuqua, David Walker and James Talbot. Signed Oct 24, 1769 and recorded same date. (Bedford DB 3:365).

Henry's marriage was proved. Recorded 1772. (Bedford OB 5:38).

Henry was the guardian of John Vance. Recorded 1775. (Bedford OB 6:119).

Henry entered military service from Bedford County. He was born Oct 25, 1759 at Prince George County VA. Pension file states that at age 72 in Campbell County VA he received a pension for service in the Revolutionary War. He married Elizabeth Jones on Aug 29, 1827 in Buckingham County, VA. His brother was Edward Brown of Campbell County VA. Reel R365 of M804, National Archives. (Wardell 1988, 1:118).

Henry witnessed a deed for 400A on Mollys Creek from Thomas Hayth et al to Sheldrake Brown and Robert Brown. Other witnesses were William Brown and Sheldrake Brown Jr. Recorded Jul 19, 1777. (Bedford DB 5:498).

Henry and his wife Alice conveyed a deed to Francis Thorp for 126A on both sides of Buffalo Creek, a branch of Otter River, patented by John Wainwright. Signed Jun 28, 1779 and recorded Aug 9, 1779. (Bedford DB6:234).

The Browns of Bedford County

Henry witnessed a deed from James Chastine to Lettice Brown for 50A on the south side of Otter River, near Thomas Robinson. Other witnesses were Francis Burks and Samuel Adams. Signed Sep 18, 1779 and recorded same date. (Bedford DB 6:310).

Henry filed a claim for supplies to Christopher Irvine for the Revolutionary army. He supplied 300 lbs beef, 4 diets, 2 pecks corn and 9 bundles fodder. Recorded Dec 23, 1782. (Bedford OB 7:17).

Henry was surety for the marriage of Jesse Witt and Aley Brown. Bond dated May 6, 1786. (Dennis 1989, 77).

Henry Sr had 1 male 16-23, 2 horses and 9 cattle. Personal Property Tax List of 1787, List B. (Schreiner-Yantis 1987, 201). He was visited on the same day as Henry Jr. (Ibid, 215).

Henry Jr had 1 slave 16+ and 5 horses. Personal Property Tax List of 1787, List B. (Schreiner-Yantis 1987, 201). He was visited on the same day as Henry Sr. (Ibid, p 215).

Henry was conveyed a deed from the guardian of Abner Early for 147A patented by Aaron Burlesson. Witnesses were Thomas Holt, William Callaway, Matthew Pate and John Pate. Signed Oct 18, 1790 and recorded Oct 25, 1790. (Bedford DB 8:337).

Henry was conveyed a deed from the guardian of Abner Early for 195A on the branches of the Little Otter River near Phelps. Witnesses were Thomas Holt, William Callaway, Matthew Pate and John Pate. Signed Oct 18, 1790 and recorded Oct 25, 1790. (Bedford DB 8:337).

Henry married Fanny Thompson, daughter of John, who gave consent. Surety was John Patrick. Bond dated Jan 7, 1792. (Dennis 1989, 8). They were married by James Mitchell on Jan 10, 1792. (Bedford PRO 1:225).

Henry was born May 16, 1792, the son of Arabia Brown and his wife Elizabeth Dooley. He and his siblings were named in his father's pension application for service in the Revolutionary War. Reel R359 of M804, National Archives. (Wardell 1988, 1:116).

The Browns of Bedford County

Henry was surety for the marriage of John McCabe and Susannah Mozeley. She was the daughter of Walter Mozeley, who gave consent. Bond dated Sep 6, 1792. (Dennis 1989, 45).

Henry married Susanna Hix. Susanna certified that she was of age. Surety was Patrick Hix. Witnesses were Patrick Hix and Caty Hix. Bond dated Nov 5, 1793. (Dennis 1989, 10).

Henry's will named his children Henry, Daniel, Samuel, Elizabeth, Alcy, Hannah, Ann, Mary and Sarah, and his wife Alice. The house at Ivy Hill was bequeathed to his wife Alice, his lands to sons Henry and Daniel, money to son Samuel, and furniture to daughters Elizabeth and Alcy. Executors were sons Henry, Samuel and Daniel. Witnesses were Abner Early, John Crumpacker and John Boblett. Will dated Jan 9, 1796, and recorded Jun 24, 1799. (Bedford WB 2:261). His will bequeathed 10 shillings each to Hannah, Ann, Mary and Sarah, his daughters by Ann Richardson, his first wife. (Merrill 1968, 15).

Henry's land was near Daniel Roberts, William Candless Jr, Abner Early, Robert Cowan, Daniel Foster and Thomas Holt, all near the Otter River. Recorded Jan 12, 1796. (Bedford PRO 1:3).

Henry's land was near Carter's orphans, William Trigg and John Phelps, all near Triggs Mill Creek. Recorded Feb 22, 1796. (Bedford PRO 1:22).

Henry's land was near James Ball and Abner Early. Recorded Mar 5, 1796. (Bedford PRO 1:46).

Henry was named as attorney to rent, lease or sell land owned by Samuel Coombs of Loudoun County VA. Witnesses were William Dobson, Samuel Hague, David Hook and Thomas Smith. Signed Mar 14, 1796 and recorded Oct 24, 1796. (Bedford DB 10:212).

Henry was recommended for lieutenant in the 91st regiment. Recorded Oct 1796. (Bedford OB 11:123). He was qualified. (Ibid, 11:342).

Henry Jr was appointed to view a road with Daniel Brown, John Crumpacker and William Austin, from William Lee's and William Austin's to the academy near New London. Recorded Feb 1797. (Bedford OB 11:152).

Henry was born Aug 25, 1797, the son of Capt Henry Brown and Frances Thompson of Ivy Cliff. (Merrill 1968, chart A). He was buried at the Thompson Brown Family Cemetery. His gravestone reads: Aug 25, 1797 - May 19, 1836. (Daughters 1970, 81).

Henry's 784A were surveyed. The land was above the Staunton River, near Crumpton on Johnson Creek, Johnson Mountain, Leftwich, Lewis, the south side of Back Creek, and Hall. He had acquired the land by virtue of land warrants: 1) 71A granted to Quarles, 2) 291A granted to Robert Pallard, and 3) 422A granted to Daniel Brown. Survey dated Apr 27, 1798. (Bedford SR 2:549).

Henry was buried at the Thompson Brown Family Cemetery. His gravestone reads: Died Nov 4, 1798, aged 86 years. (Daughters 1970, 81).

Henry, acting as attorney for Samuel Combs, conveyed a deed to Joseph Wilson for 150A on the waters of Little Otter River, near Nathaniel Tate and John Young. Signed and recorded Jan 28, 1799. (Bedford DB 11:6).

Henry, Daniel Brown, Joseph White and Roger Williams, were ordered summoned into court to show cause why a road should not be established from Blackwater River near Corams Creek, crossing the Otter River at Earlys Fork, and into the road leading to New London. Recorded Feb 25, 1799. (Bedford OB 11:311).

Henry Jr was granted a patent for 784A in Bedford and Campbell counties, on the north branches of Staunton River. Recorded Aug 8, 1799. (Bedford PB 41:370).

Henry and his wife Susanna conveyed a deed to John Garrett for 342A near Thomas Pollard and John Phelps. Witnesses were Alderson Weekes, John Trigg, M Graham and James Edgar. Signed Sep 28, 1799 and recorded Oct 28, 1799. (Bedford DB 11:121).

Henry's 1,200A were surveyed. The land was in Bedford and Campbell counties, near Austin, Johnson Mountain, Crumpton, Quarles, and Anthony. Henry had acquired the land by virtue of land warrants granted to William Calloway. Survey dated Dec 1, 1799. (Bedford SR 2:556).

The Browns of Bedford County

Henry's estate had 2 horses. Personal Property Tax List of 1800. (Dorman 1963, 7:66).

Henry had 5 males 21+, 4 horses, and 5 slaves 12+. Personal Property Tax List of 1800, District 1. (Dorman 1963, 7;66).

Henry's land was near Thomas Austin, Johnson Mountain and Orrix Creek. Recorded Mar 14, 1800. (Bedford PRO 1:66).

Henry was granted a patent for 1,200A in Bedford and Campbell counties, on or near Johnson mountain. Recorded Mar 3, 1801. (Bedford PB 48:163).

Henry was the brother of Daniel. He was conveyed a deed from Daniel Brown of Franklin County VA for 1/2 of 377A left them by their father's will. Witnesses were Thomas Clayton, Daniel Brown and Arthur Newman. Signed Sep 15, 1802 and recorded Jan 24, 1803. (Bedford DB 11:689).

Henry was qualified as magistrate. Recorded 1803. (Bedford OB 13:17).

Henry and his wife Fanny and Daniel Brown conveyed a deed to William Thorp for 336A on Orrix Creek, near Robert White and Austin. Signed Jan 20, 1803 and recorded Jan 24, 1803. (Bedford DB 11:691).

Henry witnessed the will of Robert Cowan. Other witnesses were William Cowan, Thomas Tucker and Samuel Jennings. Will dated Jan 4, 1803 and recorded Apr 25, 1803. (Bedford WB 2:413).

Henry was conveyed a deed from Christian Houtz and wife Barbara for 131A on the north side of Otter River near Henry Brown, Roberts, and the Burks Road. Witnesses were Peter Deardorf, Henry Campbell and James Hariss. Signed Jun 17, 1803 and recorded Sep 26, 1803. (Bedford DB 11:830).

Henry was appointed magistrate with Thomas Logwood, William Walker, William Irvine, Stephen Preston, Isaac Otey, and Andrew Donald, to sit in the September and October 1803 terms. (Bedford OB 13:2).

Henry resigned as captain of the second battalion of Gregory Isham's company. Recorded Nov 1803. (Bedford OB 13:267).

The Browns of Bedford County

Henry was conveyed a deed from Christian Cotty and his wife Barbary for 101A on both sides of Lick Run, on the main road from New London to Burks Ford and Island Ford on the Otter River. Witnesses were Joel Crumpacker, John Roberts Jr and John Roberts Sr. Signed Oct 4, 1805 and recorded Oct 28, 1805. (Bedford DB 11:1368).

Henry was on the list of magistrates for November 1806 Court. (Bedford OB 15:preface).

Henry, Reuben Brown and John Cobbs were appointed to be processioners in Capt William Green's company. Recorded for February 1808 Court. (Bedford OB 14:285).

Henry gave bonds to Gov Cabell that Samuel Hancock would perform the duties of sheriff. Signed Aug 22, 1808 and recorded same date. (Bedford DB 12:388-389).

Henry's land was near Roland Witt. Henry was a processioner with William Green. Recorded Mar 1809. (Bedford PRO 1:201).

Henry gave bond to Gov Tyler that Samuel Hancock would perform the duties of sheriff. Recorded 1810. (Bedford DB 13:520).

Henry was among the justices to hold court in August, June and December. Recorded Mar 1810. (Bedford OB 15:200).

Henry conveyed a deed to William Frazier for 200A at Back Creek. Signed May 25, 1810 and recorded May 28, 1810. (Bedford DB 13:520).

Henry was appointed to allot hands for surveying a road from the Burks Ford on the Otter River to Richard Lee's, and from Island Ford to the academy. Recorded Jun 1810. (Bedford OB 15:236).

Henry conveyed a deed to John Overstreet for 104A on the branches of Buck Creek, near Lewis and Leftwich. Signed and recorded May 25, 1811. (Bedford DB 13:649).

Henry gave bond to Gov Barbour that John Claytor would perform the duties of sheriff. Recorded Aug 24, 1812. (Bedford DB 13:770, 771).

The Browns of Bedford County

Henry and Daniel Brown signed bonds to Gov Barbour that John Claytor would perform the duties of sheriff. Recorded Aug 23, 1813. (Bedford DB 14:1-3).

Henry was appointed a processioner in Quarles Company, with William Green, John L Cobbs, Jesse Noell, Jabez Leftwich and David Saunders. Recorded Aug 1815. (Bedford OB 17:63).

Henry conveyed a deed to John Lee Jr for 250A near Blackwater Road and Austain. Signed and recorded May 27, 1816. (Bedford DB 15:23).

Henry was the father of Mary Brown who married Samuel Claytor. Bond dated Jul 12, 1817. (Ricks 1939, 27).

Henry was conveyed a deed from William Woodford and his wife Elizabeth for land near Henry Brown. Signed and recorded Oct 27, 1817. (Bedford DB 15:279).

Henry and Thomas R Claytor were conveyed a deed of trust from Daniel L Price, executor of Robert Price, deceased, for a debt secured by slaves Sam, Dick, Nelson and Faro. Witnesses were Alexander C Fariss, Irvine Wade and Alexander Burton. Signed Apr 10, 1818 and recorded Aug 24, 1818. (Bedford DB 15:404).

Henry and his wife Frances conveyed a deed to Henry Crumpton for 43A on Johnson Creek, at the top of Johnson Mountain. Signed Jun 10, 1818 and recorded May 27, 1820. (Bedford DB 16:184).

Henry was conveyed a deed from Rowland Witt and his wife Sarah for 109A on the north side of Otter River. Signed Jan 25, 1819 and recorded Feb 22, 1819. (Bedford DB 15:533).

Henry had 1 male 10-16, 1 male 16-26, 1 male 45+, 2 females 0-10, 1 female 10-16, and 1 female 45+. (U S Census of 1820, Southern District, p 63).

Capt Henry Brown was a trustee with Alexander Lee for a deed of trust from James Marsh to Parnell Lee, secured by farm animals and furniture. Witnesses were John G Lee, Alexander Lee Jr and Avey A Lee. Signed May 1, 1820 and recorded Jul 1, 1820. (Bedford DB 16:225).

The Browns of Bedford County

Henry and his wife Fanny conveyed a deed to James Boatright for 142A on Johnson Creek, near Henry Crumpton and David Crumpton. Signed May 20, 1820 and recorded May 27, 1820. (Bedford DB 16:29).

Henry and his wife Frances conveyed a deed to Henry Crumpton for 43A at Johnson Creek, on top of Johnson Mountain. Signed May 25, 1820 and recorded May 27, 1820. (Bedford DB 16:128).

Capt Henry Brown was a trustee with John G Lee for a deed of trust from William Marsh to John Marsh, secured by farm animals and furniture. Witnesses were James Marsh, Alexander Leftwich and Avey A Lee. Signed Jun 1, 1820 and recorded Jul 24, 1820. (Bedford DB 16:224).

Henry signed bonds to Gov Randolph that John H Otey would perform the duties of sheriff. Recorded Jul 23, 1821. (Bedford DB 17:24-26).

Henry was a partner with Samuel Claytor in the merchant firm of Brown & Claytor. They were conveyed a deed from William O Hurt for land in the estate of Garland Hurt, deceased. Signed Oct 6, 1821 and recorded Oct 8, 1821. (Bedford DB 17:87).

Henry was conveyed a power of attorney from William O Hurt and his wife Lucy to receive from Michael Graham, administrator of the estate of William O Hurt, deceased. Witnesses were Gordun Turner, James Turner and Meador Turner. Signed Oct 6, 1821 and recorded Oct 8, 1821. (Bedford DB 17:89).

Henry Brown and Samuel Claytor, as Brown & Claytor, conveyed a deed to Ira Hurt for 103A on Craddock Creek, near John Ashwell, William Dickerson and Eunice Hatcher. Land had been purchased from Daniel W Nichols. Witnesses were James Ayers, N Robertson and Harvey Layton. No signing date. Recorded Dec 23, 1822. (Bedford DB 17:347).

Henry Jr and E C L Carter were married by Rev William S Reid. Bond dated Mar 1823. From Marriage Record Book of Lynchburg. (Hinshaw 1969, 6:884).

Henry refused to accept a commission as ensign. Recorded Mar 25, 1823. (Bedford OB 18:338).

Henry was recommended to be sheriff with Stephen Preston and James Otey. Recorded Jun 1823. (Bedford OB 19:8).

Henry gave bonds to Gov Pleasants that Stephen Preston would perform the duties of sheriff. Recorded Jul 23, 1823. (Bedford DB 18:88-89).

Henry was recommended to be sheriff. Recorded Jun 14, 1824. (Bedford OB 19:164).

Henry, as justice of the peace, certified that William and Patsy Irvine were parties to a deed dated Aug 7, 1824. Signed Aug 23, 1824 and recorded Oct 25, 1824. (Bedford DB 19:47).

Henry gave bonds to Gov Pleasants that Stephen Preston would perform the duties of sheriff. Other signers to the bonds were Stephen Preston, John Headen, John H Otey, and Joseph Slaughter. Recorded Aug 23, 1824. (Bedford DB 19:48-49).

Henry, William Irvine, Alexander Austin and Samuel Crawford were appointed to view a road from Browns fork of the river to the Campbell County line near New London. Recorded Aug 24, 1824. (Bedford OB 19:179).

Henry was on the list of justices of the peace. Recorded 1825. (Bedford OB 20:1).

Henry conveyed a deed to William N Austin for 241A on Orrix Creek at Johnson Mountain, near Austin and Anthony. Signed Jun 12, 1825 and recorded Sep 12, 1825. (Bedford DB 19:275).

Henry Guilford Brown was buried at the Thompson Brown Family Cemetery. His gravestone reads: Jun 25, 1825 - Oct 12, 1845. (Daughters 1970, 81).

Henry and James Brown of Williamson County TN gave power of attorney to Henry Moss to handle the estate of their late brother Jesse Brown of Bedford County. Signed Sep 14, 1825 and recorded Oct 24, 1825. (Bedford DB 19:283).

51

The Browns of Bedford County

Henry Brown was a trustee with Tilghman A Cobbs for a deed of trust from Joel Leftwich to Garnett Lee. Witnesses were J C Steptoe, G A Wingfield and R C Mitchell. Signed Nov 25, 1825 and recorded Sep 1, 1826. (Bedford DB 20:32).

Henry Brown and Samuel Mitchell were justices of the peace who examined Gracy Dobbins, wife of Joseph Dobyns. Signed Sep 29, 1826 and recorded same date. (Bedford DB 20:98).

Henry and Fanny Thompson Brown were the parents of Locky, who married Alexander Irvine. Bond dated Mar 19, 1827. (Merrill 1968, chart A).

Henry Brown and Samuel Claytor, doing business as Brown & Claytor, were trustees for John Headen for a debt owed by Benjamin W Crouch, secured by 128A near George Weeks and Samuel Adams. Signed Oct 20, 1827 and recorded same date. (Bedford DB 20:367).

Henry Brown and John P Claytor were merchants and partners doing business as Brown & Claytor. They had been trustees for a deed of trust from Bennett M Murphy, secured by 1) 78A on Mill Creek, 2) 1/8 profits from a grist mill, 3) 50 1/2A on Goose Creek, and 4) 15A on Goose Creek. Murphy defaulted, and Claytor conveyed the land and profits to Henry Brown, who was the highest bidder. Signed Nov 19, 1827 and recorded Dec 27, 1827. (Bedford DB 20:432).

Henry gave bond to Gov Giles that Henry Brown would perform the duties of sheriff. Other signers to the bond were Samuel Hancock, Tilman A Cobbs, Joseph Slaughter, Garnett Lee, Thomas R Claytor, Samuel Mitchell and Balda McDaniel. Recorded Feb 25, 1828. (Bedford DB 20:469).

Henry appeared in court and was qualified to be sheriff. Recorded Mar 1828. (Bedford OB 22:168).

Henry Brown, Brown & Claytor, and Samuel Hancock, executors of Daniel Brown, released the indenture of Isham Lawhorn for the tract where he lived. Signed Apr 28, 1828 and recorded May 26, 1828. (Bedford DB 21:43).

Sheriff Henry Brown appointed Samuel Brown to be a deputy sheriff. Recorded Jan 26, 1829. (Bedford OB 22:201).

The Browns of Bedford County

Henry was the highest bidder for 350A at Otter River, sold by trustee Callohill Mennis for a debt Edmund Irvine owed Robert Steptoe. Signed Mar 12, 1829 and recorded Mar 23, 1829. (Bedford DB 21:342).

Sheriff Henry Brown had debtor Mark Anthony in custody for a judgment rendered by the Superior Court. Creditors mentioned were Nelson Davis, Zebedee Massey, Mary Goolsby, Edward Watts, Samuel Pannell, Daniel C Edwards, William Ray, Galt Bullock, Daniel Tompkins, John Badey, and James Bullock. Real estate parcels mentioned were 1) 42 1/2A at Terrapin Creek near James Adams, 2) 35A at McDaniels Creek near Saunders, 3) 35A near Nicholas Robertson, 4) 200A at Greasy Creek in Montgomery County VA, 5) 200A at Staunton River in Pittsylvania County VA, and 6) 442 1/2A at Staunton River in Pittsylvania County VA near George Parker. Suits mentioned were against 1) Henry Brown Jr, 2) William Fitzgerald, and 3) William Hopkins. Slaves mentioned were Ellis, Allen, Jim, Orry, Milford, David, Big Sam, Simon, James, Herbert, Peter, Randolph, Henry, Little Sam, Amos, Abram, Joe, Little Stephen, Matt, Billy, Peyton, Tom, John, Sam, Reuben, Luckey, Derry, Harry, George, Sally, Amy, Abby, Doley, Phillis, Nancy, Judy, Beckey, Milly, Rachell, Seny, Sarah, Marriah, and Juggy. Prior purchasers included Daniel C Edwards and Joshua R C Brown. Witnesses were Samuel P Mitchell, Jacob Fizer, G A Wingfield and William Goggin. Signed Apr 16, 1829 and recorded Jul 27, 1829. (Bedford DB 21:428).

Henry had 1 male 15-20, 1 male 70-80, 1 female 10-15, 1 female 15-20, and 21slaves. He was near Justinian Wills and John Fisher. (U S Census of 1830, p 176).

Henry gave bond to Gov Giles that Thomas Sale would perform the duties of sheriff. Signed and recorded Feb 11, 1830. (Bedford DB 22:67).

Henry Sr was highest bidder at a marshall's auction for 487A on Goose Creek and Mill Creek near Whitten, formerly owned by debtor Pleasants Murphy. Signed Jun 29, 1830 and recorded Aug 23, 1830. (Bedford DB 22:202).

Henry's hands, with those of William Irvine's estate, Mosly Arnold, William W Andrews, Joel Crumpacker, Peter Crumpacker, Mark Andrews, Frances Thorp, William Crouch and John Crumpacker, were ordered to assist surveyor Joel Crumpacker in viewing a road from Island Ford to "Lee's old store". Recorded Jul 1830. (Bedford OB 23:131).

Henry was trustee for a deed of trust secured by 98A at Falling Creek near Jeremiah Wade, for a debt Stephen Chaffin owed James Boatwright. Witnesses were Samuel Williams and Kenneth Urquhart. Signed Dec 18, 1830 and recorded Mar 28, 1831. (Bedford DB 22:331).

Henry was conveyed a deed from trustees William Leftwich and Thomas Preston who auctioned 150A owned by debtor Uriah Leftwich and his wife Nancy. The land was near Elijah Turner, Richard Turner, Dixon, Thadeus Miles' estate and Garland Hurt's estate. Signed Nov 17, 1831 and recorded Feb 2, 1832. (Bedford DB 22:485).

Henry was a trustee with Mosby Arnold for a deed of trust from Joel Leftwich to Garnet Lee and Frances Thorp, secured by slave Charity and three milk cows and furniture. Signed Jan 20, 1832 and recorded Jan 23, 1832. (Bedford DB 23:12).

Henry won a judgment against Nichodemus Leftwich for unlawful possession of 150A. Recorded Feb 1832. (Bedford OB 23:439).

Henry gave bonds to Gov Floyd that Joseph Slaughter would perform the duties of sheriff. Signed Feb 27, 1832 and recorded same date. (Bedford DB 23:28-29).

A justice of the peace, Henry accepted a deed from James Joplin and his wife Susan for 283 1/4A at Little Otter River for the site of a poorhouse and workhouse. Signed Aug 25, 1832 and recorded Aug 28, 1832. (Bedford DB 23:133).

Henry Brown and John Martin petitioned to erect a water grist mill, saw mill and dam on Mill Creek at Murphey's Mills. The matter was sent to jury because Henry Arthur objected on the ground that the motion was insufficient. Recorded Oct 1832. (Bedford OB 24:49).

Henry submitted to the court his application for a pension for service in the Revolutionary War, with statements by Thomas R Clayton and Thomas Andrews that they knew that he had served. The application was approved

by the court. Recorded Oct 1832. (Bedford OB 24:52). See National
Archives pension file S-8098. (Merrill 1968, 161).

Henry Brown and John Martin were granted permission to build a water
grist mill, saw mill and dam on both sides of Mill Creek, because it was
shown that they owned the lands. Recorded Nov 1832. (Bedford OB 24:64).

Henry gave bond to Gov Floyd that Joseph Slaughter would perform the
duties of sheriff. Signed Feb 25, 1833 and recorded same date.
(Bedford DB 23:267-268).

Henry Brown and Pleasant Murphy and his wife Ann, with Katharine
Murphy, widow of John Murphy, conveyed a deed to Henry Arthur for
120A on the southeast side of Mill Creek, near Goose Creek and Amos
Branch, Hackworth, and Arthur. Signed and recorded Mar 30, 1833.
(Bedford DB 23:326).

Henry conveyed a deed to John Nance for 6A in Murphy's Mill Tract.
Brown & Claytor had been conveyed the land by debtors Pleasant Murphy
and Bennett Murphy, the sons and heirs of John Murphy, deceased. Signed
and recorded Mar 30, 1833. (Bedford DB 23:346).

Henry and the heirs of John Murphy conveyed a deed to John Nance for
300A on Goose Creek near Mill Creek and Joseph Whitten. Signed
Mar 30, 1833 and recorded May 27, 1833. (Bedford DB 23:347).

Henry was exempted from paying levies for his two old slaves Joshua and
Judy, who were "infirm and unable to render service". Recorded Apr 1833.
(Bedford OB 24:128).

Henry deeded all his rights to Murphy's lands on Goose Creek near Mill
Creek to trustee Franklin Headen for Ann R Murphy and her children, to
satisfy life estate and dower rights. Signed Apr 22, 1833 and recorded
May 17, 1833. (Bedford DB 23:356).

Henry Sr conveyed a deed to Daniel Updike for 67A at Amos Creek he had
acquired at sheriff's auction from debtor Edmund Creasy, an insolvent.
Signed Feb 7, 1834 and recorded Feb 24, 1834. (Bedford DB 24:112).

The Browns of Bedford County

Henry gave bonds to Gov Floyd that Balda McDaniel would perform the duties of sheriff. Signed Feb 24, 1834 and recorded same date. (Bedford DB 24:99-100).

Henry sued Joseph Alberts and Penelope his wife, William Ray, Elijah Mitchell, William Angel, and Robert Ross and Susannah his wife, then declined to prosecute. Recorded May 14, 1834. (Bedford Chancery OB 1:170).

Henry was present in court as a gentleman justice. Recorded Nov 1834. (Bedford OB 25:14).

Henry gave bonds to Gov Tazewell that Balda McDaniel would perform the duties of sheriff. Signed Feb 23, 1835 and recorded same date. (Bedford DB 24:390-391).

Henry Brown and Peter Austin, as justices of the peace, certified that John B Witt and Plooy Crouch were parties to a deed dated Apr 11, 1835. Signed and Apr 11, 1835 same date. (Bedford DB 25:8).

Henry Jr was the eldest son of Henry Brown. He lived in Lynchburg, and died in New York after a brief illness. He was buried at Ivy Hill. He had married Eleanor Custis Lewis Carter, and they had children Henry Guilford Brown and Maria Carter Brown. (Merrill 1968, chart A). His gravestone reads: Aug 25, 1797-May 19, 1836. (Daughters 1970, 81). His obituary was printed in the "Richmond Whig and Public Advertiser" on Jun 3, 1836. (Merrill 1968, 160).

Henry was the father of Frances Brown who married Edwin Robinson. Surety was Alexander Irvine. Bond dated Oct 5, 1836. They were married by William S Reid on Oct 6, 1836. (Hinshaw 1969, 6:986).

Henry's will mentioned his children Henry (deceased), John (deceased), Samuel, Locky, Frances, Alice, son Henry's children Henry Guilford Brown and Maria Brown, grandson Edward Steptoe, son John's children (not named), and slaves Dick, Bill, John, George, Charles, Christian, Harry, Wilson, Eliza, Nancy, Mary Ann, Anna, Martha and Manda. Son Samuel was bequeathed the homeplace of 700A at Island Ford on the Otter River, daughter Locky was bequeathed 654A on Buffalo Creek, daughter Frances was bequeathed 65 shares in Virginia Bank, and daughter Alice was

56

The Browns of Bedford County

bequeathed the house in Lynchburg and 15 bank shares. His son Henry had already been given his part, and the legacies to his son John's children were revoked by a codicil dated Feb 14, 1839. The executors were directed to build a wall around the graveyard. Executors were son Samuel Brown and son-in-law Alexander Irvine. Will signed Jan 6, 1837 and recorded Sep 25, 1841. (Bedford WB 10:392).

Henry was administrator of the estate of James Ayres, deceased. He presented an account of the estate. Recorded Aug 1837. (Bedford OB 26:41).

Henry, late sheriff, was summoned to show cause why judgment should not be entered against him for $16.33, in settlement of depositions in his hands for the years 1828 and 1829. Recorded Nov 1837. (Bedford OB 26:86).

Henry was on the list of acting county justices. He had been commissioned Jan 15 1803, and qualified at July court of 1803. Recorded Jan 1, 1838. (Bedford OB 26:1A).

Henry was deceased. His executor, Micajah Davis Jr, and Mary E Brown, executor of John T Brown, deceased, sued Isham Lawhorne for $47.61. Lawhorne confessed judgment. Recorded Feb 1838. (Bedford OB 26:118).

Henry conveyed a deed of trust to trustees James S Dillard and William Leftwich for a debt owed Tilghman A Cobbs, secured by 400A at Otter River and Lick Run Creek, near Tilghman A Cobb, Peter Crumpacker, Mark Andrews, and the Island Ford Road. Signed Nov 28, 1838 and recorded Dec 4, 1838. (Bedford DB 27:350).

Henry was conveyed a deed of trust from James S Dillard and William Leftwich Jr to trustee Tilghman A Cobb, secured by 400A near Tilghman A Cobb, Peter Crumpecker, Mark Andrews, the Island Ford Road, Lick Run Creek and Otter River. Signed and recorded May 30, 1839. (Bedford DB 28:62).

Henry conveyed a deed to Tilghman A Cobbs for 229A on the northeast side of Otter River and both sides of Lick Run, near Cobbs. Signed May 30, 1839 and recorded Jun 1, 1839. (Bedford DB 28:63).

The Browns of Bedford County

Henry Sr conveyed a deed to his son Samuel T Brown for 400A at Otter River, near the Island Ford Road and Lick Run Creek. Signed Oct 22, 1839 and recorded Oct 28, 1839. (Bedford DB 28:187).

Henry Sr was age 79, head of his household, and a Revolutionary War pensioner. He had 20 slaves. He was near Thomas Hicks and Charles Crouch. (U S Census of 1840, p 39).

Henry, William Leftwich and Thomas Preston were sued by Nicodemus Leftwich for possession of land. Judgment for plaintiff. Recorded May 7, 1840. (Bedford Chancery OB 1:395).

Henry, Charles Crouch and Stephen Hicks were sued by Nicodemus Leftwich. Judgment for plaintiff for $27.73 plus interest. Recorded Sep 29, 1840. (Bedford Chancery OB 1:408).

HEZEKIAH

Hezekiah was the son of Joseph Brown and his wife Elizabeth. He and his siblings were named in his father's will dated Aug 22, 1795 and recorded Oct 26, 1795. (Bedford WB 2:163).

Hezekiah witnessed a deed from Rhodam Brown and his wife Elizabeth to Isaac James for 92 1/2 A on Beaverdam Creek. Other witnesses were Lawrence James and Joseph Brown. Signed Mar 14, 1800 and recorded Apr 28, 1800. (Bedford DB 11:205).

Hezekiah's land was processioned, with Thomas Haynes present. Recorded Feb 17, 1804. (Bedford PRO 1:133).

Hezekiah and his wife Jane conveyed a deed to John Haynes for 136A, near West, Pate and Preas. Recorded 1818. (Bedford DB 15:335).

Hezekiah was the father of Callaway who married Sarah Lawhorn. Surety was Jabez Brown. Bond dated Dec 23, 1833. (Hinshaw 1969, 6:884).

HOWELL

Howell and other justices of Amherst County VA were conveyed a release of deed of trust from trustee Robert Tinsley for debtor William P Read,

The Browns of Bedford County

secured by 160A near John Robertson in Bedford County VA, which had been devised to Read by his father Edmund Read, deceased. Signed Apr 7, 1838 and recorded Apr 30, 1838. (Bedford DB 27:163).

HUBBARD

Hubbard entered military service from Bedford County in 1781. He was born 1760 at Brunswick County VA, and was pensioned at Gibson County TN in 1834 for service in the Revolutionary War. Reel R365 of M804, National Archives. (Wardell 1988, 1:119).

Hubbard witnessed a deed from William Brown and his wife Mary to John Traylor. Recorded Feb 10, 1781. (Bedford DB 7:70).

IRENIA

Irenia Plymale was the daughter of Thomas. She married Garrett Brown, son of Joycy. Surety was Wyatt Truman. Bond dated Oct17, 1838. They were married by William Leftwich on Oct 26, 1838. (Hinshaw 1969, 6:884).

ISAAC

Isaac was paid L4.19.0 for being a Bedford soldier under the command of Lt Samuel Hairston during the French and Indian Wars. Recorded 1765. (Bockstruck 1988, 209).

ISHAM

Isham C married Nancy Pearcy, daughter of Charles. Surety was Thomas W Brown. Bond dated Jul 20, 1824. (Hinshaw 1969, 6:884).

Isham C was surety for the marriage of Thomas W Brown to Juana Tyler, daughter of Daniel. Bond dated Oct 3, 1826. (Hinshaw 1969, 6:884).

J M

J M conveyed a deed of trust to trustee William N Sherman for 1 slave and other personal property. Recorded 1827. (Bedford DB 20:332).

The Browns of Bedford County

J M conveyed a deed of trust to trustee Daniel Aunspaugh for personal property. Recorded 1835. (Bedford DB 24:455).

J M conveyed a deed of trust to trustee Daniel Aunspaugh for personal property. Recorded 1838. (Bedford DB 27:20).

J M conveyed a deed of trust to trustee Joseph Wilson for 4A near the town of Liberty on the Fancy Farm Road, and an interest in Reed Brown's estate. Recorded 1839. (Bedford DB 27:365).

J M conveyed a deed of trust to trustee James Oney for 4A near Liberty, and for personal property. Recorded 1840. (Bedford DB 28:296).

JABEZ

Jabez married Nancy Wheeler, daughter of Gabriel. Surety was Joel Wheeler. Bond dated Feb 8, 1832. They were married by Stephen Wood on Feb 16, 1832. (Hinshaw 1969, 884).

Jabez was surety for the marriage of Callaway Brown and Sarah Lawhorn. Callaway was the son of Hezekiah Brown. Bond dated Dec 23, 1833. (Hinshaw 1969, 884).

Jabez had 2 males 0-5, 1 male 20-30, 2 females 5-10, 1 female 20-30, and no slaves. He was near Edward Graham and Gabriel Heiler. (U S Census of 1840, 35).

JACOB

Jacob R was proven to be the son and one of the heirs of William Brown, deceased, "late a soldier in the 3rd regiment of Pennsylvania line on Continental establishment". Recorded Nov 21, 1828. (Bedford OB 22:166).

JAMES

James was conveyed a deed from James Buford and his wife Betty for 306A at the head of the Little Otter River. Recorded Nov 22, 1773. (Bedford DB 5:150).

The Browns of Bedford County

James was conveyed a deed from James Buford for 83A on a branch of Little Otter River at the Brambletts Road. Signed and recorded May 23, 1774. (Bedford DB 5:232).

James was appointed to survey a road from William Bramblett's to the Otter Road. Recorded May 22, 1775. (Bedford OB 6:97).

James was conveyed a deed from James Buford for 70A on Little Otter River, near Randolph and Mattathes Mount. Signed Mar 23, 1778 and recorded same date. (Bedford DB 6:20).

James witnessed a deed from George Hughes to Raba Brown for 150A on the small branch of Little Otter. James lived there near Thomas Brown Sr and Lynard Brown. Recorded Aug 18, 1778. (Bedford DB 6:94).

James lived near the Brambletts Road, Thomas Brown Sr, John Anthony, Augustine Leftwich and Raba Brown. From deed by Augustine Leftwich Sr to Thomas Brown Sr for 160A. Recorded Aug 24, 1778. (Bedford DB 6:97).

James of Botetourt County VA conveyed a deed to Adam Clement for 279A at the head of Beaver Creek at the New London Road near Adam Clement and John Thompson Brown, part of 1,116A bequeathed by John Johnson to the children of James Brown of Hanover County VA. Witnessed by Richard Stith, Joseph Anthony, Samuel Hairston, John Forbes and John Wily. Recorded Jan 1, 1780. (Bedford DB 6:428).

James Brown and Jonas Erwin qualified as executors of the estate of Thomas Murphy. Security was by William Woody and Moses Dooley. Recorded Aug 28, 1780. (Bedford OB 6:292).

James and Thomas Brown were chosen for jury, with James Wright, Henry Jeter, Charles Tate, William Cavenaugh, Rowland Wheeler, John Mead, John Bozwell, William Hancock, Marmaduke Dallis and Edward Hors. Recorded Aug 1784. (Bedford OB 8:77).

James had 1 male 16-21, 4 slaves under 16, and 15 horses. Personal Property Tax List of 1787, List A. (Schreiner-Yantis 1987, 193). He was visited on the same day as Anne Bramblett and Isham Clark. (Ibid, 211).

The Browns of Bedford County

James and his wife Jennet conveyed a deed to Joseph Fuqua for 100A on a branch of Little Otter River. Recorded Jun 27, 1787. (Bedford DB 7:531).

James and his wife Jannet conveyed a deed to Joseph Fuqua for 30A near Joseph Fuqua. Signed Feb 5, 1788 and recorded Feb 23, 1788. (Bedford DB 8:53).

James' will named his wife Jinnet, sons Thomas, David, John and James, daughters Mary, Ann, Margaret Woody, Gian Crage, Elizabeth Jones, and granddaughters Rebekah Jones, Peggy Jones and Elizabeth Woody. Executors were his son Thomas and Charles Cafferty. Witnesses were William Woody, William Hale, Charles Cafferty and Mary Thomas. Will dated Dec 3, 1789, recorded Jul 26, 1790. (Bedford WB 2:35).

James' estate was inventoried by Benjamin Rice, John Otey and Michael Graham. Recorded Feb 26, 1792. (Bedford WB 2:75).

James married Rhoda Reese. She was the daughter of Sloman Reese, who gave consent. Surety was John Reese. Bond dated Oct 2, 1792. (Hinshaw 1969, 6:884).

James and Rhoda Reese were married by Joseph Drury on Oct 4, 1792. (Bedford PRO 1:225).

James was surety for the marriage of John Reese and Ann Brown. Ann certified that she was of age. Bond dated Dec 5, 1792. (Dennis 1989, 56).

James Jr conveyed a deed to Mary Ann Brown for 31 1/2A on Little Otter River. Signed Dec 3, 1793 and recorded Dec 23, 1793. (Bedford DB 9:255).

James was the father of Tabby. He gave consent for her marriage to Stephen Smelser. Surety was Archibald Lamb. Bond dated Jan 17, 1794. (Dennis 1989, 64).

James married Elizabeth Woody, daughter of William, who gave consent. Surety by James Brown Jr. Bond dated May 13, 1794. (Dennis 1989, 10). They were married by James Turner on May 15, 1749. (Bedford PRO 1:230).

The Browns of Bedford County

James Jr and his wife Rhoda conveyed a deed to John Quin for 74A on the Brambletts Road, near John Otey. Signed and recorded Feb 23, 1795. Bedford DB 9:487).

James was a son of Jennings Brown. He and his brothers were ordered bound out by the overseers of the poor. Recorded Apr 27, 1795. (Bedford OB 10:366). James was ordered by the overseers of the poor to be bound to Joseph Patterson. Recorded Jun 1795. (Bedford OB 11:12).

James and his wife Elizabeth and Sarah Brown conveyed a deed to John Reese for 110A on the Little Otter River near Galloway. Signed Jun 22, 1795 and recorded Jun 27, 1795. (Bedford DB 9:541).

James' land was near William Thomas and John Otey, and Bramblett's Road. Recorded Feb 1796. (Bedford PRO 1:24).

James Jr's land was near James Moorman, Buford, William Thomas, John Otey, James Petross and David Brown. Recorded Feb 1796. (Bedford PRO 1:25).

James, John Reese and Frederick Gooldy gave a peace bond for John Reese. Recorded Jan 1798. (Bedford OB 11:241).

James, Mary Ann Brown, Thomas Sumpkin, William Bramblett, Walter Otey, William Haley, Charles Cafferty and George Stone gave bond for Robert Davis who was accused of larceny. Recorded Mar 1798. (Bedford OB 11:251).

James was the son of Linah. James and his wife Elizabeth conveyed a deed to his brothers Larking and John B, for 42A on Meadow Creek. Signed and recorded Jun 25, 1798. (Bedford DB 10:485).

James was the son of Linah Brown. James and his wife Elizabeth conveyed a deed to his sister Sarah for 8A on Meadow Creek. Signed Jun 25, 1798 and recorded same. (Bedford DB 10:486).

James Brown and George Baber were indicted for trespass. Recorded Nov 26, 1798. (Bedford OB 11:290).

James had 1 male 21+, and 1 horse. Personal Property Tax List of 1800, Northern District. (Dorman 1963, 7:123).

James had 2 males 21+, 2 horses, and 2 slaves 12+. Personal Property Tax List of 1800, District 1. (Dorman 1963, 7:66).

James' land was near Frederick Gooldy, William Thomas, John Otey, James Pettoross, Benjamin Rice and James L Moorman. Recorded Apr 28, 1800. (Bedford PRO 1:87).

James and his wife Jenet conveyed a deed of trust to trustee Christopher Clark for 176A on the waters of Little Otter River, near Col John Otey. Recorded 1802. (Bedford DB 11:505).

James and his wife Rhoda and Jeanet Brown conveyed a deed to William R Jones for 130A on a branch of Little Otter ("Little Auten") River, about one. mile below town of Liberty, near Randolph's old line. Witnesses were Reuben Bramblett, James Thornhill, Adam Bowyer and James Brown Jr. Signed Jan 15, 1802 and recorded Feb 23, 1802. (Bedford DB 11:535).

James' executors, Thomas Brown and Charles Caffery, were granted an injunction to stay proceedings on a deed of trust held by trustee Chris Clark for Andrew Donald. Recorded Feb 22, 1802. (Bedford OB 12:245).

James conveyed an indenture of trust to John Watson for 136A on both sides of Goose Creek which Brown had purchased from John Black, near Charles Caffey, Joseph Feezel, Jonathan Consolver and Frederick Gooldy. Witnesses were Jacob Wade, Daniel Brown and William Burnside. Signed Aug 4, 1803 and recorded Jan 23, 1804. (Bedford DB 11:913).

James conveyed a bill of sale to Jordan Reese for a cow and heifer, and furniture. Witnesses were George Baber and Charles Caffery. Signed Sep 3, 1803 and recorded Sep 27, 1803. (Bedford DB 11:860).

James was conveyed a deed from William Burton and his wife Elizabeth for 300A on Shockoe Creek near Matthias O'Brian, Reuel Shrewsbury, Callaway, Bramblett, Thomas Miller and Alexander Simmons. Signed Sep 6, 1803 and recorded Sep 26, 1803. (Bedford DB 11:851).

The Browns of Bedford County

James and his wife Elizabeth and his mother Sarah Brown conveyed a deed to Thomas Scruggs for land on the Little Otter River near Charles Marckel, Thomas, Mary Ann Brown, Sally Brown, John Fisher and Benjamin Rice. Signed Oct 1803 and recorded Jan 23, 1804. (Bedford DB 11:909).

James gave a peace bond for John Campbell. Recorded Jan 1804. (Bedford OB 13:73).

James was appointed surveyor of a road from Little Otter River to Ben Rice's. Recorded Feb 1804. (Bedford OB 13:81).

James was the eldest son of Linah Brown, per dower right which Sarah Brown conveyed to John Marrs for 110A which James Brown had conveyed to John Reese, who conveyed it to John Marrs. Witness was William Trigg. Recorded Apr 23, 1804. (Bedford DB 11:986).

James' land was processioned. Recorded May 28, 1804. (Bedford PRO 1:153).

James and his wife Betsey conveyed a deed to Adam Bowyer for 97A on Goose Creek, near Hobs, Bramblett, Callaway and Reuel Shrewsbury. Signed Sep 20, 1804 and recorded same date.(Bedford DB 11:117).

James Jr conveyed a deed of trust to trustee John Watson Sr for L200, secured by 76A near Benjamin Rice, two horses, two slaves and household furniture. Witnesses were James Miller, Josiah Auld and Moses Miller. Signed Apr 27, 1805 and recorded Sep 23, 1805. (Bedford DB 11:1320).

James was conveyed a deed from Thomas Brown and his wife Elizabeth for 70A on Little Otter River, near John Otey, Joseph Fuqua and William R Jones. Witnesses were Aaron Fuqua, John Wright and Thomas Miller. Signed Sep 1, 1805 and recorded Sep 23, 1805. (Bedford DB 11:1300).

James Jr and his wife Elizabeth conveyed a deed to Thomas Brown for a tract at Shockoe Creek, near Shrewsbury, Brian, Simmons and Hobbs. Witnesses were Thomas Miller, Aaron Fuqua and James Miller. Signed Sep 21, 1805 and recorded Sep 23, 1805. (Bedford DB 11:1299).

The Browns of Bedford County

James Jr conveyed a deed of trust to trustees Moses Miller and John Watson Sr for 70A which he had purchased from Thomas Brown, near William Jones, Joseph Fuqua and Col John Otey. Signed and recorded Nov 1, 1805. (Bedford DB 12:28).

James conveyed a deed of trust to trustee James C Steptoe for 70A, formerly the property of Thomas Brown, near William R Jones, Joseph Fuqua and John Otey, to secure a debt owed Brown McCredie & Co. Witnessses were Samuel Read, Thomas Miller and Anderson C Fariss. Samuel Read signed for Brown McCredie & Co. Signed Feb 11, 1806 and recorded Jun 23, 1806. (Bedford DB 12:74).

James was surety for the marriage of John Richardson and Priscilla Davenport. Bond dated May 26, 1806 (sic). They were married by William Leftwich on May 23, 1806. (Hinshaw 1969, 6:984).

James T married Polly Preas, daughter of Elizabeth. Surety was David Brown. Bond dated April 15, 1812. (Hinshaw 1969, 6:884).

The land of James Brown and John Lee was exonerated from erroneously assessed delinquent taxes when James showed the court a deed proving purchase prior to Jun 1, 1812. Recorded Jul 1816. (Bedford OB 17:203).

James of Franklin County VA conveyed a deed to David Quarles for 163A on Buffalo Creek near Charles Walden and Polly Brown. Witnesses were John A Leftwich, Thomas A Claytor and William Porter. Signed Sep 14, 1812 and recorded Feb 22, 1813. (Bedford DB 13:799).

James Jr was exonerated from erroneously assessed taxes for the years 1810, 1811, 1812 and 1813 on 70A which he had conveyed to James Miller in 1805. Recorded Aug 1816. (Bedford OB 17:237).

James T had 2 males 0-10, 1 male 16-26, 1 female 16-26. (U S Census of 1820, Southern District, p 61).

James of Campbell County VA was conveyed a deed from William Adams for 138A on Terrapin Creek, near E Anthony, J Brown, Rusman, Callaway and Ward. Witnesses were William Frazer and George Thomas. Signed Nov 15, 1823 and recorded Aug 9, 1824. (Bedford DB 18:397).

The Browns of Bedford County

James and Henry Brown of Williamson County TN gave power of attorney to Henry Moss to settle the estate of their late brother Jesse Brown of Bedford County. Signed Sep 14, 1825 and recorded Oct 24, 1825. (Bedford DB 19:283).

James and his Catharine of Campbell County VA, with Joshua R C Brown and his wife of Botetourt County VA, as distributors of the estate of Thomas Leftwich, conveyed a deed to James C Steptoe for 811A at Porter Mountain. Signed Jul 6, 1826 and recorded Aug 28, 1826. (Bedford DB 20:59).

James M was witness for Archibald Robertson in a deed of trust from Burwell Robertson to trustee Thomas Brown for a debt owed Archibald Robertson, secured by 178A near John Ayres, Nicholas Robertson and John Pate. Witnesses were Green B Lewellen, David M Prather and J M Brown. Signed Aug 7, 1828 and recorded Aug 25, 1828. (Bedford DB 21:148).

James T had 2 males 15-20, 1 male 30-40, 1 female 0-5, 3 females 5-10, 1 female 30-40, and no slaves. He was near Francis Pollard and Bennet M Creasy. (U S Census of 1830, p 175).

The hands of James T Brown, Thomas Preas Sr, Thomas Preas Jr, Christopher St Clair, Elizabeth Hatcher, Robert Elliott, Jesse Powell, Abram Huddleston, Ransom Jeter, Lorrin Jeter and A J Ayers were ordered to work on the road from Union Meeting House to Lorrin Jeter's. Recorded Aug 1830. (Bedford OB 23:151).

James was named as a brother of John Brown in John's pension application for service in the Revolutionary War. Reel R370 of M804, National Archives. (Wardell 1988, 1:120).

James had a survey made of 163A for land office warrant #10892 that had been granted to Hancock and Brown on Jan 8, 1833, for 350A on the south side of Terrapin Creek, a branch of Staunton River, near William Adams, James Adams, Smith and Woodson. The survey was made on Mar 18, 1833. (Bedford SR 4:91).

James and his wife Mason of Crawford County IN conveyed a deed to John Dearing for land at Orrix Creek, where Richard Dearing had lived, and was

1/5 of the land which Jeremiah Dearing owned when he died, near Warner Hewitt. Signed Apr 12, 1833 and recorded May 13, 1833. (Bedford DB 23:362).

James was granted a patent for 113A and 163A on the S side of Terrapin Creek, a branch of Staunton River. Recorded Jun 15, 1834. (Bedford PB 83:122).

James was the son of Aaron, who had entered military service from Bedford County in 1776. He was named in Aaron's death report of 1836. Reel R358 of M804, National Archives. (Wardell 1988, 1:116).

James married Martha Jane Witt, daughter of John. Surety was Wiatt Crane. Bond dated Mar 30, 1839. Married Apr 10, 1839 by Mosby Arnold. (Hinshaw 1969, 6:884).

James M had 1 male 10-15, 1 male 20-30, 2 females 5-10, 2 females 15-20, 1 female 40-50, and no slaves. He was near William R Behren and Reason Agee. (U S Census of 1840, p 33).

James M and Albert G Brown were securities for a bond for Mary Brown, who was granted a certificate to obtain letters of administration on the estate of James T Brown, deceased. Recorded May 1840. (Bedford OB 27:68).

James T's household goods and farm goods were inventoried and appraised by Jeremiah G Hatcher and Fielding H Jeter. The good were valued at $238.87. Work done on Jun 20, 1840 and recorded Jun 22, 1840. (Bedford WB10:235).

James T's inventory was ordered recorded. Proceedings recorded Jun 1840. (Bedford OB 27:88).

JANE aka Jinsey, Gian

Jane witnessed a deed from Samuel Morgan and his wife Elizabeth to Daniel Brown Jr for land near Thomas Morgan and Hinman Wooster. Other witnesses were Daniel Price, Charles Swain and John Lee. Signed Aug 28, 1779 and recorded Sep 27, 1779. (Bedford DB 6:331).

The Browns of Bedford County

Jane was the daughter of Thomas. She was born Aug 2, 1760, and married John Craig at Bedford County on Sep 17, 1780. Their children were Polly, Rachel, Anna, Rebecca, James, Robert, Nancy, John Henderson, Betsy and Linn. In 1838 she applied for a Revolutionary War widow's pension at Wayne County Ky. Reel 676 of M804, National Archives. (Wardell 1988, 1:257).

Jane Brown and John Craig were married by John W Holt. Recorded 1782. (Bedford DB 7:341).

Jane was named as Gian Crage in the will of her father James, dated Dec 3, 1789. Her siblings were also named. His will was recorded Jul 26, 1790. (Bedford WB 2:35).

Jane and her husband Hezekiah conveyed a deed to John Haynes for 136A, near West, Pate and Preas. Recorded 1818. (Bedford DB 15:335).

Jane Leftwich married Joshua Brown. Surety was Munford Stanfell. Bond dated Sep 7, 1819. (Hinshaw 1969, 6:884). She was the daughter of Thomas and Gincey Leftwich. (Hopkins 1931, 273).

Jane and her husband Joshua R C Brown of Botetourt County VA, with James Brown and his wife Catharine of Campbell County VA, were distributors of the estate of Thomas Leftwich. They conveyed a deed to James C Steptoe for 811A at Porter Mountain. Signed Jul 6, 1826 and recorded Aug 28, 1826. (Bedford DB 20:59).

Jinsey Leftwich Brown's husband Joshua R C Brown claimed right to the land of the late Thomas Leftwich, and was conveyed a deed by James Dixon and his wife Susannah of Pittsylvania County VA. Signed Dec 18, 1827 and recorded Jan 10, 1828. (Bedford DB 20:418).

Jane Brown Craig was a sister of John Brown. She and her siblings were named in his pension application for service in the Revolutionary War. Reel R370 of M804, National Archives. (Wardell 1988, 1:120).

Jane married Henry D Powell. Surety was Samuel D McCarty. Bond dated Oct 26, 1835. They were married by William Harris on Oct 29, 1835. (Hinshaw 1969, 6:979).

The Browns of Bedford County

Jane married Abner A Anthony. Jane was of Campbell County, VA.
Bond dated Feb 24, 1836. They married by William Leftwich.
(Hinshaw 1969, 6:871).

Jane L married Abner A Anthony on Feb 24, 1836. They were first cousins.
Abner was born Nov 28, 1812, the son of Mark Anthony Sr and Emily
Leftwich, and grandson of Col Thomas Leftwich and Jane Stratton.
(Hopkins 1931, 68). They were married at New Glasgow, her family home
in Campbell County, VA. (Ibid, 85).

Jane and her husband Joshua R C Brown of Laporte County IN conveyed a
deed to John B Witt for 660A at Crab Orchard Creek , near Samuel Wilkes.
Signed Nov 12, 1836 and recorded Nov 11, 1836 (sic). (Bedford DB 25:442).

Jane, wife of Joshua R C Brown, relinquished to John B Witt her dower
rights to 660A at Crab Orchard Creek. Signed Apr 12, 1837 and recorded
May 24, 1837. (Bedford DB 26:185). Also recorded at Bedford OB 26:17.

JANET aka Jennet, Jannet, Jeanet, Jinnet

Janet and her husband James conveyed a deed to Joseph Fuqua for 100A
on a branch of Little Otter. Recorded Jun 27, 1785. (Bedford DB 7:531).

Jannet with husband James conveyed a deed to Joseph Fuqua for 30A.
Signed Feb 5, 1788 and recorded Feb 23, 1788. (Bedford DB 8:53).

Janet was named in the will of her husband James, with their children
Thomas, David, John, James, Mary, Ann, Margaret Woody, Gian Crage and
Elizabeth Jones. Will dated Dec 3, 1789 and recorded Jul 26, 1790. (Bedford
WB 2:35).

Jane and Manly Brown, parents of Mary, gave consent for her marriage to
John Campbell. Surety was Isham Galloway. Bond dated Apr 26, 1790.
(Dennis 1989, 13).

Janet and her husband James conveyed a deed of trust to trustee
Christopher Clark for 176A on the waters of Little Otter River, near Col
John Otey. Recorded 1802. (Bedford DB 11:505).

The Browns of Bedford County

Jeanet conveyed a deed with James Brown and his wife Rhoda to William R Jones for 130A on a branch of Little Otter ("Little Auten") River about one mile below the town of Liberty near Randolph's old line. Witnesses were Reuben Bramblett, James Thornhill, Adam Bowyer and James Brown Jr. Signed Jan 15, 1802 and recorded Feb 23, 1802. (Bedford DB 11:535).

JENNIINGS

Jennings was conveyed a deed from John Harman for 110A on the Staunton River, Beaverdam Creek and Jumping Run, near Stephen Goggins, Spradling, James Board and Elijah Dowell. Witnesses were Elijan Dowell, James Board and Nehemiah Dowell. Signed Nov 28, 1789 and recorded Jun 28, 1790. (Bedford DB 8:283).

Jennings' son Allen was ordered bound to Caleb Browning, and son James was ordered bound to Joseph Patterson. Recorded Jun 1795. (Bedford OB 11:12).

Jennings' 100A were near James Board. Recorded Jan 12, 1796. (Bedford PRO 1:45).

Jennings' son Josiah was indentured to William Pidgeon. Recorded Feb 1796. (Bedford OB 11:62).

Jennings and his wife Elizabeth conveyed a deed to Hezekiah Meador for 100A at the mouth of Beaverdam Creek near Stephen Goggins, Spradling, James Board, Jumping Run and the Staunton River. Signed Sep 23, 1797 and recorded Sep 25, 1797. (Bedford DB 10:359).

Jennings was exonerated for taxes on 110A and 60A erroneously assessed in his name for the years 1790, 1791 and 1792. He proved to the court that he had sold to Hezekiah Meador prior to Jun 1, 1812. Recorded Jul 25, 1816. (Bedford OB 17:216).

Jennings was proved to be one of the heirs of John Brown, deceased, "a soldier of Armond's corps and Continental establishments". Recorded Aug 28, 1826. (Bedford OB 22:123).

Jennings was granted a bounty land warrant in 1828, for service in the Revolutionary War by his relative John Brown who entered service from

The Browns of Bedford County

Bedford County. Reel R369 of M804, National Archives. (Wardell 1988, 1:120).

JEREMIAH

Jeremiah's guardian was qualified. Recorded 1774-1782 at OB 6:218 per index, but text is unreadable. (Bedford OB, Index for Book 6).

Jeremiah was conveyed a deed from Benjamin Davis for 340A on the south side of Goose Creek and Reads Branch, near Charles Bunch, Womack, Ewing and Frances Read. Recorded Sep 23, 1782. (Bedford DB 7:160).

Jeremiah of Menefee County KY conveyed a deed to Jacob Feezel for 200A on the north side of Goose Creek near Callaway, Needs Branch and the Reads Road. Witnesses were Gabriel Slaughter and John Thompson. Signed May 16, 1796 and recorded Jul 25, 1796. (Bedford DB 10:183).

Jeremiah was exonerated from erroneously assessed delinquent taxes for the years 1786, 1787 and 1788, because the county clerk could find "no evidence from any records in the office". Recorded Aug 1816. (Bedford OB 17:234).

JESSE

Jesse Brown and William Geter conveyed a deed to Jonathan Davis for a slave woman named Dorcas. Witnesses were Clement Reed, George Walton and P Carrington. Recorded Aug 7, 1754. (Lunenburg DB 3:1754).

Jesse was conveyed a deed from Anthony Pate for 100A on the south branch of Beaverdam Creek near William Anderson, Holmon, Joseph Payne and Hornet's Nest branch. Witnesses were John Pate, John Payne and William Nimmo. Signed Apr 27, 1795 and recorded Oct 26, 1795. (Bedford DB 10:201).

Jesse was executor with brother Rhodham of the will of their father Joseph. Their father's will was dated Aug 22, 1795 and recorded Oct 26, 1795. (Bedford WB 2:163).

Jesse Dent Brown and Rhodham Brown qualified as executors of the will of Joseph Brown. Recorded Oct 1795. (Bedford OB 11:37).

The Browns of Bedford County

Jesse was present when his 100A were processioned. Recorded 1796. (Bedford PRO 1:41).

Jesse and his wife Dycey conveyed a deed to Samuel Oliphant for 175A on the south side of Beaverdam Creek. Signed Sep 1797 and recorded Sep 25, 1797. (Bedford DB 10:364).

Jesse D Brown, John Mays and Benjamin Stith were present when the 256A estate lands of Joseph Brown, deceased, were processioned. Recorded Dec 4, 1799. (Bedford PRO 1:99).

Jesse had 1 male 21+, and 1 horse. Personal Property Tax List of 1800, District 1. (Dorman 1963, 7:65).

Jesse was surety for the marriage of Jimmy Cundiff and Lucy Brown. Consent of Daniel Brown. Bond dated Mar 29, 1800. (Dennis 1989, 12).

Jesse married Elizabeth Payne, daughter of Thomas. Surety was Dabney Grubb. Bond dated Nov 1, 1801. They were married by John Ayers on Nov 12, 1801. (Hinshaw 1969, 6:884). Jesse Brown and Betsey Peryire were married on Nov 12, 1801 by Rev John Ayers, a Methodist minister. (Bedford PRO 1:248).

Jesse Brown and Polly George were married by George Rucker on Mar 27, 1807. (Bedford PRO 1:260).

Jesse was conveyed a deed for 65 3/4A near Payne from Judith Shands, administratrix of William Shands. Witnesses were C Blount Jr, N Robertson and John Kasey. In 1819 Judith Shands' signature was proved by John Kasey and further proved in 1833 by Nicholas Robertson. Signed and recorded Aug 26, 1833. (Bedford DB 23:431).

Jesse's administrator, Edward Lazenby, was qualified and appraisers appointed. Recorded Nov 1819. (Bedford OB 17:694).

Jesse's estate was inventoried. The inventory was returned and recorded Jan 1820. (Bedford OB 17:728).

73

Jesse qualified as the guardian of Burd, Docia, Joel and Sally Whorley. Recorded Jul 25, 1825. (Bedford OB 20:84).

Jesse's brothers Henry and James of Williamson County TN gave power of attorney to Henry Moss to handle the late Jesse's estate in Bedford County. Signed Sep 14, 1825 and recorded Oct 24, 1825. (Bedford DB 19:283).

Jesse was the father of Sinthia Brown who married Joel Worley. Bond dated Dec 30, 1826. (Hinshaw 1969, 6:1020).

Jesse was the guardian of Sarah Worley. He gave consent for her marriage to William C Martin. Thomas Martin was surety for the bond issued Oct 11, 1828. Marriage performed Oct 12, 1828 by William Leftwich. (Hinshaw 1969, 958).

Jesse had 2 males 0-5, 2 males 5-10, 1 male 10-15, 1 male 15-20, 1 male 40-50, 1 female 15-12, 1 female 40-50, and 7 slaves. He was near John Morgan and William Leftwich. (U S Census of 1830, p 184).

Jesse was granted an injunction against Thomas Stewart and Thomas Phelps to stop clearing and cutting. Recorded Sep 27, 1830. (Bedford Chancery OB 1:29).

Jesse won a judgment against Thomas Phelps for unlawful entry and detainer. Recorded Jun 15, 1833. (Bedford OB 24:163).

Jesse was a witness with George Norvell to a deed from Abraham Blankenship Sr to Polly Blankenship for household goods. Signed Jun 21, 1833 and recorded Aug 26, 1833. (Bedford DB 23:449).

Jesse J R and his wife Elizabeth conveyed a deed to John Kasey Jr for 65 3/4A on Rockcastle Creek, near Thomas Stewart. Signed Dec 21, 1833 and recorded Jan 27, 1834. (Bedford DB 24:88).

JOHN

John was paid 8 shillings for serving as a Bedford soldier in the French and Indian Wars under the command of Capt John Phelps. Recorded 1765. (Bockstruck 1988, 207).

The Browns of Bedford County

John was paid 10 shillings for serving as a Bedford soldier in the French and Indians Wars under the command of Capt Matthew Talbot. Recorded 1765. (Bockstruck 1988, 208).

John of Buckingham County VA was conveyed a deed from John Murphy for 53A on the Staunton River. Recorded Mar 27, 1770. (Bedford DB 3:421).

John was held in custody for failure to find security for his behavior. Recorded 1771. (Bedford OB 3:645).

John was the orphan of John. The church wardens were ordered to bind him out. Recorded 1772. (Bedford OB 4:29).

John's will named his wife Margaret and daughter Anne. Anne was to be given three years schooling when she reached eight years of age. Executors were Margaret Scruggs and John Holloway. Will dated Jan 13, 1774 and recorded Mar 23, 1778. (Bedford WB 1:286).

John entered Revolutionary War service from Bedford County in 1775, never married, and died Dec 22, 1832 in Wayne County KY. His siblings were David, Betsy Jones, Mary Campbell, James, Thomas, Peggy Woody, Anna Reece and Jane Craig. In 1842 his brother Thomas and sister Jane, widow of John Craig, applied from Wayne County KY for arrears of pension for service in the Revolutionary War. Reel 370 of M804, National Archives. (Wardell 1988, 1:120).

John married Ann Burnley, daughter of Israel Burnley, who gave consent. Surety was Joel Burnley. Bond dated Jan 20, 1775. (Dennis 1989, 7).

John entered military service from Bedford County in 1777, per his heir Jennings Brown's application for pension based on John's service in the Revolutionary War. Reel 369 of M804, National Archives. (Wardell 1988,120).

John's will was proved by the oath of John Hollaway that he saw Bowker Smith, deceased, subscribe his name as a witness to the will. Margaret Brown was named executrix. Recorded Mar 23, 1778. (Bedford OB 6:145).

John's estate was appraised by Thomas Watts, William Hix and Stephen Goggins. Recorded Sep 28, 1778. (Bedford WB 1:323).

The Browns of Bedford County

John Jr received a deed from John Starkey for 140A (patented by Charles Merriman in 1761) on the south side of Staunton River near Merrimans Creek near Buck Beach. Signed Oct 20, 1778 and recorded Oct 26, 1778. (Bedford DB 6:137).

John's 854A on Rockcastle Creek near Otterview was surveyed. Recorded Mar 15, 1780. (Bedford DB 7:6).

John's 35A were surveyed. The land was on the north side of Staunton River, near Canefase, Denny's Road, Alford, Thomas Vest and James Martin. Survey dated Mar 15, 1780. (Bedford SR 1:240).

John's account was allowed for 325 lbs beef he furnished to the Revolutionary army. Recorded Apr 22, 1782. (Bedford OB 6:347).

John filed claims for supplies to the Revolutionary army. (Bedford OB 7:92 and 8:47).

John Brown Esq was the clerk of general court. Recorded May 28, 1787. (Bedford OB 9:50).

John's administrator Philip Pankey was qualified and gave bond. Recorded Jul 1789. (Bedford OB 9:289).

John was the son of James and Jinnet. He and his siblings were named in his father's will dated Dec 3, 1789 and recorded Jul 26, 1790. (Bedford WB 2:35).

John and Mary, parents of Lucie, gave consent for her marriage to Edward Spradling. Surety was Joseph Wright. Bond dated Jun 14, 1791. (Dennis 1989, 64).

John was born in Bedford County in 1792, enlisted in the US Army at Botetourt County VA on May 16-17, 1812, served in 12th Infantry, and was discharged at Fort Selden, LA on May 4, 1817. (Butler 1968, 23).

John Ashwell Brown was the son of Ann, and grandson of Daniel Brown. He was bequeathed 20 shillings in his grandfather's will, which was probated in 1797. (Merrill 1968, 7).

The Browns of Bedford County

John was on the list of insolvents of the southern district for 1798, as returned by Joseph Holt. (McAllister 1986, 43).

John was the son of Linah, and brother of James and Larking. He was conveyed a deed with his brother Larking from his brother James and James' wife Elizabeth for 42A on Meaders Creek. Signed and recorded Jun 25, 1798. (Bedford DB 10:485).

John married Constant Clark. Surety was Isham Clark. Bond dated Sep 23, 1799. (Hinshaw 1969, 6:884). They were married by James Turner on Sep 24, 1799. (Bedford PRO 1:242).

John had 1 male 21+ and 1 horse. Personal Property Tax List of 1800, Northern District. (Dorman 1963, 7:123).

John, the son of Mary, was bound to John Fisher. William Brown was bound to John Wilson. Recorded Feb 22, 1802. (Bedford OB 12:248).

John and Larkin Brown conveyed a deed to John Fisher for 42A on the south side of Meadows Creek near Otey and Rice. Witnesses were William Mitchell, Francis Hopkins, Jesse Hix and Robert Mitchell. Signed Feb 1802 and recorded Jul 26, 1802. (Bedford DB 11:602).

John Thompson Brown was born Mar 7, 1802 at Ivy Cliff, the son of Henry Brown and Frances Thompson. (Merrill 1968, chart A).

John was the son of Mary. She complained of the treatment of her her son by his master John Fisher. The court rescinded the binding to Fisher, and bound John Brown to John Willson. Recorded May 1803. (Bedford OB 13:5).

John "was of full age" for that purpose, and chose Francis Calvert as his guardian. The guardian was qualified. Recorded Mar 1804. (Bedford OB 13:86).

John witnessed a deed from John Buford and William Brown to John Holliday for 139A on Beaverdam Creek near JohnWright and Walton. Other witnesses were Joseph Stith, William Holliday, William Watts and John Blankenship. Signed Mar 16, 1805 and recorded Apr 22, 1805 at Bedford

The Browns of Bedford County

DB 11:1219).

John was surety for the marriage of Joseph Wright and Aggy Brown. Bond dated Jun 26, 1805. (Hinshaw 1969, 6:1021).

John was summoned to court with his wife Edith W, the former Edith W Miner, to show cause why they should not give William Miner counter security. Edith was administratrix of the estate of Gabriel Miner. Recorded Dec 24, 1805. (Bedford OB 13:293).

John married Edith M Minor. Surety was William Minor. Bond dated Feb 6, 1806 (sic). (Hinshaw 1969, 6:884).

John was conveyed a deed from Adam Boyer and his wife Patsey for 97A near Hobbs, Bramblett and Callaway. Witnesses were Charles Patterson, Andrew B Read and Thomas Miller. Signed Jan 14, 1807 and recorded Jun 22, 1807. (Bedford DB 12:223).

John filed a complaint against Larkin Brown, who appeared in court to answer. Larkin was ordered to give a peace bond of $50, and to be kept in custody "until he find such security". Recorded Oct 1808. (Bedford OB 13:268).

John, Larkin, Mary Ann and Sarah Brown were exonerated from paying delinquent taxes on the 183A of Linah Brown, deceased. John Bowles appeared in court and proved by deed that he had purchased the land by Jun 1, 1812. Recorded July 1814. (Bedford OB 16:298).

John married Matilda Bramblett. Surety was Reuben Bramblett. Bond dated Jul 26, 1817. They were married by William Harris on Aug 3, 1817. (Hinshaw 1969, 6:884).

John W had 1 male 26-45, 1 female 16-26. (U S Census of 1820, Southern District, p 62).

John W was qualified as curator of the estate of Thomas Pullin, deceased. . Recorded Mar 1822. (Bedford OB 18:220).

John W was conveyed a deed from Thomas G Burson and his wife Sally for 120A on Goose Creek, near Israel Williams. Signed and recorded

The Browns of Bedford County

Mar 27, 1822. (Bedford DB 17:185).

John W was sworn as a juror. Recorded Nov 1822. (Bedford OB 18:310).

John and his wife Constant conveyed a deed to Moses Miller for 97A on Goose Creek, near Hobbs, Bramblett and Callaway. Witnesses were D Crescent, J Grey, Jeremiah Lockett and Joseph D Stratton. Signed and recorded Jul 22, 1822. (Bedford DB 17:235).

John was conveyed a deed from the executors of Isham Clark for 238 1/2A at Wolf Creek, conveyed to Clark by Charles Markle Sr on Jul 26, 1819. Witnesses were Robert C Mitchell, J H Otey Jr and Thomas Bell. Signed Oct 1, 1824 and recorded same date. (Bedford DB 19:40).

John and his wife Constant conveyed a deed of trust to trustee John H Otey Jr for purchase from the excutors of Isham Clark of 238 1/2A at Wolf Creek. Signed Oct 1, 1824 and recorded same date. (Bedford DB 19:44).

John C married Mary M Wood. Surety was Henry Lawhorne. Bond dated Oct 26, 1824. (Hinshaw 1969, 6:884).

John was the father of Ethelred Brown who married Anna Hopkins, dau of Price. Surety was Tilson A Pullen. Bond dated Feb 22, 1825. (Hinshaw 1969, 6:884).

John was "a soldier of Armond's corps and Continental establishments", deceased. Jennings Brown was proven to be one of his heirs. Recorded Aug 28, 1826. (Bedford OB 22:123).

John and his wife Constant were conveyed a release of indenture from John H Otey Jr as trustee for William Cook, Joseph Clark and George Stanley, the executors of Isham Clark, deceased. The indenture had been secured by 82 1/2A near Thaxton and Roy Jones. Witnesses were Jos Ferguson and Frederick Aunspaugh. Signed Jun 1, 1827 and recorded Jun 2, 1827. (Bedford DB 20:257).

John and his wife Constant conveyed a deed to William Thaxton for 83 1/2A on the heads of Wolf Creek, near Thaxton, Williams and Jones. Witnesses were Frederick Aunspaugh, Daniel Aunspaugh and Jos Ferguson. Signed Jun 1, 1827 and recorded same date. (Bedford DB 20:258).

The Browns of Bedford County

John W conveyed a deed of trust to trustee Caleb J Bramblett Jr for a debt owed Elkanor Bramblett, secured by farm animals, household furnishings and farm tools. Signed Dec 20, 1827 and recorded same date. (Bedford DB 20:233).

John W and his wife Matilda conveyed a deed to Israel Wildman for 120A on Goose Creek, near Israel Wildman. Signed May 5, 1828 and recorded Jul 1, 1828. (Bedford DB 21:87).

John complained against defendant David Farley, who was bound to keep the peace. Recorded Sep 17, 1828. (Bedford OB 22:146).

John was the father of Sarah M, who married Joel Jones on Apr 16, 1829. Surety was Thomas W Brown. (Hinshaw 1969, 6:913).

John S was attorney in fact for John Hudnall and his wife Frances McGhee, and Thomas Saunders was attorney in fact for Reuben S Brown and his wife Betsy McGhee when the McGhee heirs conveyed a deed to William McGhee for land on the north side of Little Otter River. Signed Jun 26, 1829 and recorded Mar 25, 1833. (Bedford DB 23:306).

John had 1 male 15-20, 1 male 50-60, 1 female 20-30, 1 female 50-60, and no slaves. He was near Nelson C Tyler, Thomas Brown and Walker Brown. (U S Census of 1830, p 124).

John had 1 male 40-50, 1 male 70-80, 1 female 0-5, 1 female 50-60, and 1 slave. He was near Samuel Mitchell and William Campbell. (U S Census of 1830, p 152).

John was sworn as a juror in Green trustees v Otey as sheriff. Recorded Aug 1830. (Bedford OB 23:151).

John R was sworn as a juror in Taylor v Hawkins. Recorded Aug 1830. (Bedford OB 23:151).

John R's slave Jackson was found not guilty of the rape of Nancy Jones. Recorded Sep 1831. (Bedford OB 23:359).

John S was qualified as deputy sheriff. Recorded 1832. (Bedford

OB 23:240, 469).

In the matter of John Brown v Brown in chancery court, the order requiring security for costs was set aside. Recorded Mar 1832. (Bedford OB 23:480).

John was the father of Elizabeth who married Jonas Jones. Bond dated Apr 2, 1832. They were married by William Harris on Apr 2, 1832. (Hinshaw 1969, 6:943).

John, E Gwatkin and John C Noell were witnesses for a gift of slaves Eliza, Dick and Davis, from Pleasant Jeter to trustee John Sharp for the benefit of Jeter's wife Jane and two daughters. Signed Jul 14, 1832 and recorded Jul 23, 1832. (Bedford DB 23:105).

John S was conveyed a deed from Pleasant Jeter and his wife Jane, the daughter of Jeremiah Hatcher, deceased, for 1) 62A at Hurricane Creek, near James White, formerly owned by Jeremiah Hatcher, and 2) 63 1/4A near James White. Signed Jul 16, 1832 and recorded Aug 23, 1836. (Bedford DB 25:388).

John S was qualified as deputy sheriff. Recorded Mar 1833. (Bedford OB 24:106).

"John S Brown produced in court a commission from the governor, under the seal of the Commonwealth, appointing him second lieutenant in the first regiment of cavalry, 12th brigade, 1st division of militia, and qualified to the same as the law directs". Recorded May 1833. (Bedford OB 24:137).

John was surety for the marriage of Callaway Brown, son of Hezekiah, and Sarah Lawhorn on Dec 23, 1833. (Hinshaw 1969, 6:884).

John S, Spotswood Brown, Nelson A Thompson and Balda McDaniel witnessed a deed for 362A at Elk Creek from trustee Nathaniel Mandon for debtor Mrs Euphan Logwood to William B Callaway. Signed Jan 7, 1834 and recorded Jan 27, 1834. (Bedford DB 24:73).

John S and Spotswood Brown were qualified as deputy sheriffs. Recorded Mar 1834. (Bedford OB 24:261).

The Browns of Bedford County

John S, James C Moorman, William Ownby and James Martin witnessed the relinquishment of dower rights for 900-1000A at the north fork of Otter River (purchased by her husband Henry Brown) from Judith Clark to the Bank of Virginia. Signed Oct 11, 1834 and recorded Oct 13, 1834. (Bedford DB 24:283).

John M married Sarah Ann Burson. Surety was Thomas G Burson. Bond dated Oct 20, 1834. They were married by William Harris on Oct 22, 1834. (Hinshaw 1969, 6:884).

John S and Spotswood Brown were qualified as administrators of the estate of Reuben S Brown, deceased. Recorded Nov 1834. (Bedford OB 25:14).

John S and Spotswood Brown were administrators of the estate of Reuben S Brown. They auctioned off some of his slaves on Jan 15, 1835. Recorded Sep 26, 1836. (Bedford WB 9:186).

John S and Spotswood Brown were qualified as deputy sheriffs. Recorded Mar 1835. (Bedford OB 25:51).

John S was ordered to appear and show why he should not give counter security as administrator of the estate of Reuben S Brown. Recorded Mar 1835. (Bedford OB 25:69).

John S, John S Leftwich and William B Whitton gave bond as administrators of the estate of Reuben S Brown, deceased. Recorded May 1835. (Bedford OB 25:81).

John S was the son of Reuben S Brown. He and his siblings were named in the division of his father's slaves. Division was made May 25, 1835 and recorded Jun 22, 1835. (Bedford WB 9:47).

John S and his wife Lucinda J conveyed a deed to Thomas Hatcher for 1) 62A at Hurricane Creek, near James White, and 2) 63 1/4A , near James White. Signed Jul 2, 1835 and recorded Jan 23, 1837. (Bedford DB 26:36).

John S, Betsy and Spotswood Brown gave security bonds for the guardian of Eliza Brown and William Brown. Recorded Aug 1835. (Bedford OB 25:125).

The Browns of Bedford County

John R was conveyed a deed by Tubal Early and his wife Charlotte for 214A at Echols Creek, near Nolen, Walker, and Joel Early. Signed Dec 10, 1835 and recorded Jan 30, 1836. (Bedford DB 25:297).

John R and his wife Edith conveyed a deed of trust to trustee Ludowick McDaniel for a debt owed Tubal Early, secured by 214A at Eckols Creek. Witnesss were Adam Elliott, V K Leftwich and John T Sale. Signed Dec 10, 1835 and recorded May 31, 1836. (Bedford DB 25:299).

John R and his wife Edith W conveyed a deed of trust to trustee Lodowick McDaniel for 214A on Echols Creek. Recorded 1836. (Bedford DB 25:299).

John Thompson Brown was born Mar 7, 1802 and Nov 20, 1836 died at his father Henry's home at Ivy Cliff. (Merrill 1968, 167). He had graduated from Princeton in 1820, then studied law. (Ibid, 23). He served in the Virginia State Legislature, and had given a notable speech on the abolition of slavery to the House of Delegates of Virginia. (Ibid, 28). He had married Mary Willcox, and they had three children. (Ibid, chart A).

John was the son of Aaron, who had entered military service from Bedford County in 1776. He was named in Aaron's death report in 1836. Reel R358 of M804, National Archives. (Wardell 1988, 1:116).

John S and his wife Lucinda J conveyed a deed to Thomas Hatcher for 62A near Hurricane Creek, and for 63 1/4A which was part of the estate of Jeremiah Hatcher. Recorded 1837. (Bedford DB 26:36).

John, deceased, was named in the will of his father Henry. His father's will was signed Jan 6, 1837 and recorded Sep 25, 1841. (Bedford WB 10:392).

John S and his siblings, the heirs and legatees of Reuben S Brown, deceased, were conveyed a deed from William C Leftwich for 51A at Elk Creek, near Howards Branch. Signed and recorded May 1, 1837. (Bedford DB 26:151).

John T was deceased. His administrator, Mary E Brown, acting on behalf of Micajah Davis Jr, executor of the will of Henry Brown, deceased, sued Isham Lawhorne for $47.61. Lawhorne confessed judgment. Recorded Feb 1838. (Bedford OB 26:118).

The Browns of Bedford County

John R and his wife Edith W conveyed a deed to Joseph A Brown for 214A at Echols Creek, near Walker, Joel Early and Mrs Early. Signed and recorded Aug 24, 1838. (Bedford DB 27:241).

John and his Edith his wife were sued by the administrator of Gabriel Minor, deceased. The case was dismissed. Recorded Nov 7, 1838. (Bedford Chancery OB 1:299).

John and Thomas M Brown sued William Hurt, administrator of William Brown, deceased. On the court calendar Oct 2, 1839. (Bedford Chancery OB 1:359).

John had 1 male 60-70, and 9 slaves. He was near George W Hawkins, Jonas Jones and Walker Brown. (U S Census of 1840, p 27).

John M had 2 males 0-5, 1 male 20-30, 1 female 15-20, and 11 slaves. He was near William Read and Malandor Turner. (U S Census of 1840, p 17).

John R had 1 male 50-60, 1 female 15-20, 1 female 60-70, and no slaves. He was near Moses Nelson and Thomas W Key. (U S Census of 1840, p 19)

John and Thomas M Brown sued William H Brown, deceased, by his administrator, William Hurt, and Aaron Allred and his wife Elizabeth, deceased, the late Elizabeth Brown. The case was dismissed. Recorded Oct 5, 1940. (Bedford Chancery OB 1:422).

JOSEPH

Joseph was born 1756 in Bedford County VA. In 1776 he entered Revolutionary War service from Jonesborough, TN. In 1833 he applied for a Revolutionary War pension at Lincoln County MO, where he lived with his nephew, Levi Brown. Reel R372 of M804, National Archives. (Wardell 1988, 1:121).

Joseph was conveyed a deed from Joseph Payne and wife Phebe for 238A on the east branches of Beaverdam Creek and the head branches of Stony Fork of Goose Creek, near Weaver and Pate. Witnessed by John Dent, Robert Nimmo and William Azberry. Recorded Feb 1, 1777. (Bedford DB 5:496).

84

The Browns of Bedford County

Joseph was conveyed a deed from Joseph Blankenship for 185A on Beaverdam Creek. Witnesses were Jeremiah Pate, Nathan Hunt and John Dent. Signed Nov 15, 1786 and recorded Jun 25, 1787. (Bedford DB 10:10).

Joseph's will named his wife Elizabeth and children Jesse, Rhodham, Joseph, Hezekiah, Orpah, Sarah and Margaret. Excutors were his sons Jesse and Rhodham. Witnesses were William Dent, John Dent and Sarah Dent. Will dated Aug 22, 1795 and recorded Oct 26, 1795. (Bedford WB 2:163).

Joseph's executors Jesse Dent Brown and Rhodham Brown were qualified. Recorded Oct 1795. (Bedford OB 11:37).

Joseph's estate was appraised on Jan 23, 1796 by Joseph Stith, James Board and John May. Recorded Feb 22, 1796. (Bedford WB 2:173).

Joseph was the son of Daniel and Hannah. He and his siblings were mentioned in a certificate of removal from Crooked Run Monthly Meeting to Goose Creek Monthly Meeting. Recorded at Goose Creek minutes of Mar 31, 1798. (Wright 1993, 54).

Joseph was deceased. His 256A of estate land was processioned, with John Mays, Benjamin Stith and Jesse D Brown present. Recorded Dec 4, 1799. (Bedford PRO 1:99).

Joseph had 1 male 21+, and 2 horses. Personal Property Tax List of 1800, District 1. (Dorman 1963, 7:65).

Joseph witnessed a deed from Rhodam Brown and his wife Elizabeth to Isaac James for 92 1/2A on Beaverdam Creek. Other witnesses were Lawrence James and Hezekiah Brown. Signed Mar 14, 1800 and recorded Apr 28, 1800. (Bedford DB 11:205).

Joseph was deceased. His 238A of estate lands were processioned without comments. Recorded Feb 27, 1804. (Bedford PRO 1:129).

Joseph of Cumberland County KY conveyed a deed to William Miller for 238A on the Stony Fork Branch of Goose Creek. Signed Oct 28, 1811 and recorded same date. (Bedford DB 13:634).

Joseph's estate was exonerated from erroneously assessed delinquent taxes on the 92A he had sold to William Mills (?) in 1810. Recorded Aug 1816. (Bedford OB 17:238).

Joseph M married Sally W Williamson. Surety was Leonard N Williamson. Bond dated Jan 3, 1826. They were married Jan 5, 1826 by William Harris. (Hinshaw 1969, 6:884).

Joseph had conveyed a deed of trust to Augustine Leftwich in Jun 1827 for a debt he owed Barnabas A Eidson, secured by slave Phillip, a cow, furniture, and carpenter's tools. Eidson instructed Joseph to convey the personal property to William N Sherman, to clear the debt. Joseph conveyed to a deed to Sherman for all the listed personal property. Signed Sep 5, 1827 and recorded same date. (Bedford DB 20:332).

Joseph M had 1 male 0-5, 1 male 30-40, 1 female 20-30, and 1 slave. He was near Nelson H Otey and John Robertson. (U S Census of 1830, p 127).

Joseph M served as a juror. Recorded Mar 1835. (Bedford OB 25:52).

Joseph B M conveyed a deed of trust to trustee Daniel Aunspaugh for rent and other debts owed Armistead Otey, secured by household furniture. Signed May 25, 1835 and recorded May 29, 1835. (Bedford DB 24:455).

Joseph was the son of Aaron, who had entered military service from Bedford County in 1776. He was named in Aaron's death report of 1836. Reel R358 of M804, National Archives. (Wardell 1988, 1:116).

Joseph M conveyed a deed of trust to trustee Daniel Aunspaugh for a debt owed Henry _____, secured by 700 pounds of pork, and household furniture. Trustee was to auction off the goods and repay Henry _____. Signed Jan 15, 1838 and recorded Jan 16, 1838. (Bedford DB 27:20).

Joseph A was conveyed a deed from John R Brown and his wife Edith W for 214A on Echols Creek, near Walker, Joel Early and Mrs Early. Signed Aug 24, 1838 and recorded same date. (Bedford DB 27:241).

Joseph M conveyed a deed of trust to trustee Joseph Wilson for a debt owed Vinal Smith, secured by 1) 4A near the town of Liberty, near the Fancy Farm Road, Vinal Smith and William Terry, part of the land he had purchased from the heirs of Markle, and 2) his whole interest in the estate of Reed Brown, deceased. Signed Jan 2, 1839 and recorded same date. (Bedford DB 27:365).

Joseph M was conveyed a deed from Vinal Smith and his wife Emily F for 3 1/2A near the town of Liberty, on the north side of the Peaks, which Smith had purchased from the heirs of Markle. Signed Apr 5, 1839 and recorded same date. (Bedford DB 27:463).

Joseph M was awarded an injunction to restrain Vinal Smith and Joseph Wilson from all further proceedings under a deed of trust executed by Joseph M Brown to Joseph Wilson for the benefit of Vinal Smith, dated Jan 2, 1839. Recorded Jul 1840. (Bedford OB 27:99).

Joseph had 1 male 0-5, 3 males 5-10, 1 male 50-60, 1 female 5-10, 1 female 40-50, and 4 slaves. He was near Taliaferro Owens and Thomas Heeney. (U S Census of 1840, p 31).

Joseph M's slave Phill was a pauper. The overseers of the poor had refused to send him to the poorhouse. The court ordered that they admit him as a pauper, and provide for him as in other cases. Recorded Feb 1840. (Bedford OB 27:25).

Joseph M conveyed a deed of trust to trustee James Oney for Yancy Harris, to indemnify Harris for judgment on a bond. The deed of trust was secured by 4A near the town of Liberty, which had been conveyed to him by Vinal Smith, with houses attached and all the household and kitchen furniture. Trustee to auction all to the highest bidder. Signed Apr 30, 1840 and recorded same date. (Bedford DB 28:296).

JOSHUA aka Joshua R C, J R C

Joshua R C Brown married Jane Leftwich on Sep 7, 1819. Jane was the daughter of Thomas and Gincey. Surety was Munford Stanfell. (Hopkins 1931, 273).

Joshua Robert Callaway Brown and his wife Jane lived in Salem, VA, then in La Porte, IN, and finally settled in New Buffalo, MI, where they owned the Town Hotel. (Prillaman 1995, 283).

The Browns of Bedford County

Joshua was a non-resident, but held 19 slaves in Bedford County. (U S Census of 1820, Southern District, p 7).

Joshua had 1 female 0-10, 2 females 16-26, 1 female 45+. (U S Census of 1820, Southern District, p 64).

Joshua R C conveyed title to James Woodford and his wife Lucy for 770A on Goose Creek, near John Claytor, John Scott and Milbourn Williamson. The conveyance was per order of the Chancery Court of Mar 1821, with Woodford acting on behalf of Joshua Pratt, Jesse Wilk and his wife Judith, Drury Foster and his wife Mary, and the infant heirs of Jesse Pratt, deceased. Signed May 27, 1822 and recorded Jul 22, 1822. (Bedford DB 17:238).

Joshua C was chosen as his guardian by Thomas Leftwich. Recorded Nov 1822. (Bedford OB 18:311).

Joshua was brought to court for breach of the peace. Recorded Aug 1823. (Bedford OB 19:24).

Joshua R C, guardian of Thomas Leftwich, had been awarded judgment against Matthew Bellamy. Bellamy was awarded a stay of judgment until the matter could be heard in equity. Recorded Jul 25, 1825. (Bedford OB 20:90).

Joshua R C was qualified as the administrator of Daniel Floyd. Recorded Nov 28, 1825. (Bedford OB 20:154).

Joshua and his wife Jane of Botetourt County VA, with James Brown and his wife Catharine of Campbell County VA, were distributors of the estate of Thomas Leftwich. They conveyed a deed to James C Steptoe for 811A at Porter Mountain. Signed Jul 6, 1826 and recorded Aug 28, 1826. (Bedford DB 20:59).

Joshua R C Brown of Botetourt County VA was conveyed a deed by James Dixon and his wife Susannah of Pittsylvania County VA for 700-800A at Crab Orchard Creek near Samuel Wilks. The Dixons had conveyed the land to the late Thomas Leftwich, and Joshua claimed the land in the right of his wife Jinsey, late Jinsey Leftwich. Signed Dec 18, 1827 and recorded Jan 10, 1828. (Bedford DB 20:418).

The Browns of Bedford County

Joshua R C purchased slave Derry from the assignee of insolvent debtor Mark Anthony. Recorded Jul 27, 1829. (Bedford DB 21:248).

Joshua R C and his wife Jane of Laporte County IN conveyed a deed to John B Witt for 660A on Crab Orchard Creek, near Samuel Wilkes. Signed Nov 12, 1836 and recorded Nov 11, 1836 (sic). (Bedford DB 25:442).

Joshua R C's wife Jane relinquished to John B Witt her dower rights to a deed recorded at DB 26:442. Signed Apr 12, 1837 and recorded May 24, 1837. (Bedford DB 26:185). (Also recorded at Bedford OB 26:17).

JOSIAH

Josiah was a son of Jennings Brown. He and his brothers were ordered bound out by the overseers of the poor. Recorded Apr 27, 1795. (Bedford OB 10:366.

Josiah, son of Jennings Brown, was indentured to William Pidgeon. Recorded Feb 1796. (Bedford OB 11:62).

JOYCE aka Joycy, Joicy

Joicey Snider married Daniel Brown. She was the daughter of Henry. Surety was William Snider. Bond dated Feb 12, 1802. (Hinshaw 1969, 6:884).

Joyce, widow of Daniel Brown, was alloted her dower in his real and personal property. Recorded Mar 1834. (Bedford OB 24:266).

Joyce was the mother of Garrett, who married Irenia Plymale, dau of Thomas. Surety was Wyatt Trueman. Bond dated Oct 17, 1838. (Hinshaw 1969, 6:884).

Joicy had 1 male 20-30, 1 male 30-40, 1 female 15-20, 1 female 20-30, 1 female 60-70, and no slaves. She was near Nancy Hutson and Burchy Kinnett. (U S Census of 1840, p 57).

The Browns of Bedford County

JUANA

Juana Tyler married Thomas W Brown. She was the daughter of Daniel. Surety was Isham C Brown. Bond dated Oct 3, 1826. (Hinshaw 1969, 6:884).

JUBAL

Jubal was indentured. Recorded 1820. (Bedford OB 18:20).

Jubal answered the complaint against him by Robert Carter for breach of the peace, and by consent of the parties Jubal was discharged. Recorded Feb 23, 1828. (Bedford OB 22:212).

JUDITH aka Juda

Judith married Burley Lacey, with the consent of Thomas Brown. Surety was William Woody. Bond dated Feb 9, 1786. (Dennis 1989, 41).

Judith Brown and Burnley Lacey were married by James Mitchell on Feb 10, 1786. (Bedford PRO 1:216).

Judith conveyed power of attorney to Thomas Whittington Jr for general powers. Witnesses were Nancy Whittington, John Whittington and Stark Whittington. Signed and recorded Oct 25, 1817. (Bedford DB 14:513).

Judith conveyed of a deed of gift to her nephew Thomas Whittington Jr for 13 slaves: Nat, Rose, Clara, Rachel, Maria, Linda, Juno, Richard, Julias, Henry, Granville, Mary and Lenah. Whittington was to support and provide for Judith in a genteel manner for the rest of her life. Witnesses were Dudley Jones, Balda McDaniel, Robert Tinsley and Lemuel Johnson. Susannah Cavanaugh relased her interest in the slaves. Signed Jun 14, 1819 and recorded May 27, 1822. (Bedford DB 18:129).

Judith's noncupative will was recorded, as told to Sarah A Pearman on Mar 8, 1833 when she was on her deathbed. Judith "could not write, by reason of old age". The family of Thomas Whittington lived with Judith, and his daughter Jane was bequeathed $200 for her education. Witnesses were Martha Garret, John Whittington and Oglesby Pearman. Recorded Aug 26, 1833. (Bedford WB 8:201).

Judith Brown and Susannah Cavanaugh were sued by Thomas Whittington. On calendar May 13, 1833. (Bedford Chancery OB 1:39).

Judith was deceased, dead for more than three months, and no one had asked for administration of her estate. The court found her nuncupative will to be her last will and testament, on motion of Martha Jane Whittington, with depositions by Sarah A Pearman, Martha Garritt and Oglesby Pearman. Recorded Aug 1833, (Bedford OB 24:185). Her administrator qualified. (Ibid, 189).

Judith was awarded judgment against the executor of Thomas Whittington. Recorded May 14, 1834. (Bedford Chancery OB 1:113).

Judith was deceased. Benjamin Wiggenton was sworn to settle the account current with her executor Balda McDaniel. Recorded Sep 1837 at OB 26:55. The account current was presented by her administrator, and recorded Oct 1837. (Bedford OB 26:61). The account current was ordered recorded Nov 1837. (Ibid, 70).

LARKIN aka Larking

Larking was the son of Linah. He and his brother John were conveyed a deed from their brother James Jr and his wife Elizabeth for 42A on Meadows Creek. Signed Jun 25, 1798 and recorded same date. (Bedford DB 10:485).

Larkin and John Brown conveyed a deed to John Fisher for 42A on the south side of Meadows Creek near Otey and Rice. Witnesses were William Mitchell, Francis Hopkins, Jesse Hix and Robert Mitchell. Signed Feb 1802 and recorded Jul 26, 1802. (Bedford DB 11:602).

Larkin was provided a peace bond by James Brown and Benjamin Richards. Recorded Aug 30, 1806. (Bedford OB 13:379).

Larkin appeared in court to answer a complaint of John Brown, and was ordered to give a peace bond and to be kept in custody until he made the security. Recorded Oct 1808. (Bedford OB 13:268). Bond recorded. (Ibid, p 379).

The Browns of Bedford County

Larkin was exonerated from payment of taxes erroneously assessed against the estate of Linah Brown, deceased. John Fisher appeared in court and proved by deed that he had purchased the land before Jun 1, 1812. Recorded Jun 1814. (Bedford OB 16:294).

Larkin, with John, Mary Ann and Sarah Brown, was exonerated from the tax sale against 183A of Linah Brown, deceased. John Bowles appeared in court and proved by deed that he had purchased the land by Jun 1, 1812. Recorded July 1814. (Bedford OB 16:298).

LEONARD aka Linah, Lynard, Lynee

Lynee was conveyed a deed from Augustine Leftwich Sr for 300A on Johns Creek, a branch of Little Otter River, near John Galloway. Signed Jul 26, 1773 and recorded same date. (Bedford DB 5:102).

Lynard lived near Thomas Brown Sr, James Brown and John Galawdy, per a deed from George Hughes to Raba Brown for 150A on a small branch of Little Otter. Recorded Aug 18, 1778. (Bedford DB 6:94).

Linor lived near Little Otter River, Brambletts Road and William Woody, per a deed from Thomas Brown to Thomas Jones. Signed Sep 25, 1780 and recorded Oct 23, 1780. (Bedford DB 7:28).

Leonard's administratrx, his widow Sarah Brown, was qualified and appraisers were appointed. Recorded Aug 28, 1781. (Bedford OB 6:326).

Liner's estate was inventoried and appraised on Nov 24, 1781 by Merry Carter, William Donning and William Wood. Recorded Nov 26, 1781. (Bedford WB 1:405). Also recorded at OB 6:332.

Lynee was deceased when Augustine Leftwich deeded 200A to James Moorman. The 200A adjoined the lands of Lynee Brown, deceased, and Benjamin Rice. Signed Oct 18, 1786 and recorded Oct 18, 1786. (Bedford DB 7:672).

Linah's administratrix Sarah Brown failed to give counter security, and the estate was assigned to creditors William Quarles and Boice Edson. Recorded Feb 1789. (Bedford OB 9:233).

The Browns of Bedford County

Linah was ordered by the overseers of the poor to be bound to William Powell. Recorded 1794. (Bedford OB 10:278).

Lynard had been ordered by the overseers of the poor to be apprenticed and bound to William Powell. That order was rescinded by the overseers of the poor, and he was bound to Michael Rupert. Recorded Oct 1795. (Bedford OB 11:38).

Linah was the father of James, Larking and John per a deed from son James Jr and his wife Elizabeth to Larking and John for 42A on Meadows Creek. Signed and recorded Jun 25, 1798. (Bedford DB 10:485).

Lynard's estate was settled, with Sarah Brown as administratrix. Recorded Jul 1803. (Bedford OB 13:16).

Lynard's estate and Sarah Brown conveyed a deed to John Marks for an interest in 110A on Little Otter River, which had been conveyed in 1795 by James Brown to John Reese. Recorded 1804. (Bedford DB 11:986).

Linah was deceased. His widow Sarah conveyed her dower rights to 110A to Jones Marrs, son of John Marrs, deceased. The land had been conveyed by John Reese and his wife Nancy to John Marrs in Jun 1803. Witnesses were Benjamin Rice, John McLean and Frederick Gooldy. Signed Jun 1, 1807 and recorded Jun 25, 1807. (Bedford DB 12:226).

Linah's estate was exonerated from payment of taxes erroneously assessed. John Fisher appeared in court and proved by deed that he had purchased the land by Jun 1, 1812. Recorded June 1814. (Bedford OB 16:294).

Linah's 183A, also in the names of Larkin, John, Mary Ann and Sarah Brown, were exonerated from tax sale. John Bowles appeared in court and proved by deed that he had purchased the land by Jun 1, 1812. Recorded Jul 1814. (Bedford OB 16:298).

Linah's estate lands had been billed in error for delinquent taxes, and were exonerated when proven by deed to have been purchased by Jun 1, 1812 by 1) Charles Markle who purchased 200A from Frederick Gooldy, and by 2) John Makon who purchased 240A. Recorded Sep 27, 1814. (Bedford OB 16:332).

Linah's estate was exonerated from delinquent taxes assessed on 512A for the year 1788. Recorded Jul 25, 1816. (Bedford OB 17:218).

Lenard Jr was exonerated for erroneously assessed delinquent taxes on 8A because the court could find "no such land or person". Recorded Aug 1816. (Bedford OB 17:236).

LETTICE

Lettice was born Dec 3, 1757, the eldest daughter of Henry and Alce Brown, born Dec 3, 1757. She and her siblings were mentioned when her parents' marriage was recorded. Recorded Jan 25, 1773. (Bedford DB 4:455).

Lettice was conveyed a deed from James Chastain for 50A on the south side of Otter River and Moses Run, near Thomas Robinson and Anny Witt. Witnesses were Henry Brown, Francis Burks and Samuel Adams. Signed and recorded Sep 18, 1779. (Bedford DB 6:310).

Lettice conveyed a deed to John Thompson for 50A on the south side of Otter River. Recorded Oct 23, 1785. (Bedford DB 7:580).

Lettice was buried in the Brown family cemetery at Ivy Hill. (Merrill 1968, chart A).

LEVI

Levi was the nephew of Joseph Brown. Joseph was living with him in Lincoln County MO in 1833 when Joseph applied for a pension for service in the Revolutionary War. Reel R372 of M804, National Archives. (Wardell 1988, 1:121).

LOCKY

Locky married Alexander Irvine. Bond dated Mar 19, 1827. Surety was Gustavus A Wingfield. They were married by James Mitchell on Mar 20, 1827. (Hinshaw 1969, 6:939). Locky was the daughter of Henry and Frances Thompson Brown of Ivy Cliff. Her husband was Alexander Irvine. (Merrill 1968, chart A).

The Browns of Bedford County

Locky and her siblings were named in the will of their father Henry. She was bequeathed 654A at Buffalo Creek, near David Thompson and Col Austin. Her father's will was signed Jan 6, 1837 and recorded Sep 25, 1841. (Bedford WB 10:392).

LUCINDA aka Lewcinda

Lucinda J and her husband John S conveyed a deed to Thomas Hatcher for 1) 62A at Hurricane Creek, near James White, and for 2) 63 1/4A, near James White. Signed Jul 2, 1835 and recorded Jan 23, 1837. (Bedford DB 26:36).

Lewcinda was the daughter of Aaron, who had entered military service from Bedford County in 1776. She was named in the report of his death in 1836. Reel R358 of M804, National Archives. (Wardell 1988, 1:116).

LUCY aka Lucie

Lucie married Edward Spradling. She was the daughter of John and Mary Brown, who gave consent. Surety was Joseph Wright. Bond dated Jun 14, 1791. (Dennis 1989, 64). They were on Jun 16, 1791 by Rev John Ayers, a Methodist minister. (Bedford PRO 1:223).

Lucy and her husband Daniel conveyed a deed to Hinman Wooster for 169A on Goose Creek, near Gills. Recorded 1795. (Bedford DB 10:43).

Lucy married Jimmy Cundiff, with the consent of Daniel Brown. Surety was Jesse Brown. Bond dated Mar 29, 1800. (Dennis 1989, 12). They were married on Apr 17, 1800 by Rev John Ayers, a Methodist minister. (Bedford PRO 1:245).

Lucy and her husband Daniel of Pittsylvania Co VA conveyed a deed to Thomas Stewart for 200A on both sides of the road from Hales Ford to the Meadows of Goose Creek, near Lewis Turner, David Kerson, the old mill road and Hancock. Witnesses were Arthur Goolsley, Shadrack Brown, Wiatt Brown and Samuel Murphy. Signed Jun 24, 1805 and recorded Jul 22, 1805. (Bedford DB 11:1282).

Lucy conveyed a release of dower to Thomas Stuart for 200A that was conveyed by Daniel Brown on Jun 4, 1805. Lucy was examined in

Pittsylvania Co VA because she was unable to travel to Bedford County. Signed Sep 2, 1805 and recorded Sep 28, 1807. (Bedford DB 12:250).

Lucy married Michael Vieley. Surety was Ebenizer Brown. Bond dated Sep 14, 1807. (Hinshaw 1969, 6:1009).

Lucy chose Henry Nichols to be her guardian. Recorded Sep 24, 1816. (Bedford OB 17:278).

Lucy married Edward Lazenby. Surety was Henry Moss. Bond dated Oct 20, 1817. (Ricks 1939, 90).

Lucy married John H Ferguson, son of Joseph Ferguson. Bond dated Dec 3, 1822. (Ricks 1939, 50). She was the daughter of Joyce Snider. Surety was Henry F Tate. They were married by William Leftwich on Dec 4, 1822. (Hinshaw 1969, 6:914).

Lucy Ann Moon married Daniel Brown. Surety was Thomas Steptoe. Bond dated Aug 31, 1824 (sic). They were married by John Ayres on Aug 30, 1824 (sic). (Hinshaw 1969, 6:884).

LYMAN

Lyman, Roswell and Sandford Brown, William Thornton's wards, John Davis' heirs, Joseph Reynolds and Jesse Reynolds were landowners where the James River canal was to be built. A panel was appointed to assess the damage which would be sustained by their properties. Recorded Jun 20, 1825 at OB 20:75. 40A of the lands were condemned for use of the canal and its feeds, locks and dams. Recorded Jul 22, 1825. (Bedford OB 20:93).

Lyman, Sandford and Roswell Brown were conveyed a deed from Philip Thornton and his wife Caroline for 1,924A on the James River between the Rockbridge County line and the foot of Irish Falls. The Browns were all natives of Berkshire County, MA. Signed Feb 5, 1827 and recorded Mar 10, 1828. (Bedford DB 20:476).

Lyman, Sandford Jr and Roswell Brown conveyed a power of attorney to John A Wharton to convey 1,914A on the James River to Charles B Reynolds. Signed Apr 28, 1828 and recorded same date. (Bedford DB 20:475).

The Browns of Bedford County

Lyman and his wife Frances, Sanford Brown and his wife Elvira, and Roswell Brown, of Sandsfield, Berkshire County MA, conveyed a deed to Charles B Reynolds for 924A at the James River between the Rockbridge County line and the foot of Irish Falls near Balcony Falls and Snow Creek. Signed Jul 6, 1829 and recorded Mar 9, 1830. (Bedford DB 22:75).

LYONELL

Lyonell was conveyed a deed from John McFarland Jr for 212 1/2A at the head of Meadows Creek. Signed and recorded May 25, 1778. (Bedford DB 6:48).

MANEY

Maney married James Bandy. Surety was Ebenezer Brown. Bond dated Apr 12, 1808. (Hinshaw 1969, 6:875). See NANCY.

MANLY

Manly and Janet Brown, parents of Mary, gave consent for her marriage to John Campbell. Surety was Isham Galloway. Bond dated Apr 26, 1790. (Dennis 1989, 13).

MARGARET aka Peggy

Peggy was born Aug 28, 1786, the daughter of Arabia Brown and his wife Elizabeth Dooley. Peggy and her siblings were named in her father Arabia's pension application for service in the Revolutionary War. Reel R359 of M804, National Archives. (Wardell 1988, 1:116).

Margaret was the wife of John, and mother of Anne. She was named in the will of her husband John which was dated Jan 13, 1774 and recorded Mar 23,1778. (Bedford WB 1:286).

Margaret was granted a patent for 200A on Camping Run of Lynville Creek, part of a large survey made for William Mead by Isham Talbot. Recorded Jul 5, 1780. (Bedford PB A:559).

The Browns of Bedford County

Margaret was named as Margaret Woody in the will of her father James, dated Dec 3, 1789. His granddaughter Elizabeth Woody was also mentioned. His will was recorded Jul 26, 1790. (Bedford WB 2:35).

Margaret was the daughter of Joseph Brown and his wife Elizabeth. She and her siblings were named in their father's will dated Aug 22, 1795, and recorded Oct 26, 1795. (Bedford WB 2:163).

Margaret and William McCarty were married by James Turner on Feb 1, 1803. (Hinshaw 1969, 6:953). (Also at Bedford PRO 1:253).

Peggy Brown Woody was a sister of John Brown. She and her siblings were named in his pension application for service in the Revolutionary War. Reel R370 of M804, National Archives. (Wardell 1988, 1:116).

MARIA

Maria Carter Brown was the daughter of Henry Brown and Eleanor Custis Lewis Carter. She was born in 1824. (Merrill 1968, chart A).

Maria was the daughter of Henry. She was named in will of her grandfather Henry Brown, with her brother Henry Guilford Brown. Her grandfather's will was signed Jan 6, 1837 and recorded Sep 25, 1841. (Bedford WB 10:392).

MARMADUKE

Marmaduke conveyed power of attorney to his son Enoch Brown to sell goods and chattels from the estate of Marmaduke's father George Brown of Stafford County VA. Witnesses were Jacob White and Charles Gwatkins. Signed Apr 20, 1795 and recorded Sep 23, 1805. (Bedford DB 11:1309).

Marmaduke's widow Sarah appointed Enoch Brown of Culpepper County VA as power of attorney to sell her life estate in the land in Fauquier County VA which John Davies had leased to Marmaduke Brown and his wife Sarah in 1776. Signed Dec 1812 and recorded Jan 25, 1813. (Bedford DB 13:663).

MARTHA aka Patsey

Patsey married Adam Boyer. Surety was Thomas Brown. Bond dated

The Browns of Bedford County

Oct 8, 1796. (Dennis 1989, 7). Patsey and Adam Bowyer were married by James Turner on Oct 11, 1796. (Bedford PRO 1:238).

Martha G was the mother of Tabitha who married Tyree Arthur, son of Charlotte. Marriage bond dated Dec 22, 1835. Bond dated Dec 22,1835. They were married by Abner Anthony on Dec 24, 1835. (Hinshaw 1969, 6:873).

Martha Jane Witt married James M Brown. She was the daughter of John. Surety was Wiatt Crane. Bond dated Mar 30, 1839. They were married by Mosby Arnold on Apr 10, 1839. (Hinshaw 1969, 6:884).

MARY aka Polly

Mary married Thomas Ratliffe. Surety was Alexander Dobbins. Bond dated Oct 22, 1779. (Dennis 1989, 59).

Polly Callaway married Daniel Brown on Aug 4, 1781. Surety was James Steptoe. (Hinshaw 1969, 6:883). See EMILY.

Mary and her husband William of Locust Thicket conveyed a deed to John Traylor for 1,430A. Witnesses were William Brown and Hubbard Brown. Recorded Feb 10, 1781. (Bedford DB 7:70).

Mary and her husband William conveyed a deed to Patterson Bullock for 1,900A on the north side of Whipping Creek, both sides Little Whipping Creek and on Lick Creek. Recorded Aug 27, 1781. (Bedford DB 7:71).

Mary and her husband William conveyed a deed to Josias Bullock for 1,000A near Lick Creek. Recorded Aug 27, 1781. (Bedford DB 7:72).

Mary Brown and John Frith were married by John W Holt. Recorded Oct 22, 1782. (Bedford DB 7:341).

Mary was the daughter of James Brown and his wife Jinnet. She and her siblings were named in their father's will dated Dec 3, 1789 and recorded Jul 26, 1790. (Bedford WB 2:35).

The Browns of Bedford County

Mary married John Campbell. She was the daughter of Manly and Janet, who gave consent. Surety was Isham Galloway. Bond dated Apr 26, 1790 (sic). (Dennis 1969, 13).

Mary Brown and John Campbell were married by Jeremiah Hatcher on Apr 25, 1790 (sic). (Bedford PRO 1:222).

Mary and John, parents of Lucy, gave consent for her marriage to Edward Spradling. Surety was Joseph Wright. Bond dated Jun 14, 1791. (Dennis 1989, 64).

Mary Ann received a deed from James Brown Jr for 31 1/2A on Little Otter River near James Brown. Recorded 1793. (Bedford DB 9:255).

Mary was the daughter of Henry Brown and Ann Richardson, his first wife. (Merrill 1968, 11). She and her siblings and half-siblings were named in her father's will dated Jan 9, 1796. She inherited 10 shillings by the will. His will was recorded Jun 24, 1799. (Bedford WB 2:261).

Mary Ann, James Brown, Thomas Sumpkin, William Bramblett, Walter Otey, William Halley, Charles Cafferty and George Stone gave bond for Robert Davis, who was accused of larceny. Recorded Mar 1798. (Bedford OB 11:251).

Mary was the daughter of Henry and Frances Thompson Brown of Ivy Cliff. She was born there Jan 27, 1799, died Nov 2, 1818, and was buried at Ivy Hill. Her husband was Samuel Claytor. (Merrill, chart A).

Polly L married John B Fisher. Surety was Foster Sydnor. Bond dated Nov 16, 1801. They were married by James Turner on Nov 17, 1801. (Hinshaw 1969, 6:915).

Mary's son John was bound to John Fisher, and William was bound to John Wilson. Recorded Feb 22, 1802. (Bedford OB 12:248).

Mary Ann's son Clitus Smith Brown was indentured to James McClure. Recorded Jan 24, 1803. (Bedford OB 12:341).

The Browns of Bedford County

Mary complained of the treatment of her son John by his master John Fisher. That binding was rescinded, and he was bound to John Wilson. Recorded May 1803. (Bedford OB 13:5).

Polly Hancock married Daniel Brown . She was the daughter of Samuel. Surety was James Leftwich. Bond dated Jul 15, 1803. (Hinshaw 1969, 6:884). They were married on Jul 17, 1803 by Rev John Ayers, a Methodist minister. (Bedford PRO 1:252).

Mary was a neighbor of James Brown and his wife Elizabeth per James' deed to Thomas Scruggs for land on the Little Otter River. Signed Oct 1803 and recorded Jan 23, 1804. (Bedford DB 11:909).

Mary Ann's land was processioned. Recorded May 28, 1804 at (Bedford PRO 1:153).

Mary Ann conveyed a deed to Jane Scruggs for 31 1/2A on the waters of Little Otter River, near James Brown. Witnesses were James Otey, Samuel Todd Jr and Charles Marable Jr. Signed Nov 4, 1804 and recorded Jan 28, 1805. (Bedford DB 11:1159).

Polly, Jesse Leftwich, John Lee, Lucy Pratt and James Echkols were ordered to appear in court to show cause why a road should not be established from the county line between Bedford County and Campbell County at John Lee's to Blackwater Road. Recorded Jul 1806. (Bedford OB 13:353).

Polly George and Jesse Brown were married by George Rucker on Mar 27, 1807. (Bedford PRO 1:260).

Polly's land was near William Leftwich, Jesse Leftwich and Daniel Brown. Recorded Mar 1809. (Bedford PRO 1:207).

Polly Brown was bequeathed 200A near the Staunton River, by the will of her father James Callaway dated May 2, 1809. Her siblings mentioned in the will were James, Henry T, William, John, George, Abner, Thomas, Jeremiah, Lucy, Catharine, Elizabeth Innes and Frances Steptoe. (Ackerly 1930, 298).

The Browns of Bedford County

Polly Preas married James T Brown. She was the daughter of Elizabeth. Surety was David Brown. Bond dated Apr 15, 1812. (Hinshaw 1969, 6:884).

Polly Brown and Charles Walden were property owners on Buffalo Creek when James Brown of Franklin County VA conveyed a deed to David Quarles for 163A on Buffalo Creek. Witnesses were John A Leftwich, Thomas A Claytor and William Porter. Signed Sep 14, 1812 and recorded Feb 22, 1813. (Bedford DB 13:799).

Mary Ann, Larkin, John, and Sarah Brown were exonerated from paying delinquent taxes on 183A in the estate of Linah Brown, deceased. John Bowles appeared in court and proved by deed that he had purchased the land by Jun 1, 1812. Recorded July 1814. (Bedford OB 16:298).

Mary married Samuel Claytor. She was the daughter of Henry. Bond dated Jul 12, 1817. (Ricks 1939, 27) They were married by William Leftwich on Jul 17, 1817. (Hinshaw 1969, 6:893).

Mary Brown Clayton was buried at the Thompson Brown Family Cemetery. Her gravestone reads: Jan 27, 1799-Nov 2, 1818. (Daughters 1970, 81).

Mary M Wood married John C Brown. Surety was Henry Lawhorne. Bond dated Oct 26, 1824. (Hinshaw 1969, 6:884).

Mary S Bond married Pleasant Brown. Surety was Pleasant Bond. Bond dated Dec 1, 1824. They were married by John Ayers on Dec 2, 1824. (Hinshaw 1969, 6:884).

Polly Lively married Alexander Brown. Surety was Willis B Lively. Bond dated Apr 25, 1826. They were married by William Harris on Apr 27, 1826. (Hinshaw 1969, 6:884).

Polly married Nehemiah Spradling. Surety was Rodham Brown. Bond dated Aug 19, 1826. (Ricks 1939, 145).

Mary E married James Leftwich. She was the daughter of Reuben S Brown. Surety was George W Leftwich. Bond dated Feb 4, 1830. They were married by Rev Robert Burwell on Feb 10, 1830. (Hopkins 1931, 275). (Also at Hinshaw 1969, 949).

The Browns of Bedford County

Mary and her husband Charles of Albemarle County VA to conveyed a deed to Ebenezer Watkins of Floyd County VA for 100A at Little Otter River. Signed May 3, 1831 and recorded May 11, 1831. (Bedford DB 22:349).

Mary S, Pleasant Brown and Micajah Turner witnessed a deed for slave Charlot from Wright and Martha Bond to Elizabeth A Bishop. Signed Jun 9, 1832 and recorded Aug 27, 1832. (Bedford DB 23:115).

Mary Brown Campbell was a sister of John Brown. She and her siblings were named in his pension application for service in the Revolutionary War. Reel R370 of M804, National Archives. (Wardell 1988, 1:116).

Mary E was the daughter of Reuben S Brown. She and her siblings were named in the division of her father's slaves. Her husband James Leftwich represented her at the division. Division was made May 25, 1835 and recorded Jun 22, 1835. (Bedford WB 9:47).

Mary Brown Christian was the daughter of Aaron Brown, who had entered military service from Bedford County in 1776. She was named in his death report. Reel R358 of M804, National Archives. (Wardell 1988, 1:116).

Mary Willcox Brown was the wife of John Thompson Brown who died 1836 at his father's home at Ivy Cliff. (Merrill 1968, chart A).

Mary Brown Leftwich and her siblings, the heirs and legatees of Reubin S Brown, were conveyed a deed from William C Leftwich for 51A at Elk Creek, near Howards Creek. Signed and recorded May 1, 1837. (Bedford DB 26:151).

Mary, Ammon Hancock, Lucy Hendrick and Justin Hancock, children and heirs of Samuel Hancock, deceased, were conveyed a deed from Elijah Cundiff Sr and Jamima Cundiff for 1) 5 1/4A at Rockcastle Creek, near Richard Chilton and Elijah Cundiff, and 2) land near Samuel Hancock, deceased. Signed Sep 30, 1837 and recorded Feb 26, 1838. (Bedford DB 27:54).

Mary E, administrator of the will of John T Brown, deceased, acting on behalf of Micajah Davis Jr, executor of the will of Henry Brown, deceased, sued Isham Lawhorne for $47.61. Lawhorne confessed judgment. Recorded Feb 1838. (Bedford OB 26:118).

Mary was conveyed a deed from Ammon Hancock and his wife Sarah V, Bernard G Hendrick and his wife Lucy, and Justin Hancock and his wife Harriet S, all heirs of Samuel Hancock, deceased, for 971 1/4A on both sides of Hales Ford Road at Goose Creek. Signed Oct 2, 1838 and recorded Aug 22, 1842. (Bedford DB 29:578).

Mary, Ammon Hancock and his wife Sarah V, Bernard G Hendrick and his wife Lucy conveyed a deed to Justin Hancock, all heirs of Samuel Hancock, deceased, for 339A on both sides of Rockcastle Creek, near the Meadows Road, Chilton and Jonathan Cundiff. Signed Oct 2, 1838 and recorded Aug 22, 1842. (Bedford DB 29:582).

Mary had 1 male 20-30, 1 female 50-60, 1 female 70-80, and 33 slaves. Household member Ann Hancock, age 79, was receiving a widow's pension for Revolutionary War service. They were near Josiah Crouch and Jesse Perdue. (U S Census of 1840, p 65).

Mary was bonded, and a certificate was granted her to obtain letters of administration on the estate of James T Brown, deceased. Securities were Albert G Brown and James M Brown. Recorded May 1840. (Bedford OB 27:68).

MASON

Mason and her husband James of Crawford County IN conveyed a deed to John Dearing for land at Orrix Creek, where Richard Dearing had lived, and was 1/5 of the land owned by Jeremiah Dearing when he died, near Warner Hewitt. Signed Apr 12, 1833 and recorded May 13, 1833. (Bedford DB 23:362).

MATILDA

Matilda Bramblett married John W Brown. Surety was Reuben Bramblett. Bond dated Jul 28, 1817. They were married by William Harris on Aug 3, 1817. (Hinshaw 1969, 6:884).

The Browns of Bedford County

Matilda and her husband John W conveyed a deed to Israel Wildman for 120A on Goose Creek, near Wildman. Signed May 5, 1828 and recorded Jul 1, 1828. (Bedford DB 21:87).

Matilda C was a daughter of Reuben S Brown. She and her siblings were named in the division of her father's slaves. Division was made May 25, 1835 and recorded Jun 22, 1835. (Bedford WB 9:47).

Matilda C and her siblings, the heirs and legatees of Reubin S Brown, were conveyed a deed from William C Leftwich for 51A at Elk Creek, near Howards Creek. Signed and recorded May 1, 1837. (Bedford DB 26:151).

Matilda C married Triplett E Lowry. Surety was William H Brown. Bond dated Feb 25, 1839. (Ricks 1939, 94).

MELINDA

Melinda Alford Brown was named in the will of her father Silvator Alford. Recorded Nov 24, 1777. (Bedford WB 1:264).

MILLEY

Milley Dooley and Walker Brown made a prenuptual agreement, with William Miner and Melanethon Turner to serve as trustees until the marriage. Milley's property included slaves Bett and Bett's child Jordan, horses, furniture and money from the sale of land from the estate of her late father John Dooley. Walker Brown was to share the use of the assets, but Milley was to retain sole ownership, and she could dispose of the assets as if the marriage had never been solemnized. Not dated, but recorded Jul 26, 1826. (Bedford DB 20:21).

Milly Dooley married Walker Brown. Surety was W Minor. Bond dated Jul 26, 1825. They were married by William Harris on Jul 26, 1826. (Hinshaw 1969, 6:884).

Milley and her husband Walker Brown and Sally Dooley and Polly Dooley Dodd conveyed quiet title to James Leftwich and John Leftwich for 221 3/4A on Little Otter River, as ordered by Chancery Court. Signed Apr 11, 1838 and recorded Apr 23, 1838. (Bedford DB 27:147).

The Browns of Bedford County

MOSES

Moses had one tithable. He was near John Hall and David Grifeth. List of Nicholas Haile, Lunenburg Tithe Lists of 1750. (Bell 1991, 137).

NANCY

Nancy was bound to William Halley by the overseers of the poor. Recorded Oct 1790. (Bedford OB 10:46).

Nancy Fuqua married David Brown. She was the daughter of Anna. Surety was John Fuqua. Bond dated Jan 22, 1803. Marriage return was recorded Jun 26, 1803. (Hinshaw 1969, 6:884).

Nancy married James Bandy. Surety was Ebenezer Brown. Bond dated Apr 12, 1808. (Hinshaw 1969, 6:875).

Nancy and her husband David and Thomas Brown conveyed a deed to William O'Brian for 99 1/2A on Shockoe Creek, near Preas, David Brown and Thomas Brown. Witnesses were A P Agee, Robert Campbell and John Thomas. Signed and recorded Jun 22, 1812. (Bedford DB 13:726).

Nancy and her husband David conveyed a deed to William O'Brian for 45A on Shockoe Creek, near William O'Brian and Christopher Clark. Signed Dec 16, 1814 and recorded Dec 26, 1814. (Bedford DB 14:243).

Nancy and her husband David conveyed a deed to the heirs of Jeremiah Hatcher for 45 1/2A on the waters of Boreauger Creek. Witnesses were __rin Jeter and Pleasant Jeter. Signed Oct 10, 1816 and recorded Oct 28,1816. (Bedford DB 15:95).

Nancy and her husband David conveyed a deed of trust to Peachy R Gilmer and William R Porter as trustees for a debt owed Fleming and Edwin James & Co, secured by 1) land at Boreauger Creek which was patented Oct 10, 1822, near Hatcher and O'Briant, and 2) 64A at Shockoe Creek near John Pointer, Matthias O'Bryant and the estate of Samuel Griffin. Trustees to auction the properties. Witnesses were Thomas Preston, Robert C Mitchell Jr and Charles Markle. Signed Jun 12, 1824 and recorded Jun 14, 1824. (Bedford DB 19:135).

The Browns of Bedford County

Nancy Pearcy married Isham C Brown. She was the daughter of Charles. Surety was Thomas W Brown. Bond dated Jul 20, 1824. (Hinshaw 1969, 6:884).

Nancy Wheeler married Jabez Brown. She was the daughter of Gabriel. Surety was Joel Wheeler. Bond dated Feb 8, 1832. They were married by Stephen Wood on Feb 16, 1832. (Hinshaw 1969, 6:884).

Nancy was the daughter of Aaron, who had entered military service from Bedford County in 1776. She and and his widow Nancy and other family members were named in the report of his death in 1836. Reel R358 of M804, National Archives. (Wardell 1988, 1:116).

ORPAH

Orpah was the daughter of Joseph Brown and his wife Elizabeth. She and her siblings were named in their father's will dated Aug 22, 1795 and recorded Oct 26, 1795. (Bedford WB 2:163).

PASCHAL

Paschal married Catharine Pollard, dau of Catharine. Surety was Jesse N Pollard. Bond dated Mar 2, 1824. (Hinshaw 1969, 6:884).

Paschal was in the patrol company of Samuel N Wilkes, with Gilbert Crumb, Daniel B Stephens and Abner Dobyns. They were to visit all negro quarters and other places suspected of entertaining unlawful assemblies of slaves, servants or other disorderly persons. Order dated Jul 16, 1828. (Wilkes 1949, 9). (Also at Bedford OB 22).

Paschal had 3 males 0-5, 1 male 10-15, 1 male 20-30, 1 female 15-20, and no slaves. He was near Henry Payne and Daniel Tompkins. (U S Census of 1830, p 150).

PATSEY see MARTHA

PHEBE

Phebe and her husband William conveyed a deed to John Otey for 110A where they lived, near William Woodey, Thomas Jones, Linah Brown,

The Browns of Bedford County

James Petross and Holt. Signed Feb 24, 1787 recorded Feb 26, 1787. (Bedford DB 7:685).

Phebe Brown Staples was the daughter of Aaron Brown, wo had entered military service from Bedford County in 1776. She and other family members were named in the report of his death in 1836. Reel R358 of M804, National Archives. (Wardell 1988, 1:116).

PLEASANT

Pleasant married Mary S Bond. Surety was Pleasant Bond. Bond dated Dec 1, 1824. They were married by John Ayers on Dec 2, 1824. (Hinshaw 1969, 6:884).

Pleasant was qualified as the local administrator of the will of Thomas Moore, deceased, of Madison County KY. Recorded Mar 25, 1826. (Bedford OB 20:198).

Pleasant, Mary S Brown and Micajah Turner were witnesses to a deed from Wright and Martha Bond to Elizabeth A Bishop for the sale of slave Charlot.. Signed Jun 9, 1832 and recorded Aug 27, 1832. (Bedford DB 23:115).

R

R witnessed a "bond" from William Brown of Augusta County VA to Jack Burgess for 200A on Mollys Creek. The bond functioned as an IOU, secured by the land. Other witnesses were Shildrake Brown, Sheldrake Brown Jr, Townzen Horton and Shildrake Brown Jr. Signed and recorded Jan 1, 1778. (Bedford DB 6:74).

R and Sheldrake Brown witnessed a deed from William Graham and his wife Anne to William Brown for 100A. Recorded Apr 5, 1779. (Bedford DB 6:337).

R, Shildrake, Edward and Temperance Brown witnessed a deed from James Millwood to William Brown for 100A near Thomas Hayth, William Brown, Shildrake Brown, John Simmons and Ruffin. Signed Apr 6, 1779 and recorded Oct 25, 1779. (Bedford DB 6:362).

The Browns of Bedford County

R, Richard Stith, John fitchPatrick, Brown Vineyard and Edward Brown witnessed a deed from John Simmons and his wife Elizabeth to Shildrake Brown for 100A on Mollys Creek near James Millwood, Shildrake Brown, Josias Bullock, Ajohnadab Read and John fitchPatrick. Signed Feb 5, 1778 and recorded Aug 28, 1780 at DB 7:18. Another witness was Edward Brown. Recorded Feb 5, 1780. (Bedford DB 7:18).

RABA see ARABA

RACHEL

Rachel married Ezekiel Downing. She was the daughter of Thomas, who gave consent and was surety. Bond dated Jan 30, 1778. (Dennis 1939, 17).

REED aka Read

Reed was deceased when Joseph M Brown conveyed a deed of trust to trustee for a debt owed Vinal Smith, secured by 1) 4A near the town of Liberty, Fancy Farm Road, Vinal Smith and William Terry, part of the land Smith had purchased from the heirs of Markle, and 2) all of Joseph's interest in the estate of Reed Brown, deceased. Signed and recorded Jan 2, 1839. (Bedford DB 27:365).

REUBEN aka Rubin, Reubin

Reuben married Betsey McGehee. Surety was David Saunders. Bond dated Mar 25, 1800. (Hinshaw 1969, 884). Reuben Brown and Betsy McGehee were married by James Mitchell on Mar 27, 1800. (Bedford PRO 1:246).

The overseers of the poor ordered Jabez Womer bound to Reuben Brown. Jabez had been formerly bound to Samuel Poindexter. Recorded Apr 28, 1800. (Bedford OB 12:73).

Reuben was present when the boundary lines of James Mitchell and Stith Mead were processioned. Recorded Jun 23, 1800. (Bedford PRO 1:101).

The overseers of the poor bound Susanna Roberts, George Douglas and John Roberts to Reuben Brown. Recorded Jul 1800. (Bedford OB 12:91).

109

The Browns of Bedford County

Reuben was conveyed a deed from Daniel Neal and his wife Mary for 200A at Little Otter River. Signed Jan 25, 1802 and recorded Feb 22, 1802. (Bedford DB 11:510).

The overseers of the poor ordered Philip Roberts to be bound to Reuben Brown. Roberts was formerly bound to Henry Meredith. Recorded Jan 25, 1802. (Bedford OB 12:237).

The overseers of the poor bound Matthew W Holt, son of Lucy Holt, to Reuben Brown. Recorded Jun 1803. (Bedford OB 13:9).

The overseers of the poor bound Horatio Jones to Reuben Brown. Horatio was a bastard child of Joanna Jones. Recorded Dec 24, 1804. (Bedford OB 13:162).

Reuben conveyed a deed of trust to trustee John McGhee for a debt owed David Saunders, secured by farm animals and furniture which were to be sold at the door of Walter Otey's tavern in the town of Liberty. Signed Apr 25, 1806 and recorded Sep 22, 1806. (Bedford DB 12:124).

Reuben was appointed by the overseers of the poor to apprentice James Hale, who was bound to him. Recorded Sep 1807. (Bedford OB 14:210).

Reuben was appointed with Henry Brown and John Cobbs to be processioners in Capt William Green's company. Recorded Feb 1808. (Bedford OB 14:285).

Reuben S had 2 males 0-10, 1 male 26-45, and 3 females 0-10. (U S Census of 1810).

Reuben S conveyed a deed of trust to trustee Thomas L Leftwich for four slaves and other personal property. Recorded 1819. (Bedford DB 16:87).

Reuben was conveyed a deed from James Steptoe for 398A near Leftwich's mill pond, including 107A subject to the life estate of Mrs Elizabeth Wills. Witnesses were Thomas L Leftwich, Hugh Montgomerie, William C Leftwich, Robert Lovo, Henry Stevens, Daniel Mitchell Jr and Robert C Steptoe. Signed May 25, 1819 and recorded Oct 25, 1819. (Bedford DB 16:52).

110

The Browns of Bedford County

Reuben S conveyed a deed of trust to trustees David Saunders, John S Cobb and Samuel Read for debts owed James Steptoe, secured by 1) 398A near Col William Leftwich, Capt John Leftwich, John Robinson, Richard Lee, deceased, and A E Callaway; 2) 200A near Cornelius Noell, Noell, William Booth and Mary Nance; and 3) slaves: Julia and her children Silva, Abram and Job, and by Suky and her children Archa, Flanders, Piggy and Harry. Witnesses were Thomas L Leftwich, Hugh Montgomerie, John Robinson, W C Leftwich and R C Steptoe. Signed May 26, 1819 and recorded Jul 21, 1819. (Bedford DB 15:615).

Reuben S was conveyed a release of deed of trust by trustees David Saunders, John L Cobbs and Samuel Read for 200A used as security for the purchase of 398A from James Steptoe. The 200A were near Cornelius Noell, Jesse Noell, William Boothe and Mary Nance. Witnesses were Henry Stevens, Robert C Steptoe and Thomas L Leftwich. Signed Sep 28, 1819 and recorded Oct 25, 1819. (Bedford DB 16:60).

Reuben S with his wife Elizabeth conveyed a deed to John Lowry for 168A on Big Otter River, near William Lowry, William Boothe and Jesse Noell. Witnesses were John L Cobbs, Thomas Kerr and Robert Steptoe. Signed Sep 30, 1819 and recorded Oct 25,1819. (Bedford DB 16:58).

Reuben L had 2 males 0-10, 1 male 10-16, 1 male 16-26, 1 male 45+, 1 female 0-10, 2 females 10-16, 1 female 16-26, and 1 female 26-45. (U S Census of 1820, Northern District, p 34).

Reuben S was granted an injunction to stay all proceedings against him by William Whitely until the matter could be heard in equity. Recorded May 1822. (Bedford OB 18:243).

Reuben S and his wife Betty (formerly Betty McGhee) and other heirs of Samuel McGhee, deceased, conveyed a deed to John Ryan for 70A on Little Otter River, near Lindsey Stinnett, Thomas Powell, Thomas Edgars and David Saunders. Witnesses were Daniel Hoofman, John Flower, Thomas Otey, Alexander Burton and William Cook. Signed Nov 20, 1822 and recorded Aug 9, 1823. (Bedford DB 18:229).

Reubin S was awarded an injunction in regard to a judgment against him by Samuel Phillips. Recorded Jan 14, 1825. (Bedford OB 19:265).

The Browns of Bedford County

The hands of Reuben S Brown, William Callaway, Sally Jones, Mrs Gwarfney, Robert C Steptoe, Thomas Everett, Jesse Innes and John Callaway were ordered to work on a road from Elk Creek to the academy. Recorded Aug 25, 1828. (Bedford OB 22:105).

Reuben S and his wife Betsy McGhee Brown and other McGhee heirs conveyed a deed to William McGhee for land at the north side of Little Otter River. Reuben's and Betsy's signature were signed by their attorney in fact, Thomas Saunders. Signed Jan 26, 1829 and recorded Mar 25, 1833. (Bedford DB 23:306).

Reuben S was the father of Mary E Brown who married James Leftwich. Bond dated Feb 4, 1830. (Hopkins 1931, 275).

Reuben had 2 males 15-20, 1 male 20-30, 1 male 40-50, 1 female 5-10, 1 female 15-20, 1 female 20-30, 1 female 40-50, 1 female 50-60, and 16 slaves. He was near William C Leftwich and John Robertson. (U S Census of 1830, p 133).

Reuben S' administrators John S Brown and Spotswood Brown were qualified. Recorded 1834. (Bedford OB 25:14).

Reuben's estate was accounted and expenses paid for the period Jun 6, 1834 to Sep 1, 1836. There were several payments, including $420 to Granville S Brown for his expenses in Philadelphia in the fall of 1834, $230 to Dr Thomas P Mitchell for medical care, and payments for tobacco notes. Accounting done Sep 1, 1836 and recorded Oct 26, 1836. (Bedford WB 9:199).

The slaves in Reuben's estate were inventoried and appraised. They included John, David, Jerry, Joe, Flanders, Arch, Harry, Sucky, Silvy, Peggy, Mary, Celia, Lucinda, Martha Ann, Frances and Robert. The inventory and appraisal were done on Dec 23, 1834 and recorded Jan 26, 1835. (Bedford WB 9:1).

Reuben S's slaves were auctioned by his administrators John S Brown and Spotswood Brown. Purchasers were Betsey Brown, John S Brown, William B Whitten, Frederick A Harris, William Edgars, Edmund Moss, Byrd S Leftwich, James Tankersley, Edmund Merman, William Brown, James Leftwich, Edmund Marsh and N H Price. Auction was held Jan 15, 1835,

The Browns of Bedford County

with payment due by Aug 1, 1835. Recorded Sep 26, 1836. (Bedford WB 9:186).

Reuben's widow Elizabeth was alloted her dower in his slaves, and divided the slaves among his children. Recorded Mar 1835. (Bedford OB 25:62).

Reuben S died Apr 1, 1835, leaving his widow Elizabeth and children John S, Granville S, Harriet, Matilda C, Spotswood D, William, Eliza and Mary E. His slaves were valued at $5,340. The division of slaves was made May 25, 1835 and recorded Jun 22, 1835. (Bedford WB 9:47).

Reuben S, deceased, left orphans Eliza and William, who chose Betsy Brown as their guardian. Betsy Brown, John S Brown and Spotswood Brown gave security bonds. Recorded Aug 1835. (Bedford OB 25:125).

Reuben's heirs and legatees John S Brown, Matilda C Brown, James Leftwich and his wife Mary Brown Leftwich, Spotswood D Brown, Granville Brown, William Brown and Eliza Brown were conveyed a deed from William C Leftwich for 51A at Elk Creek, near Howards Creek. Signed and recorded May 1, 1837. (Bedford DB 26:151).

James Leftwich and his wife Mary E conveyed a deed to Granville L Brown for all their interest in the estate of Reubin S Brown, deceased. Signed and recorded Jan 24, 1839. (Bedford DB 27:375).

RHODA aka Rhody

Rhoda and her husband James and Jeanet Brown conveyed a deed to William R Jones for 130A on a branch of Little Otter River, one mile below the town of Liberty. Witnesses were Reubin Bramblett, James Thornhill, Adam Bowyer and James Brown Jr. Signed Jan 15, 1792 and recorded Feb 22, 1802. (Bedford DB 11:535).

Rhoda Reese married James Brown. She was the daughter of Sloman Reese. Surety was John Reese. Bond dated Oct 4, 1792. (Hinshaw 1969, 6:884). They were married by Joseph Drury on Oct 4, 1792. (Bedford PRO 1:225).

Rhoda married Joel Chambers. She was the daughter of William and Saray. Sureties were Daniel Brown and John Bird. Bond dated Dec 9, 1811.

The Browns of Bedford County

(Hinshaw 1969, 6:891).

RHODAM aka Rodham

Rhodam married Elizabeth Eckovey. She was the daughter of Mathias Eckovey, who gave consent. Surety was John James. Bond dated Aug 24, 1795(sic). (Dennis 1989, 6). Bond dated Jun 24, 1795 (sic). (Hinshaw 1969, 6:884).

Rhodam was the son of Joseph Brown and his wife Elizabeth. He and his brother Jesse were executors for their father's will dated Aug 22, 1795. Their other siblings were named in the will. The will was recorded Oct 26, 1795. (Bedford WB 2:163).

Rhodam was qualified with Jesse Dent Brown as executors of the will of Joseph Brown. Recorded Oct 1795. (Bedford OB 11:37).

Rhodam was present when his 185A on the north side of the Pates Road was processioned. Recorded Jan 23, 1796. (Bedford PRO 1:51).

Rhodam and his wife Elizabeth conveyed a deed to Isaac James for 92 1/2A on the branches of Beaverdam Creek, near Cavender. Witnesses were Lawrence James, Joseph Brown and Hezekiah Brown. Signed Mar 14, 1800 and recorded Apr 28, 1800. (Bedford DB 11:205).

Rhodam married Frances Bruce, daughter of David. Surety was William Bruce. Bond dated Jan 17, 1801. They were married by Jeremiah Hatcher on Jan 20, 1801. (Hinshaw 1969, 6:884). They were married by Henry Hatcher on Jan 20, 1801. (Bedford PRO 1:248).

Rodham had 1 male 0-10, 1 male 26-45, 3 females 0-10, and 1 female 26-45. (U S Census of 1810).

Rodham was surety for the marriage of Nehemiah Spradling and Polly Brown. Bond dated Aug 19, 1826. (Ricks 1939, 145).

RICHARD

Richard was conveyed a deed from Justice Beech for 93A on both sides of Maggoty Cr. Witnesses were William Wright and John Clement. Signed

The Browns of Bedford County

Feb 27, 1770 and recorded May 22, 1770. (Bedford DB 3:443).

Richard was granted a patent for 80A on the south branches of Maggoty Creek. Recorded Jul 6, 1780. (Bedford PB A:580).

Richard filed a claim for 2 1/2 bushels of corn he supplied to the Revolutionary army. Recorded Feb 1783. (Bedford OB 7:27).

Richard was appointed to view a road from Maggoty Creek to a new road leading from the courthouse to James Stone's mill. Recorded Jul 1783. (Bedford OB 7:57).

Richard was appointed to survey a road from Maggoty Creek to a road by the widow Cantrel's at John Landgon's. Recorded Mar 1785. (Bedford OB 8:106).

Richard married Sarah Womax. She was the daugher of Sarah Hancock, who gave consent. Surety was John Folden. Bond dated Dec 2, 1794. They were married by James Turner on Dec 4, 1794. (Hinshaw 1969, 6:884). Richard and Sarah Womack were married by James Turner on Dec 4, 1794. (Bedford PRO 1:231).

Richard's land was processioned. Recorded Aug 28, 1800. (Bedford PRO 1:93).

Richard was conveyed a deed from James Folden and his wife Sary for 70A near Flattop Mountain. Witnesses were Edman Galloway and George Foulden. Signed May 28, 1801 and recorded Sep 28, 1801. (Bedford DB 11:422).

Richard and his wife Sarah conveyed a deed to Joseph Preast for 70A near Flat Top Mountain near Crenshaw. Witnesses were Joseph Holt, John Taylor and John W Holt. Signed Oct 12, 1802 and recorded Oct 25, 1802. (Bedford DB 11:646).

ROBERT

Robert, with Sheldrake Brown of Henrico Co VA, was conveyed a deed from Thomas Hayth and his wife Martha and William Manley and his wife Elizabeth for 400A on Mollys Creek near Thomas Hayth, James Millwood,

115

The Browns of Bedford County

John Simon and John Fitzpatrick. Witnesses were John Fitzpatrick, William Brown, John Simmons, Sheldrake Brown Jr and Henry Brown. Recorded Jul 19, 1777. (Bedford DB 5:498).

Robert and Jennings Brown were proven to be the sole heirs of Allen Brown, who had been a soldier in the Virginia Continental Line. (Bedford OB 21:60).

ROSWELL

Roswell, Sandford and Lyman Brown, William Thornton's wards, John Davis' heirs, Joseph Reynolds and Jesse Reynolds were landowners where the James River canal was to be built. A panel was appointed to assess the damages which would be sustained in the course of building the canal. Recorded Jun 20, 1825 at OB 20:75. 40A of the lands were condemned for use of the canal, its feeds, locks and dams. Recorded Jul 22, 1825 (Bedford OB 20:93).

Roswell, Sandford and Lyman Brown were conveyed a deed from Philip Thornton and his wife Caroline for 1,914A on the James River between the Rockbridge County line and the foot of Irish Falls. The Browns were all natives of Berkshire County, MA. Signed Feb 5, 1827 and recorded Mar 10, 1828. (Bedford DB 20:476).

Roswell, Sandford and Lyman Brown and John A Wharton conveyed power of attorney to Charles B Reynolds to convey 1,914A at the James River, which had been conveyed to them by Philip Thornton. Signed Apr 28, 1828 and recorded May 21, 1828. (Bedford DB 20:475).

Roswell of Sandsfield in Berkshire County, MA, with Sanford Brown Jr and his wife Elvira and Lyman Brown and his wife Frances, conveyed a deed to Charles B Reynolds for 924A at the James River between the line of Rockbridge County and the foot of Irish Falls, near Balcony Falls and Snow Creek. .Signed Jul 6, 1829 and recorded Mar 9, 1830. (Bedford DB 22:75).

RUTH

Ruth and her husband Ebenezer conveyed a deed to Alexander Brown for 100A on the north side of the Staunton River, near Caniel Corley. Signed Sep 22, 1802 and recorded Sep 27, 1802. (Bedford DB 11:606).

116

The Browns of Bedford County

Ruth and her husband Ebenezer, of Montgomery County VA, conveyed a deed to Matthew Pate and Edmund Pate for 50A on Falling Creek, near Alexander Brown and John Pate. Signed Oct 18, 1817 and recorded Oct 1817. (Bedford DB 15:254).

SAMUEL

Samuel had five tithables, was listed with William Callaway. List of Mathew Talbot, Lunenburg Tithe Lists of 1749. (Bell 1991, 101).

Samuel had five tithables, was listed with William Callaway. List of John Phelps, Lunenburg Tithe Lists of 1750. (Bell 1991, 154).

Samuel's 218A were surveyed. The land was on both sides of Cheese Creek, on a south fork of Ivy Creek, near Tullos. Survey dated Mar 29, 1756. (Bedford SR 1:34).

Samuel was paid 4 shillings for service as a lieutenant in the Bedford group during the French and Indian Wars. Recorded 1765. (Bockstruck 1988, 208).

Samuel was paid L2.14.0 for service as a soldier in the Bedford group during the French and Indian Wars. Recorded 1765. (Bockstruck 1988, 209).

Samuel was paid L2.17.0 for service as a soldier in the Bedford group during the French and Indian Wars. Recorded 1765. (Bockstruck 1988, 209).

Samuel was conveyed a deed from Charles Lynch for 40A on both sides of Burnt Bridge Creek, near Richard Tulos. Recorded June 25, 1765. (Bedford DB 2:592).

Samuel was born Nov 10, 1766, the son of Henry and Alce Brown. He and his siblings were named when their parents' marriage was recorded on Jan 25, 1773. (Bedford DB 4:455).

Rev Samuel Brown was the son of Henry Brown and Alice Beard of Ivy Hill. He was born Nov 10, 1766 and died Oct 15, 1818 at Rockbridge County VA. His wife was Mary Moore. (Merrill 1968, Chart A). Samuel's 250A were surveyed. The land was on the head branches of Ivy Creek and Judith Creek, near Anthony, Fry, Gaddy, Fleming's Mountain, Davies, and Charles Bright. Survey dated Mar 5, 1771. (Bedford SR 1:139).

The Browns of Bedford County

Samuel conveyed a deed to John Hook for 40A on Burnt Bridge Branch (part of a survey for Charles Lynch, who sold to Samuel Brown), near Richard Tullis and Richard Brooks. Recorded Oct 25, 1773. (Bedford DB 5:152).

Samuel was the son of Henry Brown and Alice Beard. He and his siblings and half-siblings were named in his father's dated Jan 9, 1796. He inherited money by the will. The will was recorded Jun 24, 1799. (Bedford WB 2:261).

Samuel Thompson Brown was the son of Henry Brown and Frances Thompson. He was born Aug 13, 1810 at Ivy Cliff, which he later inherited. His wife was Elizabeth Huger. (Merrill 1968, chart A).

Samuel married Susanna Hix. Surety was James Thomason. Bond dated Jan 7, 1814. (Hinshaw 1969, 6:884).

Samuel was appointed by sheriff Henry Brown to be a deputy sheriff. Recorded Jun 26, 1829. (Bedford OB 22:201).

Samuel applied to practice law in the Commonwealth, and the court certified that he was a county resident and "a person of honest endeavor and upwards of 21 years of age". Recorded Feb 1836. (Bedford OB 25:201).

Samuel had been licensed to practice law in the Commonwealth, took oaths and was licensed to practice in the Bedford courts. Recorded Mar 1836. (Bedford OB 25:214).

Samuel was the son of Henry. He and his siblings were named in their father's will dated Jan 6, 1837. He was bequeathed the homeplace, and named as executor with his brother-in-law Alexander Irvine. His father's will was recorded Sep 25, 1841. (Bedford WB 10:392). Samuel T Brown was bequeathed Ivy Cliff by his father Henry's will dated Jan 6, 1837. (Merrill 1968, 22).

Samuel T Brown and Tilghman A Cobbs, as commissioners, were conveyed a deed of trust by the heirs of Henry Adams for Tilchman A Cobb, secured by land near Benjamin Witt and Thomas Tucker. Commissioners were to auction off the land at the front door of the courthouse on the second court

The Browns of Bedford County

day. Signed May 18, 1837 and recorded May 22, 1837. (Bedford DB 26:174).

Samuel, Lodowick McDaniel, William Mead, John W Holet and Benjamin McDonald were appointed as commissioners to take bids and contract for the building of a bridge across Big Otter River at Burks Ford. Recorded Oct 1839. (Bedford OB 26:end of book, page not numbered).

Samuel T Brown was conveyed a deed by his father Henry Brown for 400A at Otter River, near Island Road and Lick Run Creek. Signed Oct 22, 1839 and recorded Oct 28, 1839. (Bedford DB 28:187).

Samuel T Brown conveyed a deed of trust to trustee Alexander Irvine for a debt owed Samuel H McGhee, secured by 400A at Otter River near Island Fork Road. Signed and recorded Sep 30, 1840. (Bedford DB 28:377).

SANDFORD, aka Sanford

Sandford, Roswell Brown, Lyman Brown, William Thornton's wards, John Davis' heirs, Joseph Reynolds and Jesse Reynolds were landowners where the James River canal was to be built. A panel was appointed to assess the damages which would be sustained in the course of building the canal. Recorded Jun 20, 1825 at OB 20:75. 40A of the lands were condemned for use of the canal, its feeds, locks and dams. Recorded Jul 22, 1825. (Bedford OB 20:93).

Sandford, Lyman, and Roswell Brown werre conveyed a deed from Philip Thornton and his wife Caroline for 1,1914A on the James River between the Rockbridge County line and the foot of Irish Falls. The Browns were all natives of Berkshire County, MA. Signed Feb 5, 1827 and recorded Mar 10, 1828. (Bedford DB 20:476).

Sandford, Lyman Brown, Roswell Brown and John A Wharton conveyed power of attorney to Charles B Reynolds to convey 1,914A at the James River, which had been conveyed to them by Philip Thornton. Signed Apr 28, 1828 and recorded May 21, 1828. (Bedford DB 20:475).

Sanford Jr with his wife Elvira, Lyman Brown and his wife Frances, and Roswell Brown of Sandsfield in Berkshire County MA, conveyed a deed

119

The Browns of Bedford County

to Charles B Reynolds for 924A at the James River between the line of Rockbridge Co and the foot of Irish Falls, near Balcony Falls and Snow Creek. Signed Jul 6, 1829 and recorded Mar 9, 1830. (Bedford DB 22:75).

SARAH aka Saray/Saraugh/Sally

Sarah was allowed one day's attendance in the case of Hardwick v Jackson. Recorded Sep 28, 1778. (Bedford OB 6:187).

Sarah Harmon married Clayburn Brown. Bond dated Mar 8, 1781. Surety was Peter Harmon. (Hinshaw 1969, 6:883). She was named in his pension application for service in the Revolutionary War. Reel R361 of M804, National Archives. (Wardell 1988. 1:118).

Sarah was the mother of Polly Callaway, and gave consent for her marriage to William North. Surety was Lance Woodward. Bond dated Jun 8, 1781. (Dennis 1989, 51).

Sarah was qualified as administratrix of the estate of her late husband Leonard Brown. Recorded Aug 28, 1781. (Bedford OB 6:326).

Sarah and her husband William conveyed a deed to Richard Radford for 427A, part of patent by Charles Merriman dated Feb 14, 1761, and including 287A patent to William Brown dated Dec 7, 1774. Witnesses were John Mitchell Jr, John Booth and John Camps. Signed Oct 24, 1782 and recorded Oct 28, 1782. (Bedford DB 7:164).

Sarah Brown married George Brown. She was the daughter of Sarah, who gave consent. Surety was Julius Jones. Bond dated Nov 24, 1783. (Dennis 1989, 10).

Sarah was not tithable, had 1 slave 16+, 4 horses and 4 cattle. Personal Property Tax List of 1787, List B. (Schreiner-Yantis 1987, 200). She was visited on the same day as George Brown and William Hurt. (Ibid, p 214).

Sarah was administratrix of her late husband Linah Brown. She failed to give counter security, so the estate was assigned to creditors William Quarles and Boice Edson. Recorded Feb 1789. (Bedford OB 9:233).

The Browns of Bedford County

Sarah Womax married Richard Brown. She was the daughter of Sarah Hancock, who gave consent. Surety was John Folden. Bond dated Dec 2, 1794. They were married by James Turner on Dec 4, 1794. (Hinshaw 1969, 6:884). Sarah Womack and Richard Brown were married by James Turner on Dec 4, 1794. (Bedford PRO 1:231).

Sarah, and James Brown and his wife Elizabeth, conveyed a deed to John Reese for 110A on Little Otter Creek near Galloway. Signed Jun 22, 1795 and recorded Jun 27, 1795. (Bedford DB 9:541).

Sarah was the daughter of Joseph Brown and his wife Elizabeth. She and her siblings were named in their father's will dated Aug 22, 1795 and recorded Oct 26, 1795. (Bedford WB 2:163).

Sarah was the daughter of Henry Brown and Ann Richardson, his first wife. (Merrill 1968, 11). She and her siblings and half-siblings were named in their father's will dated Jan 9, 1796. She inherited 10 shillings by the will. His will was recorded Jun 24, 1799. (Bedford WB 2:261).

Sarah was the daughter of Daniel Brown and his wife Hannah. She and her siblings were named in a certificate of removal from Crooked Run Monthly Meeting to Goose Creek Monthly Meeting. Recorded in the Goose Creek minutes of Mar 31, 1798. (Wright 1993, 54)

Sarah , daughter of Linah, was conveyed a deed from James Brown Jr and his wife Elizabeth for 8A on Meadows Creek. Signed and recorded Jun 25, 1798. (Bedford DB 10:486).

Sarah and her husband Richard conveyed a deed to Joseph Preast for 70A at the foot of Flat Top Mountain. Recorded Oct 25, 1802. (Bedford DB 11:646).

Sarah was the administratrix of the estate of Linah Brown. His estate was settled and recorded Jul 1803. (Bedford OB 13:16).

Sarah and her son James Brown and his wife Elizabeth conveyed a deed to Thomas Scruggs for land on Little Otter River near Charles Marckel, Thomas, Mary Ann Brown, Sally Brown, John Fisher and Benjamin Rice. Signed Oct 1803 and recorded Jan 23, 1804. (Bedford DB 11:909).

The Browns of Bedford County

Sarah, the widow of Linah, conveyed her dower rights to 110A which James Brown, eldest son of Linah, had sold to John Reese, who conveyed it to John Marrs. Witness was William Trigg. Signed Apr 1804 and recorded Apr 23, 1804. (Bedford DB 11:986).

Sarah married Joseph Wright. Surety was John Brown. Bond dated Jun 26, 1805. (Ricks 1939, 172). See AGGY.

Sarah, the widow of Linah, conveyed her dower rights to James Jones Marrs for 110A formerly owned by John Marrs, deceased. The 110A had been conveyed by John Reese and his wife Nancy to John Marrs. Witnesses were Benjamin Rice, John McLean and Frederick Gooldy. Signed Jun 24, 1807 and recorded Jun 25, 1807. (Bedford DB 12:226).

Sally conveyed a deed to John Bowles Sr for a tract of land near the heirs of Thomas Scruggs, formerly the land of Mary Ann Brown. Witnesses were J Floyd Teacher, Thomas Smith and William Sherman. Signed Jun 5, 1809 and recorded same date. (Bedford DB 13:432).

Sally was conveyed a deed from Joseph Flood and his wife Anne for 11 1/2A on Little Otter River at Meadows Creek. Witnesses were John Bowles, Thomas Smith and William Sherman. Signed Jun 5, 1809 and recorded same date. (Bedford DB 13:436).

Saray and William Brown gave consent for the marriage of Rhoda Brown and Joel Chambers. Sureties were Daniel Brown and John Bird. Bond dated Dec 9, 1811. (Hinshaw 1969, 6:891).

Sarah conveyed power of attorney to Enoch Brown of Culpepper County VA to sell her life estate in land in Fauquier County VA., which John Davies had leased to Marmaduke Brown and his wife Sarah in 1776. Signed Dec 1812 and recorded Jan 25, 1813. (Bedford DB 13:663).

Sarah conveyed a deed from George Brown's estate to Araba Brown for an interest in the estate of George Brown in Tennessee. Recorded 1814. (Bedford DB 13:841).

Sarah, Larkin, John and Mary Ann Brown were exonerated from erroneously assessed delinquent taxes against 183A once owned by Linah Brown, deceased. John Bowles appeared in court and proved by deed that he had purchased the land by Jun 1, 1812. Recorded July 1814. (Bedford OB 17:234).

Sarah's former 180A "at present in the possession of Littleberry Leftwich" were exonerated for delinquent taxes in her name for the year 1799. Recorded Aug 1816. (Bedford OB 17:234).

Sarah offered a security bond with Caleb Brown, William Baber, William Thomas and Gabriel Keath when Caleb Brown was indicted for arson to a corn house and a stable on the property of Joseph Flood. Recorded Nov 1816. (Bedford OB 17:283).

Sally had 2 males 10-16, 1 female 10-16, and 1 female 45+. (U S Census of 1820, Southern District, p 61).

Sarah married Elijah Hambleton. She was the daughter of Alexander. Bond dated Jan 4, 1820. (Ricks 1939, 64). Sarah married Elijah Hamilton. She was the daughter of Alexander. Surety was Thomas O Brown. Bond dated Jan 4, 1820. (Hinshaw 1969, 6:927).

Sarah Ann and her siblings were the children of Edward Brown, who qualified to be their guardian. Recorded May 1821. (Bedford OB 18:99).

Sally W Williamson married Joseph M Brown. Surety was Leonard N Williamson. Bond dated Jan 3, 1826. They were married by William Harris on Jan 5, 1826. (Hinshaw 1969, 6:884).

The hands of Sally Brown, Nancy Quarles, Francis Hopkins, James Hamilton, John Fisher, Thomas Fisher and Jacob Fizer were ordered to work on a road from Caffery's to the Meads Road near Parson Turner's. Recorded Mar 4, 1827. (Bedford OB 21:109).

Sarah M married Joel Jones. She was the daughter of John. Surety was Thomas W Brown. They were married by William Harris on Apr 16, 1829. (Hinshaw 1969, 6:943).

Sally had 1 male 20-30, 1 female 20-30, 1 female 60-70, and no slaves. She was near Becky Jones and Gideon Crews. (U S Census of 1830, p 178).

123

The Browns of Bedford County

Sarah Lawhorn married Callaway Brown, son of Hezekiah. Surety was Jabez Brown. Bond dated Dec 23, 1833. They were married by Merryman Lunsford on Dec 23, 1833. (Hinshaw 1969, 6:884).

Sarah Ann Burson married John M Brown. Surety was Thomas G Burson. Bond dated Oct 20, 1834. They were married by William Harris on Oct 22, 1834. (Hinshaw 1969, 6:884).

Sally conveyed a deed to Elliot Lowry for 11 1/2A on the waters of Little Otter River near Lowry, Fizer and Scruggs. Signed Jan 24, 1835 and recorded Jan 26,1835. (Bedford DB 24:363).

Sarah Brown Purvines was the daughter of Aaron Brown, who had entered military service from Bedford County in 1776. She and other family members were named in the report of his death in 1836. Reel R358 of M804, National Archives. (Wardell 1988, 1:116).

Sally had 1 female 30-40, 1 female 70-80. She was near Edward Estes and William Steptoe. (U S Census of 1840, p 43)..

SAWNY see ALEXANDER

SHADRACK aka Shadrock

Shadrack married Hannah Mitchell. She was the daughter of John, who gave consent. Surety was Isaac Mitchell. Bond dated Oct 15, 1787. (Dennis 1989, 10). They were married by James Mitchell on Oct 18, 1787. (Bedford PRO 1:219).

Shadrack was the son of Daniel Brown, and grandson of Daniel Brown. He was bequeathed several slaves by the will of his grandfather Daniel Brown. (Merrill 1968, 7).

Shadrack chose Daniel Brown as his guardian, who qualified and made bond. Recorded Feb 1797. (Bedford OB 11:151).

Shadrack married Tabitha Hall. She was the daughter of Magdalean Hall, who gave consent. Surety was Elisha Hall. Bond dated Oct 14, 1799. (Dennis 1989, 10). They were married on Oct 17, 1799 by Rev John Ayers, a Methodist minister. (Bedford PRO 1:243).

The Browns of Bedford County

Shadrack had 2 males 21+, 1 horse, and 2 slaves 12+. Personal Property Tax List of 1800, District 1. (Dorman 1963, 7:65).

Shadrack witnessed a deed from Daniel Brown and his wife Lucy of Pittsylvania County VA to Thomas Stewart for 200A on both sides of the road leading from Hales Ford to the Meadows of Goose Creek, near Lewis Turner, David Kerson, the old mill road and Hancock. Other witnesses were Arthur Goolsley, Wiatt Brown and Samuel Murphy. Signed Jun 24, 1805 and recorded Jul 22, 1805. (Bedford DB 11:1282).

Shadrack Brown of Bedford County TN was conveyed power of attorney by William Hall of Yahoo County MS to secure a deed in Bedford County VA (concerning the slave Rhoda) from the administrator of the estate of his father John Hall, deceased. The power of attorney was signed Apr 7, 1836, submitted to the county clerk Mar 10, 1837, and recorded Jun 7, 1837. (Bedford DB 26:190).

SHELDRAKE aka Shelldrake, Shildrake

Sheldrake was a soldier in the Revolutionary War. (Parker 1954, 39)

Sheldrake of Henrico County VA and Robert Brown were conveyed a deed from Thomas Hayth and his wife Martha and William Manley and his wife Elizabeth for 400A on Mollys Creek near Thomas Hayth, James Millwood, John Simon, and John Fitzpatrick. Witnesses were John Fitzpatrick, William Brown, John Simmons, Sheldrake Brown Jr and Henry Brown. Recorded Jul 19, 1777. (Bedford DB 5:498).

Sheldrake witnessed a deed from Joel Burgess and his wife Elander to William Brown of Augusta County VA for 200A on Mollys Creek near James Milwood, Shelldrake Brown, Thomas Hayth and Ruffen. Other witnesses were R Brown and Sheldrake Brown Jr. Recorded Jan 1, 1778. (Bedford DB 6:73).

Sheldrake witnessed a bond from William Brown of Augusta County VA to Jack Burgess for security on 200A which William Brown had purchased from Burgess. Other witnesses were R Brown, Townzen Horton and Shildrake Brown Jr. Signed Jan 1, 1778 and recorded same date. (Bedford DB 6:74).

The Browns of Bedford County

Shilldrake was the father of William who paid off the mortgage for L140 on 240A (sic) he had purchased from Joel Burgess. Witnesses were Richard Stith, Charles Talbot, William Brown and John Vest. Signed Sep 21, 1778 and recorded same date. (Bedford DB 6:109).

Sheldrake witnessed a deed from William Graham to William Brown for 333A on the south branches of Mollys Creek. Other witnesses were John Fitzpatrick, R Brown, Ruhar Thurman and Thomas Hayth. Signed Apr 5, 1779 and recorded same date. (Bedford DB 6:337).

Sheldrake witnessed a deed from James Milwood and his wife Anne to William Brown for 100A near Thomas Hayth, William Brown, Shildrake Brown, John Simmons and Ruffin. Other witnesses were R Brown, Edward Brown and Temperance Brown. Signed Apr 6, 1779 and recorded Oct 25, 1779. (Bedford DB 6:362).

Shildrake was granted permission to build a mill on Mollys Creek. Recorded Oct 1779. (Bedford OB 6:260).

Sheldrake was conveyed a deed from John Simmons and wife Elizabeth for 100A on Mollys Creek near James Millwood, Shildrake Brown, Ruffin's line, Josias Bullock, Ajohnadab Read, and John Fitchpatrick. Witnesses were Richard Stith, John Fitchpatrick, R Brown, Brown Vineyard and Edward Brown. Recorded Feb 5, 1780. (Bedford DB 7:18).

Shildrake was recommended and qualified to be an ensign in the Bedford militia. Recorded Aug 28, 1780. (Bedford OB 6:293).

SINTHIA

Sinthia married Joel Worley. She was the daughter of Jesse Brown. Surety was Henry Payn. Bond dated Dec 30, 1826. They were married by John Ayers on Jan 4, 1827. (Hinshaw 1969, 6:1020).

SMITH

Smith Brown was deceased. His administrator, Balda McDaniel, sued Susanna Cavanaugh, who was a tenant for life. Recorded May 14, 1834. (Bedford Chancery OB 1:66).

The Browns of Bedford County

SPOTSWOOD

Spotswood was qualified as deputy sheriff. Recorded 1833. (Bedford OB 24:101, 114).

Spotswood, John S Brown, Nelson A Thompson and Balda McDaniel were witnesses to a deed from trustee Nathaniel Manson to William B Callaway for 362A at Elk Creek owned by debtor Mrs Euphan Logwood. Signed Jan 7, 1834 and recorded Jan 27, 1834. (Bedford DB 24:73).

Spotswood and John S Brown were qualified as deputy sheriffs. Recorded Mar 1834. (Bedford OB 24:261).

Spotswood and John S Brown were qualified as administrators of the estate of Reuben S Brown, deceased. Recorded Nov 1834. (Bedford OB 25:14).

Spotswood and John S Brown were administrators of the estate of Reuben S Brown. On Jan 15, 1835 they conducted an auction of slaves from the estate. Recorded Sep 26, 1836. (Bedford WB 9:186).

Spotswood and John S Brown were qualified as deputy sheriffs. Recorded Mar 1835. (Bedford OB 25:51).

Spotswood was the son of Reuben S Brown. He and his siblings were named in the division of their father's slaves. Division was made May 25, 1835 and recorded Jun 22, 1835. (Bedford WB 9:47).

Spotswood, Betsy and John S Brown gave security bonds for Betty Brown, guardian of Eliza Brown and William Brown. Recorded Aug 1835. (Bedford OB 25:125).

Spotswood married Elizabeth Jane Ewing, daughter of Nancy. Surety was Richard Hobson Jr. Bond dated Nov 16, 1835. (Hinshaw 1969, 6:884).

Spotswood gave bond to Gov Tazewell that William Ewing would perform the duties of sheriff. Signed and recorded Mar 28, 1836, (Bedford DB 25:256).

The Browns of Bedford County

Spotswood D was the son of Reuben Brown. He and his siblings were conveyed a deed from William C Leftwich for 51A at Elk Creek, near Howard's Creek. Signed and recorded May 1, 1837. (Bedford DB 26:151).

Spotswood and his wife Elizabeth J conveyed a deed to Littleberry Carter for 214 1/4A on Ewing's Creek, Lot 4, which had been allotted to Elizabeth from the estate of her father Mitchell Ewing. Signed Nov 13, 1839 and recorded Nov 23, 1839. (Bedford DB 28:203).

Spotswood had 2 males 0-5, 1 male 20-30, 1 female 15-20, and 42 slaves. He was near Richard Ellis and Eli Taylor. (U S Census of 1840, p 41).

Spotswood was qualified as deputy sheriff. Recorded Apr 1840. (Bedford OB 27:63).

STARK

Stark, James Gatewood, Dudley Gatewood and Jane Wily witnessed a deed from Gilbert Harrill to William Martin for 350A. Signed Mar 3, 1779 and recorded Mar 3, 1779. (Bedford DB 6:258).

Stark married Tabitha Rigby. Surety was James Gatewood. Bond dated May 8, 1779. (Dennis 1989, 10).

Stark had appeared in court, and was allowed payment for 65 miles. Recorded May 1788. (Bedford OB 9:169).

STEPHEN

Stephen was born Jun 25, 1779, and his brother Stephen U was born Aug 17, 17--, per their father Arabia's pension application for service in the Revolutionary War. Reel 359 of M804, National Archives. (Wardell 1988, 1:116).

SUSANNA

Susanna Hix married Henry Brown. She certified that she was of age. Surety was Patrick Hix. Witnesses were Patrick Hix and Caty Hix. Bond dated Nov 5, 1793. (Dennis 1989, 10).

The Browns of Bedford County

Susanna and her husband Henry conveyed a deed to John Garrett for 342A near Thomas Pollard, Harris, Tony Thomas, Samuel Hauge, Robert Walker and David Saunders. Witnesses were Alderson Weekes, John Trigg, M Graham and James Edgar. Signed Sep 28, 1799 and recorded Oct 28, 1799. (Bedford DB 11:120).

TABITHA aka Tabby

Tabitha Rigby married Stark Brown. Surety was James Gatewood. The bond was dated May 8, 1779. (Dennis 1989, 10).

Tabby married Stephen Smelser. She was the daughter of James, who gave consent. Surety was Archibald Lamb. Bond dated Jan 17, 1794. (Dennis 1989, 64).

Tabitha Hall married Shadrack Brown. She was the daughter of Magdalean, who gave consent. Surety was Elisha Hall. Bond dated Oct 14, 1799. (Hinshaw 1969, 6:884). They were married on Oct 17, 1799 by Rev John Ayers, a Methodist minister. (Bedford PRO 1:243).

Tabitha Bundurant and Thomas Brown were married by William Harris on Dec 14, 1828. (Hinshaw 1969, 6:884).

Tabitha was the daughter of Martha G Brown. She married Tyree Arthur, son of Charlotte Arthur. Surety was Valentine Leftwich. Bond dated Dec 22, 1835. They were married by Abner Anthony on Dec 24, 1835. (Hinshaw 1969, 6:873).

TEMPERANCE

Temperance witnessed a deed from James Milwood and his wife Anne to William Brown for 100A near Thomas Hayth, William Brown, Shildrake Brown, John Simmons and Ruffin. Other witnesses were Shildrake Brown, R Brown and Edward Brown. Signed Apr 6, 1779 and recorded Oct 25, 1779. (Bedford DB 6:362).

The Browns of Bedford County

THOMAS

Thomas of Chesterfield County VA was conveyed a deed from John Fitzpatrick for 100A near John Richardson and William Hutcherson. Recorded Jul 15, 1769. (Bedford DB 3:300).

Thomas witnessed a deed from Phillip Ryan to Charles Talbot for 342A on the south side of Morton Creek, being the north fork of the south fork of Falling River, and on both sides of Naked Creek, near Burnley and Randle. Witnesses were W Talbot, Preston Gilbert, Thomas Brown, Charles Talbot and William Moore. Recorded Sep 4, 177_ (date is unreadable). (Bedford DB 4:19).

Thomas Brown, Charles Gwatkin and James Taylor witnessed the will of Col Richard Callaway in Bedford County on Dec 21, 1772. The will was recorded on Mar 1, 1784 at DB J:9&11 of Frankfort (sic) County KY. (Ackerly 1930, 320).

Thomas conveyed a deed to William Hamnack for 100A on Bear Branch near William Hutcherson and John Fitzpatrick. Recorded Aug 26, 1774. (Bedford DB 5:255).

Thomas was a soldier in the Revolutionary War. (Parker 1954, 39).

Thomas was a brother of John Brown, who entered Revolutionary War service from Bedford County in 1775. Thomas and his sister Jane (widow of John Craig) applied in 1842 for arrears to their brother John's Revolutionary War pension. Reel 370 of M804, National Archives. (Wardell 1988, 1:120).

Thomas was the father of Edy, who married Ancel Goodman in Bedford County in 1777, per John Craig's pension papers for service in the Revolutionary War. Reel R676 of M804, National Archives. (Wardell 1988, 1:257).

Thomas gave consent and was surety for the marriage of Ezekiel Downing and Rachel Brown. Bond dated Jan 30, 1778. (Dennis 1989, 17).

Thomas Sr lived at Little Otter near Araba Brown, James Brown and Lynard Brown. From a deed from George Hughes to Araba Brown, as recorded Aug 18, 1778. (Bedford DB 6:94).

The Browns of Bedford County

Thomas Sr was conveyed a deed from Augustine Leftwich Sr for 160A near John Anthony, Leftridge, Brambletts Road, James Brown, Raba Brown and William Woodley. Recorded Aug 24, 1778. (Bedford DB 6:97).

Thomas entered military service from Bedford County in 1779. He was born Feb 5, 1749 in Pennsylvania, and at age three moved to Amherst County VA with his parents. In 1832 he was living at Russell, Bedford County VA, when he applied for a pension for service in the Revolutionary War. Reel R379 of M804, National Archives. (Wardell 1988, 1:123).

Thomas was named as the father of Jane Brown who married John Craig in Bedford County on Sep 17, 1780. From John Craig's pension application for service in the Revolutionary War Reel R676 of M804, National Archives. (Wardell 1988, 1:257).

Thomas conveyed a deed to Thomas Jones for 30A on the branches of Little Otter River at Brambletts Road, near William Woody and Linor Brown. Signed Sep 25, 1780 and recorded Oct 23, 1780. (Bedford DB 7:28).

Thomas gave consent for the marriage of Burley Lacey and Judith Brown. Surety was William Woody. Bond dated Feb 9, 1786. (Dennis 1989, 41).

Thomas had 3 horses and 6 cattle. Personal Property Tax List of 1787, List A. (Schreiner-Yantis 1987, 193). He was visited on the same day as Micajah Clark Jr and Thomas Dooley Jr. (Ibid, 211).

Thomas and his wife Phebe conveyed a deed to John Otey for 110A "where Thomas Brown now lives", near William Woodey, Thomas Jones, Linah Brown, James Petross and Holt. Signed Feb 24, 1787 and recorded Feb 26, 1787. (Bedford DB 7:685).

Thomas had 2 horses and 3 cattle. Personal Property Tax List of 1787, List B. (Schreiner-Yantis 1987, 201). He was visited on the same day as Joshua Agee and Robert Lazenby. (Ibid, 216).

Thomas was the son of James Brown and his wife Jinnet. He and his siblings were named in their father's will dated Dec 3, 1789 and recorded Jul 26, 1790. (Bedford WB 2:35).

131

The Browns of Bedford County

Thomas and his wife Elizabeth conveyed a deed to James Brown for 70A on Little Otter near John Otey, Joseph Fuqua and William R Jones. Witnesses were Aaron Fuqua, John Wright and Thomas Miller. Signed Sep 1, 1795 and recorded Sep 23, 1805. (Bedford DB 11:1300).

Thomas' land was near the widow Bramblett. Recorded Mar 8, 1796. (Bedford PRO 1:36).

Thomas' land was processioned, with Alexander Brown and John Pate present. Recorded Apr 26, 1796. (Bedford PRO 1:41).

Thomas was surety for the marriage of Adam Boyer and Patsey Brown. Bond dated Oct 8, 1796. (Dennis 1989, 7).

Thomas had 2 males 21+, and 4 horses. Personal Property Tax List of 1800, Northern District. (Dorman 1963, 7:123).

Thomas Brown and Charles Caffery, executors of the will of James Brown, were granted an injunction to stay proceedings on a deed of trust held by trustee Chris Clark for Andrew Donald. Recorded Feb 22, 1802. (Bedford OB 12:245).

Thomas' land was processioned. Recorded May 28, 1804. (Bedford PRO 1:148).

Thomas was conveyed a deed from James Brown and his wife Elizabeth for a tract on the waters of Shockoe Creek, near Shrewsbury, Brian, Simmons and Hobbs. Witnesses were Thomas Miller, Aaron Fuqua and James Miller. Signed Sep 21, 1805 and recorded Sep 23, 1805. (Bedford DB 11:1299).

Thomas was conveyed a deed of trust from James Brown Jr to trustees Moses Miller and John Watson Sr for a debt owed Thomas Brown, secured by 70A on Shockoe Creek which James had purchased from Thomas Brown. The 70A were near William Jones, Joseph Fuqua and Col John Otey. Signed and recorded Nov 1, 1805. (Bedford DB 12:28).

Thomas was appointed to survey a road from the ford on Goose Creek below Caffery's mill to the fork of Boreauger Creek near the lands of Thomas Preast. Recorded Oct 1808. (Bedford OB 15:18).

The Browns of Bedford County

Thomas had 1 male 10-16, 1 male 16-26, 1 male 45+, 1 female 10-16, 2 females 16-26, and 1 female 45+. (U S Census of 1810).

Thomas, with David Brown and his wife Nancy, conveyed a deed to William O'Brian for 90 1/2A on Shockoe Creek, near Preas, David Brown and Thomas Brown. Witnesses were A P Agee, Robert Campbell and John Thomas. Signed and recorded Jun 22,1812. (Bedford DB 13:726).

Thomas had 1 male 10-16, 1 male 45+, 2 females 16-26, 1 female 26-45, and 1 female 45+. (U S Census of 1820, Southern District, p 61).

Thomas O was surety for the marriage of Elijah Hamilton and Sarah Brown, daughter of Alexander. Bond dated Jan 4, 1820. (Hnishaw 1969, 6:927).

Thomas Brown and Alexander Brown were jurors. Recorded Sep 1, 1820. (Bedford OB 18:31).

Thomas and his siblings were the children of Edward Brown, who qualified to be their guardian. Recorded May 1821. (Bedford OB 18:99).

Thomas W persuaded the court to set aside a judgment against him. Recorded Aug 1821. (Bedford OB 18:138).

Thomas W was surety for the marriage of Isham C Brown and Nancy Pearcy, daughter of Charles. Bond dated Jul 20, 1824. (Hinshaw 1969, 6:884).

Thomas Brown and Thomas A Latham, gentlemen, were attorneys in the commonwealth, and were licensed to practice law in Bedford court. Recorded Aug 28,1826. (Bedford OB 21:1).

Thomas W married Juana Tyler, daughter of Daniel. Surety was Isham C Brown. Bond dated Oct 3, 1826. (Hinshaw 1969, 6:884).

Thomas Brown and Tabitha Bundurant were married by William Harris on Dec 14, 1826. (Hinshaw 1969, 6:884).

Thomas R Brown and John D Murrell of Lynchburg were trustees for a debt owed Archibald Robertson, Hardin Murrell, David Murrell, George Morris and Lewis Davis by Robert Tinsley and his wife Judith. The debt was

The Browns of Bedford County

secured by 800 1/2A near Walker G Meriweather, and by slaves Ben, Nelson, Robin, Caleb, Moses, Edmund, Edmund (little), George, Billy, Daniel, Lewis, Abraham, Isham, Ned, Frank, Claiborn, Harry, Jenny, Mariah, Hannah, Nancy, Archy, James, Sophia, Patsy, Sarah, Kizziah, Esther, Patty and Sylvia, farm implements, household furniture, and claims against the estate of Anthony Rucker. The trustees were to sell the assets. Signed Mar 20, 1828 and recorded Mar 21, 1828. (Bedford DB 20:488).

Thomas R Brown and Samuel Garland of Lynchburg were trustees for a debt owed Archibald Robertson by Edwin D Cobbs. The debt was secured by slaves Ben, Julius, Rachel, Tom, Richard, Thompson, Anderson, Peter, William, James, Billy, Eliza and Washington. The trustees were to sell the slaves. Signed Mar 22, 1828 and recorded same date. (Bedford DB 20:510).

Thomas R was trustee for a debt owed Archibald Robertson by Robert Tinsley, secured by a tobacco crop. Signed Sep 3, 1828 and recorded Sep 5, 1828. (Bedford DB 21:162).

Thomas W was surety for the marriage of Sarah M Brown and Joel Jones on Apr 16, 1929. Sarah M was the daughter of John Brown. (Hinshaw 1969 6:943).

Thomas had 1 male 20-30, 1 female 15-20, and no slaves. He was near John Brown, Thaxton, and Walker Brown. (U S Census of 1830, p 124).

Thomas had 1 male 20-30, 1 male 80-90, 1 female 20-30, 2 females 30-40, 1 female 70-80, and no slaves. He was near Simson Powell and Robert Elliott. (U S Census of 1830, p 165).

Thomas A was trustee for a deed of trust from Henry Tate and his wife Patsy to Thomas Barbour, secured by 50A at Elk Creek. Signed and recorded Jan 16, 1830. (Bedford DB 22:95).

Thomas was surety for the marriage of William McCarty and Margaret Brown. Bond dated Feb 1, 1830. They were married by James Turner on Apr 23, 1830. (Hinshaw 1969, 6:953).

Thomas H was buried at the cemetery of St Stephen's Episcopal Church on Boonesboro Road. His gravestone reads: Sep 30, 1830 - Jun 21, 1892. (Daughters 1970, 101).

The Browns of Bedford County

Thomas filed application for a pension for service during the Revolutionary War, the application including statements by William Campbell and John Burchfield that they knew he had served. The court approved his application. Recorded 1832. (Bedford OB 24:27).

Thomas was a brother of John Brown. He and his siblings were named in John's pension application for service in the Revolutionary War. Reel R370 of M804, National Archives. (Wardell 1988, 1:120).

Thomas R, as trustee, released the deed of trust to debtor Archibald Robertson, who had paid off a debt secured by 178A near Nicholas Robertson and John Ayres. Signed Jan 25, 1833 and recorded Feb 25, 1833. (Bedford DB 23:270).

Thomas M and John Brown sued William Hurt, administrator of William H Brown, deceased. On court calendar Oct 2, 1839. (Bedford Chancery OB 1:359).

Thomas M and John Brown sued William H Brown by his administrator William Hurt, and Aaron Allred and his wife Elizabeth, deceased, the late Elizabeth Brown. The case was dismissed. Recorded Oct 5, 1840. (Bedford Chancery OB 1:422).

TUBAL

Tubal was bound to John Tyler by the overseers of the poor. Recorded Nov 1820. (Bedford OB 18:45).

VINEYARD

Vineyard witnessed a deed from John Simmons and his wife Elizabeth to Shildrake Brown for 100A on Mollys Creek, near Millwood, Shildrake Brown, Josias Bullock, Ajohnadab Read and John fitchPatrick. Other witnesses were Richard Stith, John fitchPatrick and Edward Brown. Signed Feb 5, 1778 and recorded Aug 28, 1780. (Bedford DB 7:18).

VIOLET aka Vilet, Vilett, Violett

Violet Barton and Alexander Brown wer married by William Johnson Feb 25, 1797. (Bedford PRO 1:237).

The Browns of Bedford County

Vilet and her husband Sawney conveyed a deed to Bartholomew Cary for 30A on the south side of Falling Creek, near William Pate and Ebenezer Brown. Signed Sep 24,1802 and recorded Sep 27, 1802. (Bedford DB 11:616).

Violett and her husband Sawney conveyed a deed to Ebenezer Brown for 50A on both sides of Falling Creek. Signed and recorded Sep 27, 1802. (Bedford DB 11:617.

Violet and her husband Alexander conveyed a deed to Samuel Mead for 360A on Staunton River, near Anthony Wright, Pate, Col Dickerson, Hardy, and Beverly Cawley. Signed Oct 24, 1820 and recorded Nov 27, 1820. (Bedford DB 16:352).

WALKER

Walker married Elizabeth Thornhill., daughter of William. Surety was Jacob Wade. Bond dated Feb 26, 1809. (Hinshaw 1969, 6:884). They were married by William Leftwich in Nov 1809. (Bedford PRO 1:264).

Walker had 1 male 0-10, 1 male 16-26, 1 female 0-10, 1 female 16-26, and 1 female 45+. (U S Census of 1810).

Walker was conveyed a deed of gift from his grandmother Mary Walker for slaves Lucky and Agga. Mary was the widow of William Walker. No signing date. Recorded Mar 28, 1816. (Bedford DB 14:526).

Walker relinquished claim to the two slaves given him by Mary Walker and recorded Mar 28, 1816. Several suits by other parties laid prior claim. Signed Apr 25, 1817 and recorded Apr 28, 1817. (Bedford DB 15:175).

Walker had 1 male 26-45, 1 female 10-16, and 1 female 26-45. (U S Census of 1820, Northern District, p 34).

Walker was awarded an injunction for judgment against him by Robert Lazenby until the matter could be heard in equity. Recorded May 24, 1820. (Bedford OB 17:788).

Walker, Robert Reese and James White were fined $80 each and ordered to keep the peace, and to be imprisoned until they found good security. Robert

The Browns of Bedford County

Reese, William Minor and Littleberry Leftwich gave security bonds. Recorded Sep 1, 1820. (Bedford OB 18:33).

Walker entered into a contract for marriage with Milly Wood. Recorded Jul 26, 1826. (Bedford OB 20:257).

Walker Brown and Milley Dooley made a prenuptual agreement, with William Miner and Melanethon Turner to serve as trustees until the marriage. Milley's property included slaves Bett and Bett's child Jordan, other personal property, and land she inherited from her late father John Dooley. Milley was to retain sole ownership to the properties after the marriage, and the right to dispose of them as though the marriage had not been solemnized. Not dated, but recorded Jul 26,1826. (Bedford DB 20:21).

Walker married Milly Dooley. Surety was W Minor. Bond dated Jul 26, 1826. They were married by William Harris on Jul 26, 1826. (Hinshaw 1969, 6: 884).

Walker had 1 male 0-5, 1 male 40-50, 1 female 0-5, 2 females 5-10, 1 female 30-40, and no slaves. He was near Allen Crenshaw, Samuel Jones, and John and Thomas Brown. (U S Census of 1830, p 124).

Walker was awarded an injunction to stay a judgment against him by Robert Lazenby. Recorded Dec 27, 1830. (Bedford OB 23:199).

Walker sued Robert Lazenby for money damages. An injunction was ordered on Dec 27, 1830, and was lifted after the defendant paid. Recorded Oct 17, 1832. (Bedford Chancery OB 1:19).

Walker answered a complaint by Thomas G Burson, and gave security bond secured by his chattels, lands and tenements. Recorded May 1834. (Bedford OB 24:296).

Walker released to Caleb Parker all claim to a land warrant bequeathed him by Mary Walker. This was to satisfy a money judgment against him by William George.Witnesses were D Goggin, Richard Venable, Robert Bell and Fanny Fuqua. Signed Nov 15, 1834 and recorded May 12, 1835. (Bedford DB 24:447).

137

The Browns of Bedford County

Walker and his wife Milley conveyed a deed to James Leftwich for an interest in 221 3/4A on Little Otter River. Recorded 1838. (Bedford DB 27:147.

Walker had 1 male 5-10, 1 male 10-15, 1 male 15-20, 1 male 60-70, 1 female 10-15, 1 female 60-70, and no slaves. He was near Willis Dougherty and Mary P Hopkins. (U S Census of 1840, p 27).

WILLIAM

William had 1 tithable. He was near Giles Williams and William Wiley. List of John Phelps, Lunenburg Tithe Lists of 1748. (Bell 1991, 83).

William had one tithable, and produced six squirrel heads for bounty. He was near Jacob Pyborn and Giles Williams. List of Mathew Talbot, Lunenburg Tithe Lists of 1749. (Bell 1991, 100).

William had one tithable. He was near Patrick Karr and William Briant. List of John Phelps, Lunenburg Tithe Lists of 1750. (Bell 1991, 154).

William was granted a patent for 70A on the south side of Otter River. Recorded Nov 10, 1757. (Lunenburg PB 33:411).

William's 252A were surveyed. The land was on the branches of Cubb Creek and the branches of Falling River, near Harris, Beard's Mountain, Mays, and Woolridge. Survey dated Mar 14, 1771. (Bedford SR 1:142).

William's 287A were surveyed. The land was on the south side of Staunton River, near Hogan and Clyborn. Survey dated Apr 29, 1771. (Bedford SR 2:405).

William's 373A were surveyed. The land was on the branches of the north fork of Seneca Creek and branches of Mollys Creek, near Neilson and Coffry. Survey dated Oct 30, 1771. (Bedford SR 2:141).

William's 180A were surveyed. The land was on the Staunton River, near Aquilla Greer, Reice, and Mitchell. Survey dated Mar 15, 1774. (Bedford SR 2:253).

138

The Browns of Bedford County

William was granted a patent for 287A on the south side of Staunton River. Recorded Dec 7, 1774. (Bedford PB 42:887).

William entered military service from Bedford County in 1777. He was born 1760 in Fairfax County VA, and moved to St Genevieve MO in 1818. In 1832 at Ralls County MO he applied for a pension for service in the Revolutionary War. Reel R381 of M804, National Archives. (Wardell 1988, 1:124).

William, Richard Stith and John FitzPatrick mortgaged 10 slaves as security for a bond. Signed and recorded Mar 24, 1777. (Bedford DB 5:472).

William witnessed a deed for 400A on Mollys Creek from Thomas Hayth et al to Sheldrake Brown and Robert Brown. Other witnesses were Sheldrake Brown Jr and Henry Brown. Recorded Jul 17, 1777. (Bedford DB 5:498).

William was exempt from paying a county levy. Recorded Aug 25, 1777. (Bedford OB 6:131).

William of Augusta County VA was conveyed a deed from Joel Burgess and wife his Elander for 200A on Mollys Creek near James Millwood, Shelldrake Brown, Thomas Hayth, William Brown, Ruffen, James Millwood and Joel Burgess. William gave bond to Burgess for L140, secured by the 200A. Witnesses were Shelldrake Brown, R Brown, Townzen Horton and Shelldrake Brown Jr. Signed on Jan 1, 1778 and recorded same date. (Bedford DB 6:73-74).

William's 354A. The land was on Merriman's Run, near Booth, Hadwell, and Vincent Greer. Survey dated Apr 4, 1778. (Bedford SR 2:305 and 3:95).

William witnessed a deed from George Hughes to Raba Brown for 150A on a small branch of Little Otter River. Recorded Aug 18, 1778. (Bedford DB 6:94).

William, son of Shildrake, paid off the mortgage he owed Joel Burgess for 240A. Witnesses were Richard Stith, Charles Talbot and John Vest. Signed Sep 21, 1778 and recorded same date. (Bedford DB 6:109).

The Browns of Bedford County

William Brown and Nicholas Hays and his wife Ellin conveyed a deed to Edmond Franklin for 270A on a head branch of Falling Creek near Cubb Creek. Recorded Nov 23, 1778. (Bedford DB 6:149).

William was conveyed a deed from William Graham and his wife Anne for 333A on the south branches of Mollys Creek which William Graham had purchased from William Heath on Oct 24, 1774. Witnesses were John Fitzpatrick, Sheldrake Brown, R Brown, Ruhar Thurman and Thomas Hayth. Recorded Apr 5, 1779. (Bedford DB 6:337).

William was conveyed a deed from James Milwood and wife his Anne for 100A near Thomas Hayth, William Brown, Shildrake Brown, John Simmons and Ruffin. Witnesses were Shildrake Brown, R Brown, Edward Brown and Temperance Brown. Signed Apr 6, 1779 and recorded Oct 25, 1779. (Bedford DB 6:362).

William was granted a patent for 250A on both sides of Gills Creek. Recorded Sep 1, 1780. (Bedford PB D:355).

William was granted a patent for 7,050A on both sides of Whipping Creek, Little Whipping Creek and Lick Creek, including their heads on the east side of Seneca Creek and on the branches of Mollys Creek. Recorded Sep 1, 1780. (Bedford PB E:718).

William was granted a patent for 381A on both sides of Kates Creek. Recorded Sep 1, 1780. (Bedford PB E:744).

William and his wife Mary of Locust Thicket conveyed a deed to John Traylor for 1,430A near William Brown of Locust Thicket, Josiah Bullock, "William Brown the viny", Thomas Hayth, Edmund Butler, Richard Stith, William McCloud of Blair's Order, and Benjamin Gilbert. Witnessed by William Brown, Hubbard Brown and John Phaplin. Recorded Feb 10, 1781. (Bedford DB 7:70).

William and his wife Mary conveyed a deed to Patterson Bullock for 1,900A on the north side of Whipping Creek, both sides of Little Whipping Creek and on Lick Creek. Recorded Aug 27, 1781. (Bedford DB 7:71).

The Browns of Bedford County

William and his wife Mary conveyed a deed to Josias Bullock for 1,000A near Lick Creek, part of the land that William Brown purchased from Ruffin. Recorded Aug 27, 1781. (Bedford DB 7:72).

William's account was allowed for 200 lbs beef he supplied to the Revolutionary army. Recorded Jun 21, 1782. (Bedford OB 6:359).

William's account was allowed for his service during the Revolutionary War, when he had been employed to drive cattle for the army commissary. Recorded Aug 1782. (Bedford OB 6:365).

William and his wife Salley conveyed a deed to Richard Radford for 427A, part of a patent by Charles Merriman dated Feb 14, 1761, and including a patent for 287A by William Brown dated Dec 7, 1774. Witnesses were John Mitchell Jr, John Booth and John Camps. Signed Oct 24, 1782 and recorded Oct 28, 1782. (Bedford DB 7:164).

William was appointed to survey land for two miles on each side of the roadway, from the chapel above John Payne's on Blackwater Road to Merriman's Ford of Staunton River. Recorded 1783. (Bedford OB 7:94).

William Brown and Daniel South were securities for William South, to indemnify the parish for upkeep of a bastard child born to him and Elizabeth Howerton. Recorded Mar 1785. (Bedford OB 8:108).

Williiam Brown and William South were securities for a bond for Sir John Ashwell, to indemnify the parish for upkeep of a bastard child born to him and Delilah Howerton. Recorded Mar 1785. (Bedford OB 8:108).

William had no tithables. Personal Property Tax List of 1787, List A. (Schreiner-Yantis 1987, 193). He was visited the same day as Arthur Moseley. (Ibid, p 213).

William had 2 horses and 5 cattle. Personal Property Tax List of 1787, List B. (Schreiner-Yantis 1987, 200). He was visited the same day as Thomas Cambell. (Ibid, p 214).

William J had 1 male 16-21, 1 slave 16+, 4 slaves under 16, 3 horses and 10 cattle. Personal Property Tax List of 1787, List B. (Schreiner-Yantis 1987,

201). He was visited the same day as Daniel Brown Sr and William Mitchell. (Ibid, p 215).

William, father of Elizabeth, gave consent for her marriage to William Ferguson. Surety was Jeremiah Ferguson. Bond dated Mar 7, 1787. (Dennis 1989, 21).

William married Sarah Payne. John and Sarah Payne gave consent. Surety was William Payne. Bond dated Dec 7, 1789. (Dennis 1989, 7).

William conveyed a deed to James Mayes for 50A on Kates Creek. Witnesses were Robert Nimmo, Nathan Chapman and William Nimmo. Signed Mar 19, 1790 and recorded Sep 26, 1793. (Bedford DB 8:494).

William and his brother Daniel were named in the will of their father Daniel. William was to receive the estate upon death of Anney Hastens. His father's will was dated Jan 6, 1797, and recorded Feb 27, 1797. (Bedford WB 2:193).

William was appointed as surveyor of a road from John Phelps to Ebenezer Watkins. Recorded Apr 23, 1798. (Bedford OB 11:263).

William and his wife Elizabeth were conveyed a deed from James Payne and his wife Anny for 150A near Burr Barton, Tommy Wright, John Wright, Pates Road, James Seal and William Brown. Witnesses were Robert Nimmo, Joseph Johnson, Jesse Johnson and James Johnson. Signed Aug 21, 1798 and recorded Sep 24, 1798. (Bedford DB 11:181).

William of Albemarle County SC conveyed a deed to Robert Lazenby for 100A on Fish Creek near Newland, which his father Daniel Brown Sr had bequeathed to him by will. Witnesses were Edward Hore, Julius Saunders, Daniel Brown and Jeremiah Fergis. Signed Oct 7, 1799 and recorded Oct 27, 1799. (Bedford DB 11:266).

William had 1 male 21+, and 2 horses. Personal Property Tax List of 1800, District 1. (Dorman 1963, 7:66).

William and his wife Elizabeth conveyed a deed to Charles Anthony for 150A near Pates Road, near Tommy Wright. Recorded 1800. (Bedford DB 11:181).

The Browns of Bedford County

William's land was near Randolph Bobitt, south of Pates Road. Recorded Jul 8, 1800. (Bedford PRO 1:90).

William of Lynchburg and Benjamin Hopkins were conveyed a deed from Elisha Perkins for 600A near Hawkins, Bright, Davies Ferry Road, Nichols, Richard Oglesby, Bolling Clark and Tinsley. Witnesses were Josiah Leake, Alexander Sharp, Edmund Read and J Penn. Signed Feb 10, 1802 and recorded Feb 1802. (Bedford DB 11:564).

William was bound to John Wilson. Recorded Feb 22, 1802. (Bedford OB 12:248).

William was present when his land was processioned. Recorded Jan 10, 1803. (Bedford PRO 1:114).

William's land was near Elisha Hall and Benjamin Blankenship. Recorded Feb 3, 1804. (Bedford PRO 1:131).

William of Lynchburg and Archelus Mays were conveyed a deed from Charles Jones for 734A on Ivy Creek, formerly owned by John Jones, deceased, near William Burton, George McDaniel Jr, George Cabell Sr and Henry L Davis. Witnesses were George Powell, Thomas Moorman and James Harris. Signed Sep 30, 1804 and recorded Oct 22, 1804. (Bedford DB 11:1125).

William conveyed a deed to Cornelius Pate for 165A on Kates Creek, near John Lancaster, John Holliday and George Medley. Witnesses were John Lancaster, William Turner, Matthew Pate and John Nelson. Signed Jan 10, 1805 and recorded Sep 25, 1815. (Bedford DB 14:398).

William witnessed a deed from Daniel Brown of Pittsylvania County VA to Obediah Pate for 65A on Rockcastle Creek near Hancock and Gorden. Other witnesses were Samuel Hancock, Robert Harper and Thomas Payne. Signed Mar 14, 1805 and recorded Sep 23, 1805. (Bedford DB 11:1317).

William Brown and John Buford conveyed a deed to John Holliday for 139A on Beaverdam Creek, near John Wright and Walton. Witnesses were Joseph Stith, William Holliday, William Watts, John Blankenship and John Brown. Signed Mar 16, 1805 and recorded Apr 22, 1805. (Bedford DB 11:1219).

The Browns of Bedford County

William conveyed a deed of trust to trustee John Claytor and Benjamin Mead for L100, secured by three slaves. The slaves were to be sold to repay a debt owed Brown Leftwich & Co. Signed Sep 15, 1805 and recorded Sep 23, 1805. (Bedford DB 11:1303).

William and his wife Elizabeth conveyed a deed to John Blankenship for 116A on the head branches of Kates Creek, near Robert Nimmo. Witnesses were William Halladay, William H Maddera and John Dent. Signed Jan 14, 1806 and recorded Feb 24, 1807. (Bedford DB 12:184).

William was surety for the marriage of John Bird and Elizabeth Brown. Bond dated Nov 9, 1810. They were married by John Ayers on Nov 15, 1810. (Hinshaw 1969, 6:879).

William and Saray were the parents of Rhoda who married Joel Chambers. Sureties were Daniel Brown and John Bird. Bond dated Dec 9, 1811. (Hinshaw 1969, 6:891).

William Bramblett Brown was indentured by the overseers of the poor, and bound over to Joseph Flood. Recorded March 1812. (Bedford OB 16:49).

William's former 181A were exonerated for erroneously assessed delinquent taxes for years 1796 and 1806. Matthew Pate, administrator of Comet Pate Sr, showed the deed at court. Recorded Jul 23, 1816. (Bedford OB 17:208).

William's former 70A "conveyed to Mayre Blankenship in 1791" were exonerated from erroneously assessed delinquent taxes in his name for the years 1791, 1796, 1797, 1809, 1811 and 1814. Recorded Aug 1816. (Bedford OB 17:235).

William H married Elizabeth Hurt. Surety was A I Agee. Bond dated Sep 27, 1819. (Hinshaw 1969, 6:884).

William H had 1 male 26-45, and 1 female 16-26. (U S Census of 1820, Southern District, p 62).

The Browns of Bedford County

William was "deceased, late a soldier in 3rd Regiment of Pennsylvania Line on Continental establishments". Jacob R Brown was proven to be his son and one of his heirs. Recorded Nov 21, 1828. (Bedford OB 22:166).

William H Brown, deceased, had been dead for more than three months, and no person had applied for administration of his estate, so the court ordered sheriff Thomas Sale as administrator. Recorded Jul 1831. (Bedford OB 23:337).

William was named as a purchaser at auction of slaves from the estate of Reuben S Brown. The auction was held on Jan 15, 1835 and recorded Sep 26, 1836. (Bedford WB 9:186).

William was the son of Reuben S Brown. He and his siblings were named in the division of their father's slaves. Division was made May 25, 1835 and recorded Jun 22, 1835. (Bedford WB 9:47).

Wiilliam and Eliza, orphans of Reuben S Brown, deceased, chose Betsy Brown as their guardian. Betsy Brown, John S Brown and Spotswood Brown gave security bonds. Recorded Aug 1835. (Bedford OB 25:125).

William was allowed $4.62 for performing public service. Recorded Jun 1836. (Bedford OB 25:107).

William and his siblings were conveyed a deed from William C Leftwich for 51A at Elk Creek, near Howards Creek. Signed and recorded May 1, 1837. (Bedford DB 26:151).

William H was surety for the marriage of Thomas Robinson and Harriett Brown. Bond dated Jan 3, 1838. (Hinshaw 1969, 6:986).

William H was surety for the marriage of Triplett E Lowry and Matilda C Brown. Bond dated Feb 25, 1839. (Ricks 1939, 94).

William H was deceased. His administrator, William Hurt, was sued by John Brown and Thomas M Brown. On court calendar Oct 2, 1839. (Bedford Chancery OB 26:359).

The Browns of Bedford County

William H was deceased. His administrator, William Hurt, and Aaron Allred and his wife Elizabeth, deceased, the late Elizabeth Brown, were sued by Thomas M Brown and John Brown. The case was dismissed. Recorded Oct 5, 1840. (Bedford Chancery OB 1:422).

WILLIAM BROWN & CO

William Brown & Co did business in Bedford County and in Lynchburg. William was burned in a theater fire in Richmond in 1811. (Chalkley 1989, 192).

WILSON

Wilson was the son of Aaron, who had entered military service from Bedford County in 1776. He and other family members were named in Aaron's death report of 1836. Reel R358 of M804, National Archives. (Wardell 1988, 1:116).

WYATT aka Wiatt

Wyatt witnessed a deed from Daniel Brown and his wife Lucy of Pittsylvania County VA to Thomas Stewart for 200A on both sides of the road leading from Hales Ford to the meadows of Goose Creek, near Lewis Turner, David Kerson, the old mill road and Hancock. Other witnesses were Arthur Goolsley, Shadrack Brown and Samuel Murphy. Signed Jun 24, 1805 and recorded Jul 22, 1805. (Bedford DB 11:1282).

Wyatt had 2 males 0-5, 1 male 20-30, 1 female 20-30, and no slaves. He was near Nancy Leftwich and Nancy Hutson. (U S Census of 1840, p 57).

ZACHARIAH

Zachariah's former 185A were surveyed. The land was near Hutton and Pate. Zachariah had transferred the land to George Nathan, who had it surveyed on Mar 17, 1775. (Bedford SR 3:141).

Zachariah, Aaron Brown and Absalom Adams were sureties on a peace bond for Aaron Brown, in the matter of Peter Dent and Micajah McCormack v Aaron Brown. Recorded Aug 1782. (Bedford OB 6:368).

The Browns of Bedford County

Zachariah had 2 horses and 1 head of cattle. Personal Property Tax List of 1787, List B. (Schreiner-Yantis 1987, 200). He was visited on the same day as Peter Dent. (Ibid, p 213).

Zachariah and Betty Brown gave consent for the marriage of Betty Brown and William King. Surety was James King. Bond dated Feb 26, 1788. (Dennis 1989, 38).

Zachariah's former 90A "supposed to be conveyed to Isaac James in 1800" were exonerated from erroneously assessed delinquent taxes in his name for the year 1791. Recorded Aug 1816. (Bedford OB 17:235).

****

Notes

The Browns of Bedford County

BIBLIOGRAPHY

ORIGINAL SOURCES
(Letters in parentheses indicate abbreviations
used within the text to cite references)

Bedford County Virginia records
Chancery Court Order Book 1, 1831-1841 (ChOB)
Court Order Books (OB)
Books 1A-3, 1754-1771
Books 4-6, 1772-1782
Books 7-10, 1782-1795
Books 11-13, 1795-1806
Books 14-16, 1806-1815
Books 17-18, 1815-1823
Books 19-22, 1823-1829
Books 23-25, 1829-1837
Books 26-29, 1837-1848
Patents and Land Grants, Index (PB)
Processioners Book (1), 1796-1812 (PRO)
Real Estate Conveyances (DB)
General Index Grantees
General Index Grantors
Deed Books 3-5, 1766-1778
Deed Books 6-7, 1778-1787
Deed Books 8-10, 1787-1798
Deed Book 11,1799-1806
Deed Books 12-13, 1806-1813
Deed Books 14-15, 1813-1818
Deed Books 16-18, 1819-1824
Deed Books 19-21, 1824-1829
Deed Books 22-24, 1829-1835
Deed Books 25-27, 1835-1839
Deed Book 28, 1839-1840
Surveyor's Records (SR)
Book 1, 1754-1781
Book 2, 1754-1795
Book 3, 1774-1782
Book 4, 1811-1881

Will Books (WB)
    Books 1-3, 1763-1811
    Books 4-6, 1811-1828
    Books 7-9, 1828-1838
    Book 10-11, 1838-1845

United States Federal Census
    Census of 1810, Bedford County VA
    Census of 1820, Bedford County VA
    Census of 1830, Bedford County VA
    Census of 1840, Bedford County VA

SECONDARY SOURCES

Ackerly, Mary D. Our Kin. Lynchburg, VA: J P Bell Co Inc, 1930.

Bell, Landon C. Sunlight on the Southside. Philadelphia, PA: np, 1931; reprint, Baltimore, MD: Clearfield Co Inc, 1991.

Bockstruck, Lloyd DeWitt. Virginia's Colonial Soldiers. Baltimore, MD: Genealogical Publishing Co, 1988.

Butler, Stuart Lee. Virginia Soldiers in the United States Army, 1800-1815. Athens, GA: Iberian Publishing Co, 1968.

Chalkley, Lyman C. Chronicles of the Scotch-Irish Settlement in Virginia: Extracted from the Original Court Records of Augusta County, 1745-1800. np: 1912; reprint, Baltimore, MD: Genealogical Publishing Co, 1989.

Chilton, Ann. Bedford County, Virginia, Deed Book A-1, 1754-1762. Signal Mountain, TN: Mountain Press, 1987.

Chilton, Ann. Bedford County, Virginia, Will Book I 1759-1787, and Will Book II 1787-1803. Signal Mountain, TN: Mountain Press, 1988.

Daughters of the American Revolution, Peaks of Otter Chapter, comp. Tombstone Inscriptions of Bedford, Virginia. 1970. (Family History Library, microfilm 0849494).

The Browns of Bedford County

DeLorme Mapping Company. Virginia Atlas and Gazeteer. Freeport,
ME: DeLorme Mapping Company, 1989.

Dennis, Earle S and Jane E Smith, comps. Marriage Bonds of Bedford
County, Virginia 1755-1800. Bedford, VA: np, 1932; reprint,
Baltimore, MD: Genealogical Publishing Co, 1989.

Dorman, John Frederick, comp. Bedford County, Virginia, Personal
Property Tax List of 1800. Vol 7, The Virginia Genealogist.
Washington, DC: John Frederick Dorman, 1963.

Evans, June Banks, Lunenburg County, Virginia, Deed Book 3,
1752-1754. New Orleans, LA: Bryn Ffyliaid Publications, 1990.

Hinshaw, William Wade, ed. Marriage Bonds of Bedford Co.,
Virginia. Vol 6, Encyclopedia of American Quaker Genealogy.
Ann Arbor, MI: Edwards Brothers, 1936; reprint, Baltimore, MD:
Genealogical Publishing Co, 1969.

Hopkins, Walter Lee, Leftwich-Turner Families of Virginia and Their
Connections. Richmond, VA: J W Fergusson & Sons, 1931.

Kegley, F B. Kegley's Virginia Frontier. Roanoke, VA: The
Southwest Virginia Historical Society, 1938; reprint, Bowie, MD:
Heritage Books, Inc, 1993.

McAllister, Ann , comp. "Bedford County, Virginia, Insolvent Lists
for 1797 and 1798 Filed in Bedford County Courthouse". Virginia
Appalachian Notes, August 1986.

Merrill, Eleanor Brown. A Virginia Heritage. Richmond, VA: Press
of Whittet & Shepperson, 1968.

Parker, Lula Jeter. The History of Bedford County, VA. Bedford,
VA: The Bedford Democrat, 1954.

Prillaman, Helen R, Places Near the Mountains, np, 1985; reprint,
Baltimore, MD: Clearfield Co, Inc, 1995.

Ricks, Joel. Bedford County VA Marriage Bonds, 1800-1853. TS; np, 1939. (Family History Library, microfilm 0896772).

Schreiner-Yantis, Nettie and Florene Love. The Personal Property Tax Lists for the Year 1787 for Bedford County, Virginia. Springfield, VA: Genealogical Books in Print, 1987.

TLC Genealogy, Bedford County, Virginia, Deeds, 1761-1766. Miami, FL: TLC Genealogy, 1991.

Wardell, Patrick G. VA/WV Genealogical Data from Revolutionary War Pension and Bounty Land Warrant Records. Vol 1, A-C. Bowie, MD: Heritage Books, Inc, 1988.

Wilkes, Harry, comp. Letters, Day Books and Records of the Wilkes Family of Bedford County, Virginia, abt 1790-1871. TS; np, 1949. (Family History Library, microfiche 6018438).

Wright, F Edward. Quaker Records of South River Monthly Meeting, Virginia, 1756-1800. Westminster, MD: Family Line Publications, 1993.

INDEX

Adams 4
 Absalom/Absolom 1, 146
 Henry 118
 James 53, 67
 Samuel 44, 52, 94
 William 66, 67
Agee
 A 23, 34, 133, 144
 Joshua 130
 Reason 68
Alberts
 Joseph 55
 Penelope 55
Alexander
 Thomas 18
Alford 76
 Melinda 105
 Silvator 105
Allen
 Robert 43
 William 9
Allred
 Aaron 36, 84, 135, 146
 Elizabeth 36, 84, 135, 146
Anderson
 Nelson 3
 William 72
Andrews
 Mark 53, 57
 Thomas 31, 54
 William 53
Angel
 William 54
Anthony 46, 51, 117
 Abner 22, 70, 99, 129
 Charles 32, 142
 E 66
 Emily 70

Jane 70
John 7, 61, 131
Joseph 61
Mark 21, 53, 70, 89
Armond 71, 79
Arnold
 Eliza 23, 29
 Mosby 23, 29, 54, 68, 99
 Mosly 53
Arthur 55
 Charlotte 99, 129
 Henry 54, 55
 Lewis 22
 Tabitha 99, 128
 Tyree 99, 128
Ashwell
 John 50
 Sir John 140
Auld
 Josiah 19, 65
Aunspaugh
 Daniel 13, 60, 79, 86
 Frederick 13, 79
Austin/Austain 18, 37, 46, 47, 49,
  51
 Alexander 51
 Col 95
 Peter 56
 Thomas 47
 William 16, 45
Ayers
 A 67
 James 9, 22, 50, 57
 John 16, 18, 21, 27, 30, 32, 33,
  39, 67, 73, 95, 96, 101,
  102, 108, 124, 126, 129,
  135, 144
Azberry

William 84

Baber
  George 63, 64
  Wiatt 28
  William 10, 123
Badey
  John 53
Ball
  James 45
Bandy
  James 27, 97, 106
  Maney 95
  Nancy 27, 106
Banks
  Samuel 15
Barberry
  James 22
Barbour
  Thomas 134
Barton
  Brer 2
  Burr 32, 142
  David 3
  Vilet 2, 134
  Violet 2, 134
Beard 8
  Alice 4, 13, 15, 31, 41, 116
  Alce 4, 40
Beech
  Justice 114
Behren
  William 68
Bell
  Robert 137
  Thomas 79
Bellamy
  Matthew 88
Bentley
  Banner 15

Best
  Druzilla 30, 39
  Elizabeth 30, 39
  Levi 30, 39
Bird
  Elizabeth 32, 144
  John 20, 33, 113, 122, 144
Bishop
  Elizabeth 103, 108
Bitz
  Abraham 8
Black
  John 64
Blankenship
  Abraham 74
  Benjamin 14, 15, 143
  John 33, 77, 143, 144
  Joseph 85
  Mayre 144
  Polly 74
Blount
  C 73
Board
  James 31, 71, 85
Boatright
  James 38, 50, 54
Bobitt
  Randolph 143
Boblett
  John 45
Bond
  Isaak 1
  Martha 103
  Mary 102, 108
  Pleasant 102, 108
  Wright 103, 108
Booth/Boothe 139
  John 120, 141
  William 22, 34, 111
Bouty

James 24
Bowles
  Greenbury 9, 11
  John 78, 92, 93, 102, 122
Bowyer
  Adam 64, 65, 71, 99, 113
  Patsey 99
Boyd 22
  James 19
  Milley 19
Boyer
  Adam 33, 78, 98, 132
  Patsey 78, 98, 132
Bozwell
  John 14, 61
Bramblett 12, 23, 33, 64, 65, 78,
    81, 132
  Anne 61
  Caleb 80
  Elkanor 80
  Matilda 78, 104
  Reuben 64, 71, 78, 104, 113
  William 61, 63, 100
Branch
  James 18
Brian 23, 33, 65, 132
Briant 138
Bright 143
  Charles 117
  Edward 11
  Mary Ann 11
Brooks
  Richard 118
Brown 67
  Aaron 1, 26, 35, 39, 68, 83, 86,
    95, 103, 107, 108, 123,
    124, 146
  Aggy 1, 78
  Albert 1, 68, 104
  Alce 4, 13, 29, 42, 94, 117

Alexander 2, 3, 26, 102, 117,
    123, 130, 132, 133, 135,
    136
Aley 4, 44
Alcy 4, 45
Alice 4, 5, 13, 15, 31, 36, 41-43,
    45, 56, 117, 118
Allen 5, 71, 116
Ann/Anne 5, 6, 16, 40, 41, 62,
    70, 75, 76, 97, 100, 121
Anna 6, 37, 75, 79
Araba/Arabia 6-8, 25, 30, 39,
    44, 97, 122, 128, 130
Archibald 8
Benjamin 9
Betsy/Betsey 1, 29, 32-35, 65,
    73, 75, 80, 82, 109, 112,
    113, 127, 145
Betty 30, 33, 110, 127
Bramble 9, 11
Caleb 9-11, 123
Callaway 11, 58, 60, 81, 124
Catharine 11, 67, 69, 89, 107
Celia 11
Charles 11, 103
Claiborn/Clayburn 12, 41, 120
Clara 12, 28
Clitus 12, 100
Constant/Constance 12, 13, 77,
    79
Daniel 4, 10, 13-22, 29, 31, 36,
    37, 40-42, 45-47, 49, 52,
    64, 68, 73, 76, 85, 89, 95,
    96, 99, 101, 113, 121,
    122, 124, 125, 142, 143,
    146
David 23-25, 62, 63, 66, 70, 75,
    102, 105, 106, 133
Doshy 6, 25
Douglas 25, 28

Dycey/Dicey 1, 25, 26, 73
E C L 29
Ebenezer/Ebenizer 23, 26, 27, 96, 106, 116, 117, 136
Edith/Edy 27, 28, 78, 83, 84, 86, 130
Edward 12, 25, 28, 29, 33, 34, 108, 109, 123, 126, 129, 133, 135, 140
Eleanor 29, 56, 98
Eliza 23, 29, 35, 82, 113, 127, 145
Elizabeth 1, 4, 6, 7, 15, 16, 28-36, 39, 40, 42-45, 58, 62, 63, 65, 70, 71, 73, 74, 77, 81, 84, 85, 91, 93, 97, 98, 101, 107, 111, 113, 114, 118, 121, 127, 128, 131, 132, 135, 136, 142, 144, 146
Elvira 36, 38, 97, 116, 119
Emily 14, 36
Enoch 36, 98, 122
Esther 4, 36
Ethelred 6, 37, 79
Frances/Fanny 5, 18, 36-38, 44, 46, 47, 49, 50, 52, 56, 77, 94, 97, 100, 114, 116-119
Francis 38
Garrett 39, 59, 89
George 1, 8, 30, 36, 39, 98, 120, 122
Gian 62, 69, 70
Granville 35, 40, 112, 113
Hannah 16, 20, 31, 40, 41, 45, 85, 121, 124
Harmon 41
Harriet 35, 41, 113, 145

Henry 4-6, 10, 13, 15-18, 20, 22, 28, 29, 31, 36-38, 40-58, 67, 74, 77, 82, 83, 94, 95, 98, 100, 102, 103, 109, 116, 117, 119, 121, 125, 129, 139
Hezekiah 11, 31, 32, 58, 60, 69, 81, 85, 114, 124
Howell 58
Hubbard 59, 99, 140
Irenia 39, 59, 89
Isaac 59
Isham 59, 90, 107, 133
J 59, 66
Jabez 11, 58, 60, 107, 124
Jacob 60, 143
James 1, 5, 7, 10, 11, 14, 18, 23, 30-32, 60-71, 74-77, 88, 91-93, 98-102, 104, 113, 121, 122, 120, 129-132
Jane 11, 14, 58, 68-70, 75, 87-89, 130, 131
Janet/Jannet 62, 70, 71, 97, 100
Jeanet/Jenet/Jennet/Jinnet 23, 61, 62, 64, 76, 99, 113, 131
Jennings 5, 31, 63, 71, 75, 79, 89, 116
Jeremiah 72
Jesse 25, 31, 32, 34, 51, 67, 72-74, 85, 95, 101, 114, 126
Jinnet 23, 61, 76, 99, 131
Jinsey 69, 88
John 1, 5, 6, 12, 13, 16, 25, 27-29, 32, 34, 35, 37, 56, 57, 61, 62, 67, 69-71, 74-84, 86, 91-93, 95, 97, 98, 100-105, 112, 113, 123, 124, 125, 127, 134, 135, 137, 143, 146

Joseph 1, 16, 28, 31, 32, 40, 58, 72, 73, 84-87, 94, 98, 107, 109, 112, 114, 121, 123
Joshua 11, 53, 67, 69, 70, 87-89
Josiah 71
Joyce/Joycy/Joicey 22, 39, 59, 89
Juana 59, 90, 133
Jubal 90
Judith 82, 90, 91, 131
Larkin/Larking 32, 63, 77, 78, 91-93, 102, 122
Leonard 92, 120
Lettice 4, 42, 44, 94
Lenard 94
Levi 84, 94
Lewcinda 1, 95
Linah 32, 63, 65, 77, 78, 91-94, 102, 107, 120-122, 131
Liner 92
Linor 92, 131
Locky 52, 56, 94, 95
Lucinda 82, 83, 95
Lucy/Lucie 15, 17, 19, 21, 27, 73, 76, 95, 96, 100, 125, 146
Lyman 36, 38, 96, 97, 116, 119
Lynard 61, 92, 93, 130
Lynee 92
Lyonell 97
Maney 97
Manly 70, 97, 100
Margaret 5, 31, 62, 70, 75, 85, 97, 98, 134
Maria 56, 98
Marmaduke 36, 98, 122
Martha 68, 99, 129
Mary 1, 11-13, 32, 35, 45, 49, 57, 59, 62, 63, 65, 68, 70,

75-79, 83, 92, 95, 97, 99-104, 108, 111-113, 117, 121, 122, 140, 141
Mason 67, 104
Matilda 35, 78, 80, 104, 105, 113, 145
Melinda 105
Milley/Milly 105, 137, 138
Moses 106
Nancy 1, 5, 23, 24, 27, 59, 60, 106, 107, 133
Orpah 31, 85, 107
Paschal 11, 107
Patsey 98, 99, 132
Peggy 6, 75, 97, 98
Phebe 1, 107, 108, 131
Pleasant 102, 103, 108
Polly 3, 14, 18, 20, 23, 66, 73, 99, 101, 102, 114
R 28, 108, 109, 125, 126, 129, 139, 140
Raba 7, 30, 61, 92, 131, 139
Rachel 109, 130
Reed 60, 87, 109
Reuben 29, 32, 33, 35, 40, 41, 48, 80, 82, 83, 103, 105, 109-113, 127, 128, 144, 145
Rhoda 20, 62-64, 71, 113, 122, 144
Rhodam/Rhodham 31, 32, 37, 58, 72, 87, 102, 114
Richard 114, 115, 120, 121
Robert 5, 43, 115, 116, 125, 139
Roswell 36, 38, 96, 97, 116, 119
Ruth 2, 3, 26, 116, 117
Samuel 4, 16, 40, 42, 45, 52, 56-68, 117-119
Sally/Salley 32, 86, 121-124, 141

Sanford/Sandford 36, 38, 96, 97, 116, 119
Sarah/Saray 1, 3, 8, 10-12, 20, 28, 31, 32, 36, 41, 45, 58, 60, 63, 65, 78, 80-82, 85, 92, 93, 98, 102, 113, 115, 120-124, 133, 134, 142-144
Sawney 2, 26, 27, 124, 136
Shadrack 16, 19, 40, 95, 124, 125, 129, 146
Sheldrake/Shildrake 28, 43, 108, 109, 115, 116, 125, 126, 129, 135, 139, 140
Sinthia 74, 126
Smith 125
Spotswood 29, 35, 81, 82, 112, 113, 127-128, 145
Stark 128, 129
Stephen 6, 128
Susanna 45, 46, 118, 128, 129
Tabitha/Tabby 62, 99, 124, 128, 129, 133
Temperence 28, 108, 126, 129, 140
Thomas 2-4, 7, 23, 27, 28, 36, 42, 59, 61, 62, 64-67, 69, 70, 75, 80, 84, 90, 92, 98, 106, 107, 109, 123, 129-132, 134, 135, 144, 145
Tubal 135
Vineyard 28, 135
Violet/Vilet 1-3, 26, 27, 135, 136
Walker 33, 80, 84, 105, 134, 136-138
Wiatt/Wyatt 19, 95, 125, 146
widow 26
William 7, 14-16, 20, 28-30, 32, 33, 35, 36, 41, 43, 59, 60, 77, 82, 84, 99, 100, 105, 107, 108, 113, 116, 120, 122, 125-127, 129, 135, 138-146
Wilson 1, 146
Zachariah 1, 30, 146
Brown & Claytor Co 9, 10, 22, 50, 52, 55
Brown Leftwich & Co 10, 144
Brown McCredie & Co 10, 66
Browning
  Caleb 5, 71
Bruce
  David 37, 114
  Frances 37, 114
  William 37, 114
Brumfield 8
Buford 23, 63
  Betty 60
  James 60, 61
  John 77, 143
Bullock
  Galt 21, 53
  James 25, 53
  Josiah 140
  Josias 28, 99, 109, 126, 135, 141
  Patterson 99, 140
Bunch
  Charles 72
Bundurant
  Tabitha 129, 123
Burchfield
  John 135
Burgess
  Elander 125, 139
  Jack 108, 125
  Joel 125, 126, 139
Burks
  Francis 44, 94
Burlesson

Aaron 44
Burnett
  Samuel 17
Burnley 130
  Ann 75
  Israel 75
  Joel 75
Burnside
  William 18, 19, 64
Burson
  Sally 78, 122
  Sarah 82
  Thomas 78, 82, 124, 137
Burton
  Alexander 34, 49, 111
  Elizabeth 64
  William 64, 143
Burwell
  Robert 102
Butler
  Edmund 140

Cabell
  George 143
Cadwallader
  Jesse 34
Cafferty/Caffery 123, 131
  Charles 62-64, 100, 122, 132
Caffey
  Charles 18, 64
Callaway 12, 33, 43, 64-66, 72,
      78, 79
  A 111
  Abner 101
  Catharine 101
  Elizabeth 40, 101
  Emily 14, 36
  Frances 101
  George 101
  Henry 101

James 14, 36, 101
Jeremiah 101
John 40, 101, 112
Lucinda 40
Lucy 101
Polly 99, 101, 120
Richard 130
Sarah 36
Thomas 101
William 42, 44, 81, 101, 112,
      117, 127
Calloway
  William 46
Calvert
  Francis 77
Cambell
  Thomas 141
Campbell
  Henry 47
  John 65, 70, 97, 100
  Mary 75, 97, 100, 103
  Robert 23, 106, 133
  William 80, 135
Camps
  John 120, 141
Candless
  William 44
Canefase 76
Cantrell
  widow 115
Carrington
  P 72
Carson
  Daniel 17
  Robert 23, 29
Carter 45
  E C L 29, 50
  Eleanor 29, 98
  Littleberry 35, 128
  Merry 92

159

Robert 90
Cary 8
Bartholomew 2, 26, 136
Cavanaugh/Cavenaugh
  Susannah 90, 91, 126
  William 14, 34, 61
Cavender 32, 114
Cawley
  Beverly 3, 136
Chaffin
  Stephen 54
Chambers
  Joel 20, 113, 122, 144
  Rhoda 20, 113, 121, 144
Chapman
  Nathan 142
Chastain/Chastine
  James 44, 94
Chilton 104
  Richard 103
Christian
  Mary 1, 103
Clark
  Bolling 143
  Christopher/Chris 24, 25, 64,
        70, 106, 132
  Constant 12, 13, 77
  Elizabeth 15
  Henry 22
  Isham 12, 13, 61, 77, 79
  Joseph 13, 79
  Judith 82
  Micajah 131
  Robert 15
Clayton
  Mary 102
  Samuel 15
  Thomas 18, 47, 54
Claytor
  John 19, 20, 48, 49, 52, 88, 144

Mary 100, 102
Samuel 9, 49, 50, 52, 100, 102
Thomas 49, 52, 66, 102
Clement
  Adam 61
  John 114
Clyborn 138
Cobbs 57
  Edwin 134
  John 34, 48, 49, 110, 111
  Tilghman/Tilman 52, 57, 118
Coffrey 138
Consolve/Consolver
  John 11
  Jonathan 18, 64
Cook
  William 13, 34, 79, 111
Coombs/Combs
  Samuel 45, 46
Corley
  Caniel 2, 26, 116
  William 1, 33
Cotty
  Barbary 48
  Christian 48
Cowan
  Robert 45, 47
  William 47
Cowley
  Caniel 26
  Kary 26
Craig/Crage
  Anna 69
  Betsy 69
  Gian 62, 69, 70
  James 69
  Jane 69, 75, 131
  John 27, 69, 75, 131
  Linn 69
  Nancy 69

Polly 69
Rachel 69
Rebecca 69
Robert 69
Crane
  Wiatt 68, 99
Crawford
  Samuel 51
Creasy
  Bennet 67
  Edmund 55
Crenshaw 115
  Allen 137
Crescent
  D 12, 79
Crews
  Gideon 123
Crouch
  Benjamin 9, 52
  Charles 58
  Josiah 104
  Plooy 56
  William 53
Crum
  Elizabeth 15
Crumb
  Gilbert 107
Crumpacker
  Joel 48, 53, 54
  John 16, 45, 53
  Peter 53, 57
Crumpton 46
  David 38, 50
  Henry 38, 49, 50
Cundiff
  Benjamin 15
  Elijah 17, 103
  Elisha 17
  Jamima 103
  Jimmy 17, 73, 95

John 17
Jonathan 20, 22, 104
Lucy 17, 73, 95
Mary 22
Currey
  Bartholomew 27
  Razene 27

Dabney
  Chiswell 21
Dallis
  Marmaduke 14, 61
  Robert 17
Davenport
  Priscilla 66
Davies 117
  John 36, 98, 122
Davis
  Benjamin 72
  George 6, 37
  Henry 19, 143
  John 6, 37, 96, 116, 119
  Jonathan 72
  Lewis 133
  Micajah 57, 83, 103
  Nelson 53
  Robert 63, 100
  Samuel 19
  William 19
Deardorf
  Peter 47
Dearing
  Jeremiah 68, 104
  John 67, 104
  Richard 67, 104
Dent
  John 33, 84, 85, 144
  Peter 1, 146
  Sarah 85
  William 3, 85

Dickerson
  Col 3, 136
  William 20, 41, 50
Dickinson 37
  Pleasant 6, 37
  William 22
Dillard
  James 57
Dixon 54
  James 69, 88
  Susannah 69, 88
Dobbins/Dobyns
  Abner 107
  Alexander 99
  Gracy 52
  Joseph 52
Dobson
  William 45
Dodd
  Polly 103
Donald
  Andrew 47, 64, 132
Donning
  William 92
Dooley 8
  Elizabeth 6, 30, 44, 97
  George 8
  Janey 8
  John 8, 105, 136
  Milley/Milly 105, 137
  Moses 61
  Polly 105
  Sally 105
  Thomas 131
Dougherty
  Willis 138
Douglas
  George 109
Dowell
  Elijah 31, 71

Nehemiah 71
Downing
  Ezekiel 109, 130
  Rachel 109, 130
Drury
  Joseph 62, 113

Eads 23
Early
  Abner 15, 44, 45
  Charlotte 83
  Joel 28, 83, 84, 86
  Mrs 28, 84, 86
  Tubal 28, 83
Echkols
  James 101
Eckovey
  Elizabeth 31, 114
  Mathias 31, 114
Edgar
  James 46, 127
Edgars
  Thomas 34, 111
  William 112
Edson
  Boice 92, 120
Edwards
  Daniel 53
Eidson
  Barnabas 86
  Thomas 7
Eitson
  Elebeth 7, 30
Elliott
  Adam 28, 83
  Robert 67, 134
Ellis
  Richard 128
English
  James 20

Parmenas 23
Permenus 22
Erwin
Jonas 61
Estes
Edward 124
Everett/Everitt
Anderson 35
Thomas 109
Ewing 72
Elizabeth 35, 127
Mitchell 35, 128
Nancy 35, 127
William 127

Farley
David 80
Farris/Fariss
Alexander 49
Anderson 10, 66
John 10
Feezel
Jacob 72
Joseph 18, 64
Fergis
Jeremiah 17, 141
William 17, 142
Ferguson
Elizabeth 30, 142
Jeremiah 30, 142
John 22, 96
Jos 13, 79
Joseph 96
Lucy 96
Mary 22
William 30, 142
Finley
Sally 3
Fisher

John 32, 53, 65, 77, 92, 93, 100,
101, 121, 123, 133
Polly 100
Thomas 122
FitchPatrick/fitchPatrick/Fitch-
patrick/Fitzpatrick
John 28, 43, 109, 116, 124-126,
130, 135, 139, 140
Fitzgerald
William 53
Fizer 124
Jacob 53, 123
Fleming and Edwin James & Co
24
Flood
Anne 122
Joseph 9-11, 122, 124, 143
Flower
John 33, 111
Floyd
Daniel 89
Folden
James 115
John 121
Sary 115
Forbes
John 61
Foster
Daniel 45
Drury 88
Mary 88
Foulden
George 115
Frazer
William 47, 66
Frazier
William 48
Franklin
Edmond 140
Freeman

Nancy 21
Robert 21
French
James 43
William 7, 8, 30
Frith
John 99
Fry 117
Fuqua
Aaron 33, 65, 131, 132
Anna 23, 106
Fanny 137
John 23, 106
Jos 14
Joseph 33, 62, 65, 66, 70, 132
Moses 17, 19, 43
Nancy 23, 106
William 25
Furgerson
Jeremiah 21
Furguson
Jeremiah 21
Joseph 21

Gaddy 117
Galawdy
John 92
Gallaway
John 7, 43
Galloway 31, 63, 121
Edman 115
Isham 70, 97, 100
John 30, 92
Garland
Samuel 134
Garrett/Garritt
John 46, 129
Martha 90, 91
Gatewood
Dudley 128

James 128, 129
George
Polly 73, 101
William 137
Geter
William 72
Gibson
William 5
Gilbert
Benjamin 140
Preston 130
Gills 95
Gilmer
Peachy 24, 106
Gilpin
Francis 19
Goggins/Goggin
D 137
Stephen 31, 71, 75
William 53
Goodman
Absalom 7
Ancel 27, 130
Ansalom 30
Edy 27, 130
Lucy 27
Gooldy
Frederick 19, 63, 64, 93, 122
Goolsby
Mary 53
Goolsley
Arthur 19, 95, 125 146
Gorden 15, 143
Governors of Virginia
Barbour 20, 48, 49
Cabell 48
Floyd 54-46
Giles 52, 53
Pleasants 51
Randolph 50

164

Tazewell 56, 1267
Tyler 48
Graham
  Anne 108, 140
  Edward 60
  M 46, 129
  Michael 50, 62
  William 108, 126,140
Grant
  Edy 27
  John 27
Green 80
  William 48, 49, 110
Greer
  Aquilla 138
  Vincent 139
Grey
  J 12, 79
Gribb
  Jesse 15
Grifeth
  David 106
Griffin
  Samuel 24, 106
Grubb/Grubbs
  Dabney 32, 73
  Jesse 15, 17
Grundy
  George 43
Gwarfney
  Mrs 112
Gwatkins/Gwatkins
  Charles 36, 98, 130
  E 81

Hackworth 55
  Joseph 17
  William 10, 18
Hadwell 139
Hague

Samuel 45
Haile
  Nicholas 106
Hairston
  Samuel 59, 61
Hale
  James 110
  William 62
Haley
  William 63
Hall 46
  Elisha 17, 124 129 143
  John 13, 15, 106, 125
  Magdalene 15, 124, 129
  Tabitha 124, 129
  widow 17
  William 125
Halladay
  William 33, 144
Halley
  William 100, 106
Halsey
  Thomas 43
Hambleton
  Elijah 123
  Sarah 123
Hamilton
  Elijah 3, 133
  James 123
  Sarah 3, 133
Hamnack
  William 130
Hancock 15, 19, 67, 95, 125, 143,
    145
  Ammon 103, 104
  Ann 104
  Harriet 104
  Justin 103, 104
  Lucy 103, 104
  Mary 13, 103, 104

165

Polly 18, 101
Samuel 10, 15, 16, 18, 22, 48,
    52, 101, 103, 104, 1423
Sarah 104, 115, 121
William 14, 61
Hanes
    Hanner 7, 30
Hardwick 120
Hardy 3, 136
    Solomon 20
Harman
    John 71
Harmon
    Peter 12, 120
    Sarah 12, 41, 120
Harper
    Robert 15, 143
Harrill
    Gilbert 128
Harris/Hariss 129, 138
    Frederick 112
    James 47, 143
    William 3, 34, 69, 78, 81, 82, 86,
        102, 104, 105, 123, 124,
        129, 133, 137
    Yancy 87
Hastens
    Anney 16, 142
Hatcher 24, 106
    Benjamin 16
    Elizabeth 67
    Eunice 50
    Henry 37, 114
    Jane 81
    Jeremiah 24, 68, 81, 83, 100,
        106, 114
    Thomas 82, 83, 95
Hauge
    Samuel 129
Hawkins 80, 143

George 26, 84
    John 26
Haynes
    John 58, 69
    Thomas 58
Hays
    Ellin 140
    Nicholas 140
Hayth
    Martha 115, 125
    Thomas 28, 43, 115, 126, 129,
        139, 140
Headen
    Franklin 55
    James 22
    John 9, 21, 51, 52
Heath
    William 138
Heeney
    Thomas 87
Heiler
    Gabriel 60
Heisel
    Dicey 1
Hendrick
    Bernard 104
    Lucy 103, 104
Henry
    Alexander 21
Hewitt
    Warner 68, 104
Hicks
    Thomas 58
    Stephen 58
Hill
    Jane 17
    John 17
Hix
    Caty 45, 128
    Jesse 77, 91

Patrick 45, 128
Susanna 45, 118, 128
William 75
Hoard
  Solomon 20
Hobbs/Hobs 12, 33, 65, 78, 79,
    132
Hobson
  Richard 35, 126
Hogan 138
Holet
  John 119
Hollaway/Holloway
  John 5, 75
Holliday
  John 77, 143
  William 77, 143
Holmon 72
Holt 108, 131
  John 69, 99, 115
  Joseph 77, 115
  Lucy 110
  Matthew 110
  Thomas 44, 45
Homan
  Elizabeth 20
Hoofman
  Daniel 34, 111
Hook
  David 45
  John 20, 118
Hopkins
  Ann 6
  Anna 6, 37, 79
  Benjamin 143
  Elizabeth 6
  Francis 77, 91, 123
  John 6
  Martha 6
  Mary 138

Price 6, 37, 79
Sally 6
William 6, 53
Hore/Hors
  Edward 14, 17, 61, 142
Horton
  Townzen 108, 125, 139
Houtz
  Barbara 47
  Christian 47
Howerton
  child 141
  Delilah 141
  Elizabeth 141
Huddleston
  Abram 67
Hudnall
  Frances 80
  John 80
Hudson
  Alexander 21
  Joel 20
Huger
  Elizabeth 118
Hughes
  Daniel 16
  David 16
  George 7, 61, 92, 130, 139
Hundley/Hunley
  Betsy/Betsey 33
  Elizabeth 1, 35
  Jordan 1, 33
Hunt
  Nathan 85
  Wilkins 3
Hurt
  Elisha 18-20, 41
  Elizabeth 34, 144
  Garland 9, 50, 54
  Ira 9, 50

John 3
Lucy 450
William 3, 9, 36, 50, 84, 120,
    135, 145, 146
Hutcherson
    William 128, 130
Hutson
    Nancy 89, 146
Hutton 146
Hylton
    John 19

Innes
    Elizabeth 101
    Jesse 112
Irvine
    Alexander 38, 52, 56, 57, 94,
        118-119
    Christopher 14, 44
    Edmund 53
    Elizabeth 42
    Locky 52, 94
    Patsy 51
    William 42, 47, 51, 53
Isham
    Gregory 47

Jackson 120
James
    Edwin 24, 106
    Fleming 24, 106
    Isaac 32, 58, 85, 114, 145
    John 31, 114
    Lawrence 32, 58, 85, 114
Jarred/Jared
    Elizabeth 30
    Israel 30, 33
Jennings
    Samuel 47
Jeter/Geter

Elliott 25
Fielding 68
Henry 14, 61
Jane 81
Lorrin 67
Pleasant 24, 81, 106
Ransom 67
__rin 24, 106
William 71
Johnson 22, 37
    James 3, 32, 142
    Jesse 33, 142
    John 61
    Joseph 32, 142
    Judith 21
    Lemuel 90
    Polly 21
    Thomas 6, 37
    William 2, 134
Jones 13, 79
    Becky 123
    Betsy 75
    Charles 143
    Dudley 90
    Elizabeth 30, 34, 43, 62, 70, 81
    Horatio 110
    Joanna 110
    Joel 80, 123, 134
    John 143
    Jonas 4, 81, 843
    Julius 39, 120
    Nancy 80
    Peggy 30, 62
    Rebekah 30, 62
    Roy 13, 78
    Sally 112
    Samuel 24, 137
    Sarah 80, 123, 134
    Seay 24
    Solomon 24

Thomas 92, 107, 131
William 33, 64, 65, 71, 113, 132, 135
Joplin
James 54
Susan 54
Jordan
Leroy 3

Karr
Patrick 138
Kasey
John 34, 73, 74
William 21
Keath
Gabriel 11, 123
Kerr
Thomas 34, 111
Kerson
David 19, 95, 125, 146
Kesson
David 17, 123
Key
Thomas 84
King
Betty 30, 145
James 30
William 30, 145
Kinnett
Burchy 89

Lacey
Burley/Burnley 90, 131
Judith 131
Lamb
Archibald 62, 129
Lancaster
John 143
Landon
John 19

Landsdown
Trifene 18
William 18
Langdon
John 115
Latham
Thomas 133
Lawhorn/Lawhorne
Henry 79, 102
Isham 10, 2, 52, 57, 83, 104
Sarah 11, 58, 60, 81, 124
Layton
Harvey 9, 50
Lazenby
Edward 73, 96
Lucy 94
Robert 17, 130, 136, 137, 142
Leake
Josiah 143
Lee
Alexander 49
Avey 49, 50
Garnett 52, 54
John 14, 49, 50, 66, 68, 101
Parnell 49
Richard 10, 48, 111
William 15, 16, 45
Leftridge 131
Leftwich 46, 48
Alexander 50
Augustine 7, 61, 86, 92, 131
Byrd 112
George 102
Ginsey/Jinsey 69, 87
J 19
Jabez 49
James 17, 18, 40, 101-103, 105, 112, 113, 138
Jane 69, 70, 87
Jesse 20, 101

169

Jinsey 69, 88
Joel 52, 54
John 31, 66, 82, 102, 105, 111
Littleberry 121, 137
Mary 113
Nancy 54, 146
Nichodemus 54, 58
Thomas 11, 67, 69, 70, 87, 89,
    110, 111
Uriah 54
V 28, 83
Valentine 129
W 111
William 10, 17, 20, 29, 33, 39,
    40, 54, 57-59, 66, 70, 74,
    96, 101-103, 128, 136,
    145
Lewellen
Green 67
Lewis 46, 48
Lisle
James 18
Lively
Polly 3, 102
Willis 3, 102
Lockett
Jeremiah 12, 79
Logwood
Euphan 81, 127
Thomas 47
Lovo
Robert 110
Lowry 124
Elliot 124
John 34, 111
Matilda 105, 145
Triplett 105, 145
William 34, 111
Lunsford
Merryman 11, 124

Lusk
Jane 7
Lynch
Charles 117, 118

MacPherson
John 1
Maddera
William 33, 144
Maglothlin
John 1
William 1
Makon
John 92
Mandon
Nathaniel 81
Manley
Elizabeth 115, 125
William 115, 125
Manson
Nathaniel 21, 127
Marable
Charles 101
Markham 14
Markle/Marckle/Marckel 107
Charles 8, 24, 32, 65, 79, 93,
    106, 121
Marks
John 93
Marr/Marrs
Elizabeth 3
James 3, 122
John 65, 93, 122
Jones 92
Marsh
Edmund 110
James 49, 50
John 50
William 50
Martin

Dabney 37
James 76, 82
John 54, 55
Sarah 74
Thomas 74
William 22, 74, 128
Massey
Zebedee 53
May
John 73
Mays/Mayes 138
Archelus 143
James 142
John 85
McCabe
John 45
Susannah 45
McCarty
Margaret 98, 134
Samuel 69
William 98, 134
McCloud
William 140
McClure
James 12, 100
McCormack
Micajah 1, 146
McCraw
Edward 8
Benjamin 8
McDaniel
Balda 52, 56, 81, 90, 91, 126, 127
George 143
Lodowick 28, 83, 119
McDonald
Benjamin 119
McFarland
John 97
McGhee/McGehee

Betsy/Betty 32, 34, 80, 109, 111, 112
Frances 80
John 110
Samuel 34, 111, 119
William 34, 112
McLean
John 93, 122
Mead
Benjamin 15, 31, 144
Elizabeth 15, 31
John 14, 61
Samuel 3, 136
Stith 109
William 18, 19, 97, 119
Meador
Hezekiah 31, 71
Medley
George 143
Mennis
Callohill 53
Meredith
Henry 110
Meriweather
Walker 134
Merman
Edmund 112
Merriman
Charles 76, 120, 141
Miles
Thadeus 54
Miller
James 33, 65, 66, 132
Moses 12, 65, 66, 79, 132
Thomas 10, 33, 64, 65, 78, 131, 132
William 34, 85
Mills
William 85, 86
Millwood/Milwood 135

Anne 28, 126, 129, 140
James 28, 108, 109, 115, 125,
    126, 129, 139, 140
Miner/Minor
  Edith 27, 28, 78
  Gabriel 27, 28, 78, 84
  W 105, 136
  William 27, 78, 105, 137
Mitchell 15, 138
  Daniel 110
  Elijah 55
  Hannah 40, 124
  Isaac 124
  James 5, 32, 37, 40, 44, 90, 94,
      109, 124
  John 14-16, 120, 124, 141
  R 25, 52
  Robert 7, 24, 77, 79, 91, 106
  Samuel 52, 53, 80
  Thomas 112
  William 77, 91, 142
Montgomerie
  Hugh 110, 111
Moon
  Lucy 21, 96
Moore
  Christopher 10
  Mary 117
  Thomas 108
  William 130
Moorman
  James 23, 63, 64, 82, 92
  Thomas 143
Morgan
  Elizabeth 14, 68
  John 74
  Samuel 2, 14, 68
  Thomas 14, 68
Morlan
  Stephen 19

Morris
  George 133
Moss
  Edmund 112
  Henry 9, 51, 67, 74, 96
Mount
  Mattathes 61
Moseley/Mozeley
  Arthur 141
  Susannah 45
  Walter 45
Murdock
  Elijah 22
Murphy 7, 8, 54
  Ann 55
  Bennett 9, 10, 52, 55
  John 10, 55, 75
  Katharine 55
  Pleasant/Pleasants 10, 53, 55
  Samuel 19, 95, 125, 146
  Thomas 61
Murrell
  David 133
  Hardin 133
  John 133

Nance
  John 10, 43, 55
  Mary 111
Nathan
  George 146
Neal
  Daniel 109
  Mary 109
Neilson 138
Nelson
  John 143
  Moses 84
Newland 17, 142
Newlin/Newline 43

The Browns of Bedford County

John 15
Newlon
  John 10, 16, 18
Newman
  Arthur 18, 47
Nichols 143
  Daniel 50
  Henry 96
Nimmo
  Robert 32, 84, 142, 144
  William 72, 142
Noell 111
  Cornelius 111
  Jesse 34, 49, 111
  John 81
Nolen 83
North
  William 120
Norvell
  George 74
Nowlin
  John 13

O'Brian
  Matthias 634
  Rhoda 23
  William 23, 106, 133
O'Briant 24, 106
O'Bryant
  Matthias 24, 106
Oglesby
  Richard 143
Oliphant
  Samuel 25, 73
Oney
  James 25, 60, 87
Orick 14
Ornsby
  John 43
Otey 77, 80, 91

Armistead 86
Isaac 47
J 79
James 51, 101
John 12, 13, 23, 33, 50, 51, 62-
  66, 70, 107, 131, 132
Nelson 86
Thomas 34, 111
Walter 63, 100, 110
Overfelt 21
  Nicholas 20
Overstreet
  Archibald 22
  John 48
Owens
  Taliaferro 87
Ownby
  William 82

Pallard
  Robert 46
Pankey
  Anne 5
  Philip 5, 76
Pannell
  Samuel 53
Parker
  Caleb 137
  George 53
Pate 3, 58, 69, 84, 136, 146
  Anthony 72
  Comet 144
  Cornelius 143
  Edmund 3, 27, 117
  Jeremiah 85
  John 2, 3, 27, 44, 67, 72, 117,
    132
  Matthew 2, 3, 26, 27, 117, 143,
    144
  Obediah 143

William 27, 136
Patrick
John 37, 44
Patterson
Charles 78
John 3
Joseph 7, 63, 71
Payne/Payn 73
Anny 32, 142
Archer 10
Elizabeth 32, 73
Henry 107, 126
James 32, 114
John 72, 141, 142
Joseph 72, 84
Phebe 84
Sarah 142
Thomas 15, 32, 73, 143
William 142
Pearcy
Charles 59, 107, 133
Nancy 59, 107, 133
Pearman
Oglesby 90, 91
Sarah 90, 91
Penn
J 143
Perdue
Jesse 104
Perkins
Elisha 143
Perrin
widow 17
Peryire
Betsey 73
Elizabeth 32
Petross/Petoross
James 23, 63, 64, 108, 131
Phaplin
John 140

Phelps 44, 45
John 46, 74, 117, 138, 142
Thomas 74
Phillips
Edw 25
Edward 25
Samuel 111
Pidgeon
William 71, 89
Pike
William 13
Pleasants
Thomas 15
Plymale
Amy 22
Irenia 39, 59, 89
Thomas 39, 59, 89
Poindexter
Samuel 109
Pointer
John 24, 106
Pollard
Catharine 11, 107
Francis 67
Jesse 11, 107
Thomas 46, 129
Pope
Richard 1, 33
Porter
William 24, 25, 66, 102, 106
Powell
George 143
Henry 69
Jane 69
Jesse 67
Simson 134
Thomas 34, 111
William 93
Prather
David 67

Pratt
  Jesse 88
  Joshua 88
  Lucy 101
Preas 23, 58, 69, 106, 133
  Elizabeth 66, 102
  Henry 30
  Polly 23, 66, 102
  Thomas 67
Preast
  Joseph 115, 121
  Thomas 132
Preston
  Mary 43
  Phillip 43
  Pleasant 6, 37
  Stephen 47, 51
  Susanna 22
  Thomas 24, 54, 58, 106
  William 22
Price 14
  Daniel 14, 49, 68
  N 112
  Robert 49
Pullen
  Tilson 6, 37, 79
Pullin
  Thomas 78
Purvines
  Sarah 1, 122
Pyborn
  Jacob 137

Quarles 46, 49
  David 66, 102
  Nancy 123
  William 92, 120
Quin
  John 63

Radford
  Richard 120, 141
  Randle 130
  Randolph 7, 61, 64, 71
Ratliffe
  Thomas 99
Ray
  William 53, 56
Read
  Ajohnadab 109, 126, 135
  Andrew 78
  Edmund 59, 143
  Frances 72
  Samuel 10, 66, 111
  William 10, 58, 84
Reed
  Clement 2
Reece
  Anna 75
Reese
  Ann 5, 62
  John 5, 31, 62, 63, 65, 113, 121,
    122
  Jordan 64
  Nancy 92, 122
  Rhoda 62, 113
  Robert 136, 137
  Sloman 62, 113
Reice 138
Reid
  Alexander 15
  William 29, 38, 50
Reynolds
  Charles 36, 38, 96, 97, 116, 118-
    120
  Jesse 96, 116, 118, 119
  Joseph 96, 116, 118, 119
Rice 77, 91
  Benjamin 32, 62, 64, 65, 92, 93,
    121, 122

Richards
  Abijah 20, 41
  Benjamin 91
  John 19
Richardson
  Ann 6, 40, 41, 100, 121
  John 66, 130
  Priscilla 66
Rigby
  Tabitha 128, 129
Roberts 47
  Daniel 45
  John 48, 109
  Philip 110
  Susanna 109
Robertson
  Archibald 67, 133-135
  Burwell 67
  Harriett 34
  James 10
  John 59, 86, 112
  N 9, 50, 73
  Nicholas 53, 67, 73, 135
  Thomas 35
Robinson
  Edwin 38, 56
  Frances 56
  Harriett 41, 145
  James 35
  John 111
  Thomas 41, 44, 94, 145
Ross
  Robert 55
  Susannah 55
Rucker
  Anthony 134
  George 73, 101
  Ruffen/Ruffin 28, 108, 125, 126, 129, 139-141
Rupert

Michael 91
Rusman 66
Ryan
  John 34, 111
  Phillip 130

Sale
  John 28, 83
  Thomas 53, 145
Saunders 22
  David 32, 34, 49, 109-111, 129
  James 8
  Julius/Julious 17, 21, 22, 142
  Lucinda 40
  Thomas 80, 112
Scott
  John 88
Scruggs 124
  Gross 5, 13
  Jane 101
  Margaret 5, 75
  Thomas 32, 65, 101, 122
Seal
  James 32, 142
Shands
  Judith 73
  William 73
Sharp
  Alexander 143
  John 81
  Sampson 24, 25
Sherman
  William 59, 86, 122
Shrewsbury/Shrewsberry/
  Shewsbury 33, 34, 65, 132
  N 32
  Nathaniel 16
  Reuel/Ruel 23, 33, 64, 65
  Sally 23
Simon

John 116, 125
Simmons 33, 65, 132
  Alexander 64
  Elizabeth 109, 126, 135
  John 28, 43, 108, 109, 116, 125,
    126, 129, 135, 140
Slaughter
  Gabriel 72
  Joseph 51, 52, 54, 55
Smelser
  Stephen 62, 129
  Tabby 62, 129
Smith 67
  Bowker 75
  Emily 87
  John 43
  Thomas 44, 122
  Vinal 86, 87, 109
Snider
  Henry 18, 89
  Joyce/Joicey 18, 89, 96
  William 18, 89
South
  child 141
  Daniel 141
  William 141
Spradling 31, 71
  Edward 76, 95, 100
  Lucy/Lucie 95, 100
  Nehemiah 102, 114
  Polly 102
St Clair
  Caleb 3
  Christopher 67
Stanfell
  Munford 69
Stanley
  George 13, 79
  Jesse 37
Staples

Phebe 1, 107
Starkey
  John 74, 76
Stephens
  Daniel 107
Steptoe
  Ann 5
  Edward 56
  Frances 101
  J 8, 39, 52
  James 11, 14, 66, 67, 69, 88, 99,
    110, 111
  Nancy 5
  R 111
  Robert 34, 53, 110, 112
  Thomas 21, 96
  William 5, 124
Stevens
  Henry 110, 111
Stewart
  Thomas 19, 21, 34, 74, 95, 125,
    146
Stinnett
  Lindsey 34, 111
Stith
  Benjamin 73, 85
  Joseph 77, 85, 143
  Richard 28, 61, 109, 126, 135,
    139, 140
Stone
  George 63, 100
  James 115
Stratton
  Jane 70
  Joseph 12, 79
Stuart
  Thomas 95
Sumpkin
  Thomas 63, 100
Swain/Swayn

Charles 14, 19, 68
Sydnor
  Foster 100

Talbot
  Charles 126, 130, 139
  Isham 97
  James 43
  Matthew 75, 117, 138
  W 130
Tankersley
  James 112
Tate
  Charles 14, 61
  Henry 96, 134
  Nathaniel 46
  Obediah 15
  Patsy 134
  Sarah 14, 36
Taylor 80
  Eli 128
  Henry 13
  James 130
  John 115
  William D 11
Teacher
  Floyd 121
Terry
  William 109
Thaxton 12, 13, 79, 133
  William 12, 79, 86
Thomas 32, 65, 120
  George 66, 127
  John 23, 106, 131
  Mary 62
  William 10, 23, 63, 64, 121
Thomason
  James 117
Thompson
  David 95

Fanny 37, 44, 52
Frances 5, 46, 77, 100, 117
John 15, 37, 44, 72, 94
Nelson 81, 125
Thornhill
  Elizabeth 33, 135
  James 64, 71, 113
  William 33, 135
Thornton
  Caroline 96, 118
  Philip 96, 118
  William 96
Thorpe/Thorp
  Frances 53, 54
  Francis 4, 43
  William 18, 37, 47
Thurman
  Ruhar 126, 140
Tinsley 143
  Judith 133
  Robert 58, 90, 133, 134
Todd
  Samuel 101
Tompkins
  Daniel 53, 107
Traylor
  John 59, 99, 140
Trent
  John 19
Trigg
  John 46, 129
  William 45, 122
Truman
  Wyatt 39, 59, 89
Tucker
  Thomas 47, 118
Tullis/Tulos/Tullos 117
  Richard 117, 118
Turner 8
  Elijah 10, 18, 54

Elizabeth 6
Gordun 50
James 6, 8, 12, 30, 50, 62, 77,
   98-100, 115, 121, 134
Lewis 19, 95, 125, 146
Malandor 84
Meador 50
Melanethon 105, 137
Micajah 103, 108
Parson 123
Richard 54
William 143
Tyler
   Daniel 59, 90, 133
   John 135
   Juana 59, 90, 133
   Nelson 80

Updike
   Daniel 55
Urquhart
   Kenneth 54

Vance
   John 43
Venable
   Richard 137
Vest
   John 126, 139
   Thomas 76
Vieley
   Lucy 27, 96
   Michael 27, 96
Vineyard
   Brown 106, 126

Wade
   Irvine 49
   Jacob 19, 33, 64, 136
   Jeremiah 54

Waggoner 22
Wainwright
   John 43
Walden
   Charles 66, 102
   John 6, 37
   Patsy 37
Walker 28, 83, 84, 86
   David 43
   Elizabeth 31
   John 31
   Mary 136, 137
   Robert 129
   Sally 6
   Thoma 4, 42
   William 47, 136
Walton 8, 14, 77, 143
   George 72
Ward 66
   John 43
Watkins
   Ebenezer 11, 103, 142
Watson
   John 18, 64, 66, 132
Watts
   Edward 53
   Thomas 75
   William 77, 143
Weaver 26, 84
Weekes/Weeks
   Alderson 31, 46, 129
   George
West 58, 69
Wharton
   John 96, 118
Wheeler
   Gabriel 60, 107
   Joel 60, 107
   Nancy 60, 107
   Rowland 14, 61

White
  Jacob 36, 98
  James 81, 82, 95, 136
  Jane 7
  Joseph 17, 46
  Robert 18, 37, 47
  Thomas 7
Whitely
  William 11
Whitten
  Joseph 53
  William 55
Whittington
  Jane 90
  John 90
  Martha 91
  Nancy 90
  Stark 90
  Thomas 90, 91
Whitton
  William 82
Whorley
  Burd 74
  Docia 74
  Joel 74
  Sally 74
Wiggenton
  Benjamin 91
Wildman
  Israel 80, 105
Wiley
  William 138
Wilk
  Jesse 88
  Judith 88
Wilkes/Wilks
  Samuel 19, 70, 88, 89, 107
Willcox
  Mary 83, 103
William Brown & Co 146

Williams 12, 79
  Giles 138
  Israel 78
  James 24
  Roger 15, 17, 46
  Samuel 54
Williamson
  Leonard 86, 123
  Milbourn 88
  Sally 86, 122
Wills
  Elizabeth 110
  Justinian 53
Wilson
  John 77, 100, 101, 143
  Joseph 46, 60, 86, 87
Wily
  Jane 128
  John 61
Wingfield
  G 25, 52, 53
  Gustavus 94
  Lewis 22
Witt
  Aley 4, 44,
  Anny 94
  Benjamin 118
  Jesse 4, 44
  John 56, 68, 70, 89, 99
  Martha 68, 99
  Roland/Rowland 48, 49
  Rowland
  Sarah 49
Womack 43, 72
  Sarah 119
Womax
  Sarah 115, 121
Wood
  Francis 17, 19
  Mary 79, 102

Milly 137   Stephen 60,
107
William 92
Woodford
  Elizabeth 49
  James 88
  Lucy 88
  William 49
Woodley
  William 7, 131
Woodson 67
  Obediah 43
Woodward
  Celia 11
  Lance 120
  Samuel 11
Woody/Woodey
  Elizabeth 30, 62, 98
  George 17
  Margaret 62, 70, 98
  Peggy 75, 98
  William 30, 61, 62, 90, 92, 107,
    131
Woolridge 138
Wooster
  Hinman 14, 15, 68, 95
Worley
  Joel 74, 126
  Sarah 74, 125
  Sinthia 74, 126
Worner
  Jabez 109
Worthington
  William 5
Wright
  Aggy 78
  Anthony 2, 3, 26, 136
  James 14, 61
  John 33, 65, 77, 132, 142, 143
  Joseph 32, 122

Sarah 120
Tommy 32, 142
William 114

Young
  John 46

SLAVES

Abby 53
Abraham 134
Abram 53, 111
Agga 136
Allen 53
Amos 53
Amy 53
Anderson 134
Anna 56
Arch 112
Archa 11
Archy 134

Becky 53
Ben 134
Bett 105, 137
Big Sam 53
Bill 56
Billy 53, 134

Caleb 134
Celia 112
Charity 54
Charles 56
Charlot 103, 108
Christian 56
Claiborn 134
Clara 90

181

Daniel 1324
David 53, 112
Davis 81
Derry 53, 89
Dick 49, 56, 81
Doley 53
Dorcas 72

Edmund 134
Eliza 56, 81, 134
Ellis 53
Esther 134

Faro 49
Flanders 111, 112
Frances 112
Frank 134

George 53, 56, 134
Granville 90

Hannah 134
Harry 53, 56, 111, 112, 134
Henry 53, 90
Herbert 53

Isham 134

Jackson 80
James 53, 134
Jenny 134
Jerry 112
Jim 53
Job 111
Joe 53, 112
John 53, 56, 112
Jordan 105, 137
Joshua 55
Judy 53, 55
Juggy 53

Julia 111
Julias 90
Julius 134
Juno 90

Kizziah 134

Lenah 90
Lewis 134
Linda 90
Little Edmund 134
Little Sam 53
Little Stephen 53
Lucinda 112
Luckey 53
Lucky 136

Manda 56
Maria 90
Mariah 134
Marriah 53
Martha 56
Martha Ann 112
Mary 90, 112
Mary Ann 56
Matt 53
Milford 53
Milly 53
Moses 134

Nancy 53, 56, 134
Nat 90
Ned 134
Nelson 49, 134

Orry 53

Patsey 134
Patty 134
Peggy 112

Peter 53, 1324Peyton 53
Phill 87
Phillip 86
Phillis 53
Piggy 111
Polly 16

Rachel 53, 90, 134
Randolph 53
Reuben 53
Rhoda 125
Richard 90, 134
Robert 112
Robin 134
Rose 90

Sally 53
Sam 49, 53
Sarah 53, 134
Seny 53
Silva 111
Silvy 112
Simon 53
Sophia 134
Sucky 112
Sulky 111
Sylvia 134

Thompson 134
Tom 53, 134

Washington 134
William 134
Wilson 56

BUILDINGS

Brown Leftwich store 10
Chapel 141

Lee's store 54
Poorhouse 54, 87
St Stephen's Episcopal Church
    134
Union Meeting House 67
Workhouse 54

CEMETERIES

St Stephen's Episcopal Church
Cemetery 133
Thompson Brown Family
Cemetery 21, 22, 38, 42, 46, 51,
    102

COMMUNITIES

Missouri
    St Genevieve 139
North Carolina
    Guilford 42
Pennsylvania
    Philadelphia 40, 112
Tennessee
    Jonesborough 84
Virginia
    Liberty 60, 64, 71, ,86, 87, 109,
        113
    Lynchburg 4, 13, 22, 50, 56, 57,
        133, 143, 146
    New London 16, 17, 21, 45, 46,
        48, 51
    Otterview 76
    Portsmouth 42
    Richmond 146
    Roanoke 13
    Russell 13

COUNTIES

Indiana
  Crawford 67, 104
  Laporte 70, 87
Kentucky 8
  Caldwell 8, 39
  Cumberland 85
  Frankfort (sic) 130
  Garrard 6
  Madison 108
  Menefee 72
  Wayne 69, 75
Massachusetts
  Berkshire 36, 38, 96, 97, 116
Mississippi
  Yahoo 125
Missouri
  Lincoln 84, 94
  Ralls 139
New Jersey 41
New York 56
Pennsylvania 131, 145
South Carolina
  Albemarle 17, 142
Tennessee 122
  Bedford 125
  Gibson 59
  Jefferson 8, 39
  Monroe 1
  Williamson 9, 51, 67, 74
Virginia
  Albemarle 103
  Amherst 58, 131
  Augusta 36, 42, 108, 125
  Botetourt 2, 11, 61, 67, 69, 88
  Brunswick 59
  Buckingham 43, 75

Campbell 11, 28, 43, 46, 47, 51, 67, 70, 88, 101
Chesterfield 130
Culpepper 36, 98, 122
Cumberland 1
Fairfax 139
Fauquier 98, 122
Floyd 11, 103
Franklin 6, 15, 18, 19, 20, 47, 66, 102
Hanover 61
Henrico 115, 125
Loudoun 45
Lunenburg 106, 117, 138
Montgomery 27, 53, 117
Pittsylvania 15, 19, 53, 69, 88, 95, 125, 143, 146
Prince George 43
Rockbridge 36, 38, 96, 97, 116, 117, 119, 120
Stafford 36, 98

ESTATES

Blair's Order 140
Ivy Cliff 5, 46, 77, 83, 94, 99, 113, 118
Ivy Hill 4, 6, 13, 41, 94, 99, 117
Locust Thicket 99, 140
Mount Pleasant 15
New Glasgow 70

MILLS

Brown's 19
Caffery's 132
Grist mill 52, 54, 55
James Stone's mill 115

Leftwich's 110
Merchant and saw mill 19
Mill dam 19, 41, 54, 55
Mills 20, 41
Mollys Creek 125
Murphy's 10, 54, 55
Saw mill 54, 55
Trigg's 45

MOUNTAINS

Beards 137
Flat Top 115, 121
Flemming's 117
Johnson 38, 46, 47, 49, 50, 51
Porter 67, 69, 88
The Peaks 87

ROADWAYS

Blackwater 17, 49, 101, 141
Boonsboro 134
Brambletts 7, 61, 63, 92, 131
Burks 47
Davies Ferry 143
Dennys 76
Fancy Farm 60, 86, 109
Hales Ford 104
Island 119
Island Ford 57, 58
Island Fork 119
Meadows 104
Meads 20, 41, 123
New London 61
Old mill road 19, 95, 123, 145
Pates 26, 32, 114, 142, 143
Reads 72

WATERWAYS
Spellings have been edited

Amos Creek 55
Anthonys Ford 21
Back Creek 46, 48
Balcony Falls 36, 97, 120
Bear Branch 130
Beaver Creek 61
Beaverdam Creek 16, 25, 31, 32,
      58, 71-73, 77, 84, 85,
      114, 143
Big Otter River 111, 119
Blackwater River 46
Borams Creek 17
Boreauger Creek 23-25, 106, 132
Browns Fork 51
Buck Beach 76
Buck Creek 48
Buffalo Creek 4, 43, 56, 95, 102
Burks Ford 48, 119
Burnt Bridge Creek 1167, 118
Camping Run 97
Cheese Creek 117
Corams Creek 46
Crab Orchard Creek 70, 88, 89
Craddock Creek 9, 19, 21, 22, 50
Cubb Creek 138, 140
Earlys Ford 17
Earlys Fork 46
Echols Creek 11, 28, 83, 84, 86
Elk Creek 29, 40, 81, 103, 105,
      112, 113, 127, 128, 134,
      145
Ewings Creek 35, 128
Falling Creek 2, 3, 26, 27, 54, 136,
      138, 140
Falling River 117, 130, 137
Fish Creek 17, 142

Fuquas Branch 14
Gills Creek 13, 15, 140
Gladys Creek 42
Goose Creek 4, 9, 10, 12, 15, 17,
    19, 20, 33, 34, 41, 42, 52,
    53, 55, 65, 72, 78-80, 84,
    85, 95, 104, 105, 125,
    132, 146
Greasy Creek 53
Hales Ford 19, 95, 104, 125, 146
Hornets Nest Branch 72
Howards Branch 29, 40
Howards Creek 103, 105, 113,
    128, 145
Hurricane Creek 81-83, 95
Irish Falls 36, 38, 96, 97, 116, 120
Island Creek 43
Island Ford 48-54-56
Ivy Creek 117, 143
James River 36, 38, 96, 86, 116,
    119, 120
Johns Creek 92
Johnsons Creek 38, 46, 49, 50
Judith Creek 21, 117
Jumping Run 31, 71
Kates Creek 33, 140, 142-144
Lick Creek 13, 99, 140, 141
Lick Run Creek 4, 36, 42, 48, 57,
    58, 119
Little Whipping Creek 99, 140
Little Otter 7, 8, 11, 14, 30-34, 44,
    46, 54, 60-65, 70, 71, 80,
    92, 93, 99, 101, 103, 105,
    110-113, 121, 122, 124,
    130-132, 138, 139
Lynville Creek 97
Maggoty Creek 114, 115
McDaniels Creek 53
Meadows Creek 32, 68, 77, 91,
    93, 97, 121, 122

Merrimans Creek 76
Merrimans Ford 141
Merrimans Run 139
Mill Creek 9, 52-55
Mollys Creek 28, 43, 108, 109,
    115, 125, 126, 135, 138,
    139, 140
Morton Creek 130
Moses Run 94
Naked Creek 130
Needs Branch 72
Orrix Creek 18, 37, 47, 51, 67,
    104
Otter Creek 4
Otter River 15, 17, 22, 42-49, 53,
    56, 57, 61, 82, 94, 119,
    138
Reads Branch 72
Roanoke River 4, 36, 41
Rockcastle Creek 15, 34, 74, 76,
    103, 104, 143
Seneca Creek 138, 140
Shockoe Creek 23-25, 33, 64, 65,
    106, 132, 133
Sick Run 43
Snow Creek 36, 38, 97, 116, 120
Staunton River 2, 3, 13-15, 21,
    26, 31, 46, 53, 67, 68, 71,
    74, 101, 135, 138, 141
Stony Creek 6
Stony Fork 6, 34, 37, 84, 85
Terrapin Creek 53, 66-68
Triggs Mill Creek 45
Weavers Creek 2
Whipping Creek 99, 140
Wolf Creek 12, 79

www.ingramcontent.com/pod-product-compliance
Lightning Source LLC
Chambersburg PA
CBHW070916270326
41927CB00011B/2591